THE BEAUTIFUL AND THE DANGEROUS

With her husband, Dennis (the translator of *The Popol Vuh*), Barbara Tedlock has lived among the Mayan Indians of Guatemala and Belize and the Zuni of New Mexico. She has written three previous books and is a professor of anthropology at the State University of New York at Buffalo.

THE
BEAUTIFUL
AND THE
DANGEROUS

Dialogues with the Zuni Indians

BARBARA TEDLOCK

PENGUIN BOOKS

PENGUIN BOOKS

Published by the Penguin Group

Penguin Books USA Inc., 375 Hudson Street, New York, New York 10014, U.S.A.

Penguin Books Ltd, 27 Wrights Lane, London W8 5TZ, England

Penguin Books Australia Ltd, Ringwood, Victoria, Australia

Penguin Books Canada Ltd, 10 Alcorn Avenue, Toronto, Ontario, Canada M4V 3B2

Penguin Books (N.Z.) Ltd, 182–190 Wairau Road, Auckland 10, New Zealand

Penguin Books Ltd, Registered Offices: Harmondsworth, Middlesex, England

First published in the United States of America by
Viking Penguin, a division of Penguin Books USA Inc., 1992
Published in Penguin Books 1993

1 3 5 7 9 10 8 6 4 2

AUTHOR'S NOTE

Out of respect for privacy, personal names, with the exception of Barbara and
Dennis, are pseudonyms, and some of the incidents have been rearranged.

Section of a draft of a letter from Frank Hamilton Cushing to Sylvester Baxter
reprinted courtesy of the Southwest Museum, Los Angeles,
Hodge-Cushing Collection (97).

THE LIBRARY OF CONGRESS HAS CATALOGUED THE HARDCOVER AS FOLLOWS:
Tedlock, Barbara.
The beautiful and the dangerous: Encounters with the Zuni Indians/Barbara Tedlock.
p. cm.
Includes bibliographical references and index.
ISBN 0-670-84448-9 (hc.)
ISBN 0 14 01.7812 0 (pbk.)
1. Zuni Indians—Social life and customs. 2. Zuni (N.M.)—Social life and customs.
3. Ethnology—New Mexico—Zuni—Field work. 4. Tedlock, Barbara. I. Title.
E99.Z9T425 1992
978.9´004974—dc20 91–41836

Printed in the United States of America
Set in Garamond #3
Designed by Jessica Shatan

To
DENNIS TEDLOCK
husband, friend, and colleague

ACKNOWLEDGMENTS

■ ■ ■ ■

MY RESEARCH AT ZUNI PUEBLO, begun in 1968, was undertaken with the permission of the head of the Zuni civil government, Robert Lewis. The fieldwork, library research, and writing have been supported, on separate occasions, by Wesleyan University in Middletown, Connecticut; Tufts University in Medford, Massachusetts; the Wenner-Gren Foundation for Anthropological Research in New York City; the National Endowment for the Humanities in Washington, D.C.; the School of American Research in Santa Fe, New Mexico; and the Institute for Advanced Study in Princeton, New Jersey. I am most grateful to all of the people and institutions that have made this long-term project possible.

I started on the path to this book in 1981 with a slide lecture at the Indian Arts Research Center of the School of American Research. Two years later, the poet Jerome Rothenberg invited me to present my work during his conference, "The Symposium of the Whole," held at the Humanities Center at the University of Southern California. The unexpected enthusiasm with which the poet Robert Duncan greeted my presentation, together with subsequent positive responses from other writers, encouraged me to continue using a narrative format in presenting my research at Zuni Pueblo. In 1987 I read a section from what has since become chapter 7, at the invitation of Clifford Geertz, in the Thursday social science lecture series at the Institute for Advanced Study. Subsequently, I gave readings and slide lectures based on the manuscript at Rutgers, University of Texas at Austin, University of Michigan at Ann Arbor, University of Wisconsin at Madison, McMaster University, University of Western Ontario, University of British Columbia, The Visual Studies Workshop in Rochester, Bard, Brown, University of Rochester, and Vassar. Segments of chapters 3, 7, and 14 were published in somewhat different formats in the literary journal *Conjunctions,* and an earlier version of chapter 16 was published in *Anthropology and Humanism Quarterly.*

An earlier stage of the book manuscript was carefully read and sensitively critiqued by Scott Edward Anderson, Deborah Baker, Ruth Behar, Billie Jean Isbell, Bruce Jackson, Marla Powers, and Dan Rose. Their perceptive comments and questions were crucial to my final rewriting.

For opening their homes and sharing their life stories with us, despite distances of language and culture, I say *elahkwa* to those Zuni individuals who have been so kind to us over these past twenty years. To my husband and colleague, Dennis Tedlock, I say both *elahkwa* and *maltiox,* not only for sharing these field encounters with me but also for providing continuing support in seeking new ways of writing about these most human of experiences. Without his constant encouragement and criticism this book would be less than it should be.

CONTENTS

■ ■ ■ ■

CONTENTS

PREFACE

■ ■ ■ ■

Everything is always the same
and everything is always different.
—GERTRUDE STEIN

AT THE BEGINNING OF THIS STORY, I fall in love with the beauty
of the high desert and the native peoples of the American Southwest. The pueblos of Arizona and New Mexico have long provided
an alternative world, a vast psychic oasis for photographers, paint-
ers, sculptors, poets, novelists, collectors, yearners, and sojourn-
ers of many a stripe. But as for me, it is only a short while before
I shift from painting and sculpting this bewitching land to doing
field research at Zuni Pueblo. In my person as an ethnographer,
I record ancient myths, rituals, and ceremonies, of course, but
there is more to life at Zuni than that. It brings the joys of
romance, marriage, and birth together with the tragedies of
alcoholism, chronic illness, and premature death. My account
hinges on a shift in attention from a distanced aesthetic enchant-
ment with Southwestern landscapes to a more intimate knowledge
of what Zunis refer to as the beautiful (*tso'ya*) and the dangerous
(*attanni*) within and between all lives.

The ethnographer inside me—that strange blend of privileged refugee, advanced tourist, and trained observer—compulsively records, on odd scraps of paper, hundreds of samenesses and differences. But why this drive to offer up yet another witnessing? After all, my husband, Dennis Tedlock, and I have also done ethnographic fieldwork in Guatemala, Belize, Nigeria, and Brazil. Perhaps it is because Zuni was, for both of us, our first serious encounter with Otherness. But this encounter was so strong, and by now has lasted so long, that we have also learned the important lessons of nearness and sameness. By this time, I can no longer simply walk away from my many experiences with Zuni individuals, since their lives have become the weft in the fabric of my own life. Always there are my notes, diary entries, slides, photos, tapes, and texts. And always I am obsessed by more, far more, than they contain; for ethnography is a privileged refugee's suitcase crammed with jumbled experiences, impressions, ideas, and mementos from time spent not so much in the living of a particular life, but rather in the searching for an alternative life. Ethnography is a work of art, a shimmering brocade interwoven with dense strands of dark discomfort knotted in brightening desire.

In today's rapidly changing multicultural world we are all becoming ethnographers, gathering, inscribing, and interpreting what Others say and do in order to make sense of our own sayings and doings. Within this new social context the inquiring Self is as problematic as the cultural Other. While some progress has been made in understanding certain cultural Others, we still lack an adequate understanding of the culture of ethnographic inquiry. My account of learning the craft of ethnography is at least a beginning, revealing how an ethnographer is created, motivated, and then goes about creating personal, gendered cultural and intercultural portraiture. The explicitly narrative structure of my text is an intentional break with an older, more static manner of representing and typifying other peoples and cultures. In this older tradition, the firsthand experiences that take place during what is set aside and labeled as "fieldwork" become mere anecdotes reserved for informal occasions among family and friends. Topics such as kinship, gender relations, economics, and politics are abstracted from the matrix of experience and formally presented as "objective data" to colleagues at professional meetings in the expensive hotels of distant cities. Because ethnography is not only a product but also a process, our lives as ethnographers are embedded within experience in such a way that all of our interactions involve choices and thus have a moral dimension. When we see or fail to see, report a particular misunderstanding or embarrassment or ignore it, we make choices. We also make a choice when we edit ourselves out of our books.

Recently there has been a subtle yet profound shift in ethnographic methodology, from the oxymoronic concept of "participant observation" toward the observation of participation. During participant observation, ethnographers move back and forth between being emotionally engaged participants and coolly dispassionate observers of the lives of others. This strange procedure is not only emotionally upsetting but morally suspect in that ethnographers carefully establish intimate human relationships and then depersonalize them—all, ironically, in the name of the social or human sciences. In the observation of participation, on the other hand, ethnographers use their everyday social skills in simultaneously experiencing and observing their own and others' interactions within various settings. This important change in procedure has resulted in a representational transformation where, instead of a choice between writing a personal memoir portraying the Self (or else producing a standard ethnographic monograph portraying the Other), both Self and Other are presented together within a single multivocal text focused on the character and process of the human encounter. This emergent form of writing is known as "narrative ethnography."

The world, in a narrative ethnography, is re-presented as perceived by a situated narrator, who is also present as a character in the story that reveals his or her own personality. This enables a reader to identify the consciousness that has selected and shaped the experiences within the text. In contrast with confessional memoirs in which the ethnographer becomes a superhero (with legendary linguistic and interactional skills) or else a slapstick anti-hero (stumbling through field research), narrative ethnographies focus not only on the ethnographer's Self but also on ethnographic Others and the precise nature of the interaction between Self and Other.

What follows, then, is a multitude of voices and textures, each revealing human experience centering on events recorded in field notes, letters, tape recordings, slides, and the very heart and memory of the narrator who, while she is a character in the narrative, is also the author of this account. And although I sometimes speak as an omniscient, distanced, and authoritative narrator, I am also a voice among other voices submerged within the narrative flow I myself created, a startled witness to the events recorded herein.

—B.T.

· T H E ·
BEAUTIFUL
· A N D T H E ·
DANGEROUS

1

YOU'RE OUR GUEST, TODAY

■ ■ ■ ■

Up the dirt road under a turquoise sky past a row of adobe ovens and on into the Old Pueblo, we arrived at a huge stone house. Dennis pushed open the great wooden door to reveal a room as large as any New York City artist's loft: bare light bulbs dangling from a twelve-foot ceiling supported by hand-hewn beams, whitewashed walls, turquoise drapes with crimson tie-backs, jewelry benches covered with tools and materials—an electric grinding wheel with buffer attachment, metal anvil, vise, long-nosed pliers, tweezers, wax-tipped wooden sticks, acetylene torches, metal-shears, stamps, dies, emery paper, fine-gauge wire, silver bezels and beads, scattered bits of jet, coral, abalone, mother-of-pearl, and spiny oyster shell, petrified wood, turquoise and malachite gemstones—a wide plank dining table surrounded by ten plastic-covered aluminum chairs, and a television console tuned to a *Star Trek* rerun, *The City on the Edge of Forever*.

We were well within the threshold when a woman of about

thirty-five dressed in a spotless, but badly faded, house dress, ripped cotton hose, and tattered tennis shoes spun around toward us, emitting a tiny shriek. She had burnt-almond eyes rimmed by long black lashes, a large flat nose, warm rose-brown skin, and wavy black hair pulled back softly with a pair of silver-and-turquoise barrettes. Recovering her composure, speaking rapidly in Zuni, she presented her right hand to Dennis. Grasping her chafed but nonetheless delicate palm, lifting it to his lips, he breathed in deeply while replying in very formal Zuni.

Peering around him, smiling broadly at me, she said, "Come in, please, dear, my name is Sadie and you must be Dennis' good friend."

Sadie's husband, Sabin, who looked somewhat younger than she in his snappy cobalt cowboy shirt, leather dress-belt with fancy carved alabaster bear buckle (his CB name was "Polar Bear"), and square-toed spit-shined boots, ambled across the room, and exchanged another, more elaborate, set of greetings with Dennis. Pointing with puckered lips toward me, Sabin seemed to be asking a question. Dennis responded by grasping my hand, hard, and presenting me as "hom il'ona/*the one who has me.*"[1]

Sadie giggled. "So the world has ended; Kyamme/*Uncle* has gone and gotten himself married!"[2] She had long ago placed him, together with her bashful younger brother Albert, in the highly-unlikely-to-marry category.

"We did it the Zuni way first," Dennis replied, slyly winking.

"That's good," she quipped, "because then, when you get divorced, you won't have to pay anything. Seriously, did you hear about my baby?"

"No, you didn't notify me," he said in a slightly hurt tone.

Sabin sauntered over to the eastern wall, and gingerly lifted down an old pine plank with a swaddled infant strapped onto it with leather laces. Sadie commented that her father made the cradleboard when her older brother, Kwinsi, was born, and that all the children, including herself, as well as many grandchildren, had spent time stretched out on it. "Look here, you can tell by the back of my head, still flat."

The two-month-old baby boy, who twittered the moment his father unlaced him, was as yet unnamed. When Sabin handed his son over to Dennis the baby didn't cry, even though, as far as he was concerned, the blond-haired man was a total stranger.

Dennis passed the infant over to me and I fondled, bounced, and tickled him until a boy in a Beatles hair cut, who appeared from a back room, protectively gathered up the baby in a tiny yellow blanket. Cuddling, tickling, bouncing, and swinging him round and round his head, humming "All You Need Is Love," the young man, who turned out to be the baby's brother Shawiti, quickly noticed that the baby was wet, and expertly set about changing his diapers.

Since his last visit Dennis had acquired both a blond mustache and wire-rimmed glasses. Sabin asked where his old glasses were as Shawiti remarked on his mustache, "You change yourself," adding, "Maybe I'll raise one up." When Sadie inquired whether or not we had eaten, Dennis shook his head no.

"Get yourselves right on over and sit down," she said authoritatively, entering her kitchen and then returning with an enormous enameled bowl overflowing with purple tamales. Dennis remembered his gift and bolted out to the car as Sadie brought out homemade chile sauce, scallions, jerked venison, radishes, cucumbers, cilantro, wild mint, raw jalapeño peppers, iced tea, and a dish of salt crystals.

Upon his return Sadie smiled at the bulging bushels of peaches and apricots Dennis carried into her kitchen and, sinking down into a dinette chair with a sigh, announced, "Itonaawe/*Let's eat!*" Passing the food around, I remembered Dennis' instructions to take only a little at a time, and to eat slowly: a bite of tamale, chewing deeply and deliberately, keeping my eyes down, like a character in a folktale. Grabbing a scallion, I stirred the bulb round and round in the salt crystals, slowly savored it, munched a fistful of cilantro followed by a radish, lingered over the iced tea with wild mint; then more tamale, more scallion, more salt, more cilantro, more radish, more tea, more mint.

Dennis inquired politely after Sadie's parents: They were fine, well, aging some; you know Mother has had a little rheumatism? But they were still pretty active: Hapiya had planted corn, rye, and wheat, and Tola had a big garden full of squash, broccoli, carrots, scallions, cilantro, and radishes. When school let out Sadie sent her middle children, Ramona and Seff, up to her mother's to keep the old lady company. She thought the country would be good for them, give them the opportunity to learn how to care for animals, but, most important, she herself needed the rest. Shawiti and his baby brother were enough to handle for the summer.

When Dennis asked after the news around Zuni, Sadie at first replied, "Nothing." But then, casting about for a juicy tidbit, she remarked that the ruined church was being restored, but that only "Catholics" were employed on the project.[3]

I sucked on the salt crystals, noticing they were weaker and less bitter than Morton's salt; took a bite of jalapeño, chewing slowly, breaking into a sweat; then a nibble of cooling cilantro, scallion, radish, more chile. Dennis nudged me under the table, encouragingly.

Watching me bite into a fiery-hot pepper, Sadie said, with delight, "You married yourself some mean lady!"

Turning toward me with a grin, Dennis said, "My dear, how did you enjoy your first raw chile pepper?"

"Sure was hot, but good."

"You're one mean lady, all right. Wouldn't catch me, or any other male around here, eating those yellow ones," he replied, beaming.

So, I had behaved properly, for a woman, and it was sheer beginner's luck. But when Sadie asked me what I did for a living, and I answered truthfully that I was a painter, she rolled her eyes, smothered a giggle, then blurted out, "No. *Seriously,* you can't sell very many. I can sell all the jewelries I make, and there's nothing ever left over. That's where the *money* is. Someday I'll teach you the jewelry making, and you can support your husband, just like me."[4] The men chuckled at the thought of being supported by their women; then Dennis, as he rose to leave, nodded toward me.

It was late, and we were tired from our long drive across the state, so we left for a nearby motel. By morning, when Dennis decided to drive up to the country place to visit the Old Ones, thunderheads were stacking themselves along the horizon. Everything was fine till the storm broke, and the red clay roadbed softened into what some Southwesterners call greased owl shit; we were sucked in, then slipped and nearly slid off into a ditch. The bridge below the house creaked and swayed under the weight of our old Volvo, but somehow stayed together.

We passed a row of beehive-shaped adobe ovens and big bunches of fresh corn ears that were strung up between two wooden posts to dry. Dennis explained that the largest oven was for roasting corn, the medium one was for baking bread, and the smallest was for roasting meat. The house, a rain-softened adobe with crumbling mud-and-straw plaster, had window sashes with traces of pink paint, wavy purplish panes, and no screens. To the left of the front door sat an upholstered chair with coiled springs piercing through the seat and a cuddly black puppy sleeping on its single arm; on the right side of the door, a pair of mallards ambled aimlessly, stopping every now and again to preen one another.

A robust man in his early sixties, with deeply sunburnt skin, etched crow's-feet, networks of lines around the corners of his mouth, and not a trace of gray hair, emerged from the house and

DENNIS TEDLOCK

walked toward the car, oblivious to the rain. It was Hapiya, Sadie's father, dressed in a homemade long-sleeved plaid shirt, washed-out blue jeans, and muddy work boots. As Dennis and he exchanged greetings at the threshold, Tola emerged from her kitchen, wiping her hands on her apron. She was a heavyset woman with almost square mahogany eyes, long graying hair, bushy salt-and-pepper eyebrows, and dozens of laugh lines.

Dennis introduced me once again as "hom il'ona/*the one who has me.*" Tola smiled, tipping her head slightly, as Hapiya stretched out his callused hand in welcome. I bowed at Tola and brushed Hapiya's open palm with mine. Dennis looked relieved that I was not overly bold in giving my greetings. During the subsequent conversation I found no way to contribute, even though at one point Hapiya apparently asked Dennis where I was raised, for Washington, D.C., leapt out of the surrounding Zuni language, and if I had ever been to New Mexico before—No.

As we entered the two-room house and walked around the edge of the fireplace I noticed a little girl, about five—Ramona, Sadie's only daughter—in a turquoise-colored turtleneck, white overalls, white socks, and scuffed brown oxfords sitting on a tiny rocking chair near the empty fireplace. Yellow rayon ribbons, braided into her long blue-black pigtails, wiggled as she rocked, singing to her favorite toy, a bedraggled monkey:

Monkii ts'a$_{naaaa}$ monkii ts'a$_{naaaa}$

ehe$_{ee}$haaaa eheee haaaa.

Little mon$_{keeey}$ *little mon*$_{keeey}$

ehe$_{ee}$*haaaa eheee haaaa.*

When Dennis appeared around the edge of the adobe fireplace Ramona squealed with delight, since she knew that whenever *he* came around her grandpa told old-time stories: wonderful stories about a little girl who went out hunting in wintertime, for rabbits; about a little boy who was abandoned by his mother and raised by deer; about miraculous twin boys who helped people; about silly coyote trying to learn bird songs.

Dennis surveyed the room, noting that the walls had been freshly whitewashed. Hapiya said that Tola told him she had to get the house ready soon because she dreamed that her kyamme/ *uncle* was coming to visit. The linoleum was washed and waxed but badly cracked, occasionally revealing the packed earthen floor beneath. The mantel was cluttered with wrenches, pliers, ammunition, matches, letters, comics, a pottery owl, and two tiny paint pots. Thumbtacked to the wall was a slick magazine photograph of President Kennedy with Pope Paul VI. On the facing wall was a faded reproduction of the flogging of Christ, surrounded by matchbook-cover illustrations of deer and trout, and various family photos. Next to this display was a framed 1961 citation from the commissioner of Indian affairs, Phileo Nash, recognizing Hapiya's years of community service.

Furnishings included a big lumpy bed with brass posts, two iron cots, a rough farm table with picnic benches, an oak clothes cabinet, a wooden high chair, two easy chairs with worn covers, a nonfunctioning icebox, and two kerosene lamps. In the kitchen were a dry sink, iron cookstove, a Styrofoam cooler, plastic buckets, aluminum kettles, cast-iron frying pans, and a wood-and-cardboard cupboard filled with assorted cups, plates, and jelly jars.

On wires stretching across the room fresh venison was drying, and on the hearth, a nighthawk, a Western tanager, and two other birds had been laid out, all sprinkled with cornmeal. Heaped up in the center of the battered oak table were freshly painted feathered sticks, which Dennis picked up and methodically examined. Noticing his interest, Hapiya commented that the full moon was approaching. Then, when Dennis asked him whether there weren't supposed to be four turns of cord between each feather, he replied in a half-joking tone, "Supposed to be, but sometimes I might make mistake; maybe they reject it."

Dennis asked for news, and Hapiya said that his son Joe was married and had a job working the 6:00-P.M.-to-6:00-A.M. night shift on the oil and gas rigs out behind the hogback. When the sheep herders, Albert and Ramona's brother Seff, arrived together with Joe, Tola immediately disappeared into her kitchen, leaving me momentarily confused.

Should I offer to help out, or not? After all, Tola didn't seem to have anyone else to help her. But as I made a move toward the kitchen door she shook her head, saying, "No, you're our guest, today; later on, you can be family."

Relieved not to have to haul water or cook on a wood stove, I settled into my chair, listening. There was talk of the heavy summer rains, during which people had gotten stuck on the road. Four nights ago Sabin was stuck in the mud with Kwinsi, Tola's eldest son, and had to walk more than ten miles to the pavement, where they hitched a ride to the village. But the guy who gave them the lift didn't take them to their doorsteps, just left them by the side of the highway, and they had to walk through the streets in the middle of the night. If they'd been seen, people would have thought they were out witching; or, if they weren't doing the witching themselves, then a witch might run into them, capture them, and take them along on the witch's path.

For lunch there were fried chicken parts, reheated pinto-bean stew, paperbread made from blue cornmeal, sourdough bread, roasted green chile peppers, clumps of salt crystals, and—fresh from Tola's garden—scallions, carrots, radishes, and cilantro. Albert talked about Joe's car; how during the first week they had had to replace both the hand brake and clutch cable; how it had to be jump-started whenever it rained; how they had to pull it out of the mud with Hapiya's tractor twice last week; how, in light of all of this, the pathetic vehicle should be named "Pushmobile." Joe ignored his older brother, who had no woman and no car and, since he still lived with his parents, no money of his own, and thus no independence at all.

Occasionally Hapiya looked at me intently and asked whether I liked chile, or paperbread, or Zuni Salt Lake salt, and when I said I did, he replied with obvious pleasure, "That's our Indian way." He seemed relieved that I took whatever was offered, commenting that some people didn't like to eat the Indian way.

Ramona, who had chosen to sit right next to me, spent her

dinner hour making eyes, giggling, and touching—first with a scallion and later with a carrot—my long stringy strawberry-blond hair. Seff spent his time building a tiny house from chicken bones, bread crumbs, and salt. Dessert included thin wedges of honeydew melon and watermelon.

When we were finished eating, Hapiya took Dennis and me for a walk out behind the house. As we neared the top of the hill, overlooking the valley, he pointed out various abandoned homes: one had the remains of a roof on top of a brass bedstead, and men's clothing still hanging on the wall, stained with mud and bird droppings. It must have been a gradual abandonment, I thought, rather than an abrupt departure. Was this a clue to the way things were left behind in prehistoric ruins?

Hapiya gestured toward two rock-and-cement foundations, where he and his father had lived before they built his present home back in the teens. "Old Man cut all the sandstone on the hogback right over there." Turning, then puckering his lips as if to whistle at the tilted cliffs, he continued, "Wet sandstone's pretty easy to cut with an ax, you know. I helped Old Man lay blocks with small slices of sandstone for chinking. They were real skillful back in them days; didn't use mortar or nothing. Mom did all the plastering. The house belongs to me, just like it did my dad. Someday it'll be Albert's."

"What about Kwinsi?" Dennis asked in a surprised tone.

"He's got his own place already, his wife's place, over there near that Gallup road. Albert's the one in charge around here now. He's the main one that runs the rams year-round."

"But what about Tola? Isn't this *her* place?" I asked, pointedly. In an anthropology class I had taken the previous spring I had learned that Zuni was a matrilineal society, which meant that women inherited important material possessions, such as houses.

"No. Tola's is that old Shalako place in the village."

This caused me to review my knowledge of Zuni property ownership. Each year between five and eight new houses were constructed for the great fall masked dances, known as Shalako. After the ceremony the house became the property of the woman whose husband's masked-dance group, or kiva, constructed the new home. Other, smaller homes were also built, both in the pueblo and in the countryside, that also became the property of women. There were some complexities to this pattern; but one thing was clear, a house and its dooryard belonged to a woman, *always*.

Thus, the country house, as well as the house in the village, should be Tola's to pass on to her daughters. But Hapiya had apparently inherited this country place from his father, and was determined to pass it along to, of all people, a middle son. Farmlands at Zuni were also in the female line, at least traditionally. Dennis had heard that more recently some people were dividing these lands equally among their daughters and sons, while others were giving their farms to the eldest son. But there was no precedent for Hapiya's choice. Stranger still was his link-ing of sheepherding to inheritance, since lambing and grazing lands were never owned by individuals, always by the tribe. Dennis decided not to question him about it—not right then, at least.[5]

Hapiya pointed to the ruins of a house where a Rain Priest had once lived with his five sisters, and explained that none of them ever married. The women worked like men in the fields, and they always had stacks and stacks of corn. During the famine, back in the 1880s, many people came out from the village to their farm for corn. They brought along woven belts, sashes, and blankets to exchange for corn, and the brother and his sisters grew rich. "Old-timers worked hard, not like these up-to-date kids. Old Man woke us up before it got light, sent us out to herd sheep, or cultivate the corn, without breakfast, or nothin'. It suuuure was hard, back in them days.

"Once, when we was up in the country with the whole family, our next-door neighbor, down in the village, saw a light inside our house.[6] Next day, somebody came and brought the word. My father went down there and checked the house; nobody was in there.

"That same fall, my brother and his wife fell sick. I was herding sheep, and in the evening I had my supper. When I finished supper my dog was right at my door.

"I had the sheep camp over there in the west; the sheep was outside, and the dog was herding towards the east. Just a little ways from my door he started whining.

" 'What the heck,' I said.

"I look up, see he was waiting there facing east, and said, 'What's wrong?' He started whining. I get the stick and hit the dog. The moon was just about out.

"My brother's wife was sick. By the time my father told me, she was in pretty bad shape, sick, sick, you know. Well, I got the notion that dog was giving me the story, telling me what was happening. So I put my hat on, put my coat on, start walking up from the sheep camp. When I got here the lady was pretty sick. Then I ask that sick person how she felt.

" 'Serious?'

"She said, 'Yes.' Then she told me she might kick the bucket.

" 'No, I don't think so, you better go to hospital now.'

" 'No. I don't want to go to hospital. I rather stay here with family,' that's what she said.

" 'Well, I'm sorry I can't stay overnight. I have to go back, there's nobody at sheep camp, just the dog,' I said.

"So I went. Probably I went about two or three o'clock in the morning. When I got to camp the sheep was laying down. The dog jump up and met me there, where that family is living over there right now. That's where my dog met me. I said, 'What's wrong?' That dog just ran all around.

"Next morning—well, I didn't go to sleep at all, you know, because I worried and worried about this woman. Next morning, before sunrise, before dawn, I build a fire and start to cook. Then I finish cooking, finish eating, and the sun was just about up. The sheep start grazing. I went towards south, and was around there till evening.

"When I got to camp that dog was going round and round. I didn't know why he was going around, four times he went, then he quit; and I don't see anything. Nothing.

"The sheep come around and when they got to where they spend the night, I build a fire. I was sitting there for a while, and them sheep was sound asleep. They chew, you know, but I couldn't hear anything. Nothing. They was sleeping, real silently.

"Then I felt somebody coming. I heard somebody coming. You could hear the tramps, you know, steps. Then I kind of got scared, a little bit. I got my gun. I got my .30/30 and sit down right at the door. Whoever comes, then I might see him.

"Pretty soon, the sheep, moving little bit, they got scared and move a little bit. Then they comes quite a ways, to where that turkey, about from that distance, I see something black moving.

"Later, about two or maybe three minutes, where that black spot was, the light come up: like you put up the match, you know, a spark went up, then it fall down on the east side. And I think that woman give me a sign she pass away. That black spot didn't move after that light pop up, fall down on east side.

"I went to bed, finally, but couldn't sleep, just roll and roll. So I build a fire.

"Next day, my uncle came and told me. 'Well, she pass away. I'll take your place so you can rest now,' he said.

"And when I got here to the house, my mother told me to go to Zuni, check up on my brother. So I went down there. They ask me if I see anything on the night that lady passed away.

" 'No, until the next night, and then I saw the light,' I said.

" 'Probably that was notifying you that she pass away,' that's what they told me.

"Then I told my grandfather about it and my grandpa said, 'Well, it's not right, but I think I'll take you over there, where you saw that light. We'll put it in the Indian way and try to protect you, or save you,' that's what the Old Man, my grandpa, said.

"So we came up here, and next day went over there, where I saw that light. Then we put that cornmeal and turquoise and coral, we put it all in there. Well, probably for that reason, nothing's been happening to me, yet.

"Let's go back now," he said abruptly, and the three of us walked down below to his house.

It was threatening to rain again, and there was a growing sense of the need to rush, insofar as Zunis are capable of rushing. Try to imagine a relaxed rush.

As the early big drops began to fall, Tola and the grandchildren walked down to the gardens to get some things for us to take back home. Then, as we climbed into the car and reversed to turn around, Dennis saw that the rain was quite heavy further down the road.

"Goodbye for now," he yelled, "but we might be back in five minutes." Everyone laughed.

The ride down was easier than the ride up, even though it was raining hard, because now we knew where the soft spots were. When we hit the pavement Dennis turned left, heading for Ramah, where we would spend the night. We stopped at the Johnson Guest Ranch, which, like most of the local businesses, was owned by Mormons. The Johnsons were a wonderful family, though they had their problems, especially with their sons-in-law. The last one had tried to burn the family auto business to the ground.

Dennis was offered, and accepted, a Margarita. But he was alert, so that if the doorbell sounded we should tuck our drinks under the flowery flounces of the sofa. The community was "Jack Mormon"; many people drank but none of them wanted to be caught drinking. Dinner consisted of baked potatoes, broccoli, and steak—all with only a whisper of either salt or pepper. As the grandmother in the family put it, "If you can taste spice, then you've used too much."

The conversation focused on our mutual friends, Hapiya and his family. We were regaled with stories of how they were "model Americans," always managing to pay off their debts, or if they couldn't, for some unexpected reason, they sent over one of their kids to work at the grocery store or gas station till they were clear. For that matter, most Zunis were pretty good about debts, except perhaps for Old One-O-One and his Navajo in-laws. Navajos were the biggest problem, the Johnsons reported; many of them were on the food stamps, and whenever they weren't they'd take out a loan and make the first payment, but by the time of the second payment the whole family, except for a poor old blind grandma or grandpa, would split for Mexican Hat or some other remote area on the Big Reservation. It was easier to do business with the local Zunis and the dirt-poor farmers from Texas and Oklahoma; they were hard workers who needed the credit and were good for the finance charges.

On and on they complained about problems in wheat farming—the investment in land and machinery, pests, weather; about running a gas station—how hard it was to find good people to work, how help stole from you. . . . Until the daughters, in self-defense, started swapping Navajo taboos.

Did you know that if you sleep too much you'll get spots on your face?

No. But if you leave your shoes under your pillow when you go to sleep you'll have nightmares.

If you sleep with a dog you'll have stomach trouble.

If you chew your fingernails you'll go broke.

If you let a baby's head stay to one side in the cradleboard too long, it'll have a wide head.

Don't eat with your hat on, or you won't get full.

Don't eat chicken, you'll get boils.

Don't eat twin corn ears, you'll have twins.

Don't eat frog, you'll get bad breath.

We took our leave and walked back to the cinder-block motel, where we found a small, modest, but spotless room. The only curious thing about it was the ceiling over the bed: a former guest had used it for target practice, shooting out a deer silhouette so precise that we could count the number of tines on each antler.

Before falling asleep, Dennis jotted down notes concerning Hapiya's strange ideas about property ownership, and typed the following observations in his field notes:

AUGUST 13, 1968 (cont.)   P. 1477

Some of my wife's comments about this day are worth noting. She finds the Zunis (or at least my families) to be a very sensual people, and that strikes me as correct: one can be sensual, after all, without being Dionysian about it; this is an easygoing sensuality, expressed, for example, in the fondling of small children and in the slow savoring of even the simplest meal. She also noted that children spent most of the day in the company of adults: they didn't go off by themselves; she contrasted this with the situation of the Western child, who has a whole world of his own from which adults are excluded. I think that the contrast is a valid one, though down in the village children do spend some of their time in play groups. Certainly Zuni adults, for their part, do not enforce a separation of worlds: I don't think I've ever heard a Zuni order a child "to go out and play."

The next morning, when we drove back to the village to take our leave of Sadie, she dashed into a back room, then returned holding a gorgeous ring: a robin's-egg-blue gemstone set in a silver bezel surrounded by twisted wire and small balls of silver, called "raindrops." As she slipped it gently on my finger she told me that it had won first prize in last year's Gallup Ceremonial. I grasped her hands, softly, acknowledging her gift with the one Zuni word I knew, "Elahkwa/*Thanks*," then abruptly turned away, afraid to show her my tears. None of my Albuquerque in-laws had given me anything at all to remember them by, and here this wonderful Zuni woman, who had only just met me, gave me a prize-winning ring! I was entranced, emotionally tied to Sadie and her family; I could leave the pueblo, of course, whenever I wished, but I knew I would always return.

SHEEPHERDING DAYS

■ ■ ■ ■

SAUNTERING OVER FROM THE SHEEP PENS in the harsh winds of late March, Hapiya gently touched our hands, grinned, and said, "Thought you two might come earlier today and help out in the fields." We'd been living in Berkeley, California, for more than a year and had moved back to Santa Fe, New Mexico—for good, we hoped.

"Sorry, Old Man, but I've got a mess of fleece-strings and some Emps branding liquid for you," replied Dennis.

"Good, at least Kyamme does what I want him to," he said, casting a meaningful look at Kwinsi, his eldest son, who shrugged. Hapiya brought up the subject of the drought, saying that the Navajos must have known it was going to be bad, since they hadn't bothered to plant anything. He'd planted his corn, early as usual, so if it didn't rain soon, there wouldn't be much of a harvest. Dennis suggested that the weather might change and Hapiya replied that some people can really dream the way it's going to happen.

One time, late at night, he dreamed he saw an old, old man with long white hair, pure white. He was walking in handmade moccasins, bent over with a cane, shaky, wearing a bright-red headband, carrying a basketful of prayer sticks. The old man stopped, stood there right in front of him, and he recognized him, Leonard's father. He had passed away some time ago. He told him his son had changed, quit the hard drinking and carrying on. Returned to the old ways, you know, dancing with his group and healing in his society, that Ant Medicine group. Then he felt kind of a cool breeze, heard wind in the junipers, smelled piñon pines, and woke up. It was all cloudy, so he went outside to see if it was raining, but it wasn't.

After a moment's pause he smiled and pushed open the screen door, and we entered the house. A handsome young male sparrow hawk, the American kestrel, skittered out from under Albert's iron cot, and across the bumpy linoleum floor. Tola picked him up and placed him gently on Ramona's clenched fist, stroking his head. He beat his wings wildly, shrilling "killy-killy-killy-killy," and pecked at her wrist. When he stopped flapping Ramona said, "K'okshi tsililik'o/*Handsome sparrow hawk*," and presented him to me. I gasped and drew back in shock.

I had heard that bird lice caused histoplasmosis, a disease affecting the lymph nodes of the trachea and bronchi. But since I had clearly shown an interest in the hawk, I decided to be a sport and clenched my right fist, holding it thumb up, as I had seen on the television series *Nature*. The bird stepped gingerly onto my fist and pecked once, experimentally. Gazing at this falconers' delight—with black-and-white face, blue-gray crown and wings, whitish underparts, rust back and tail—I tried to stroke his head, but at the sound of an arriving pickup, he leapt to the floor and darted under the bed.

Through the open door I studied the strange pickup; it was a brown camper-back with narrow red pin-striping, gun rack, Roswell tags, and a bumper-sticker proclaiming "SEMI-NATIVE." Two men, one young and one old, jumped down out of the cab and opened the screen door. Entering the low-beamed room, they removed their mahogany-brown felt hats and walked over in their tight jeans and pointy Tony Lama cowboy boots, with fancy initialed-silver toe caps, to shake hands with Hapiya.

Pumping his hand enthusiastically, the younger man said, "Buenos díííías, les de Dííííoooos. Cómo le va?" He had the slight drawl and singsong intonation that identified him as a native of northern Sonora, or possibly southern Arizona.

Dropping his hand, Hapiya replied flatly, in the standard Mexican Spanish he had picked up locally, "Muy bien y muy buenos días, amigos." Turning toward us, he said, "Kyamme, Tsilu,[1] may I present you my good friends Vicente and Ondelace?" We smiled, shyly, and shot out our hands for a stiff shake. Hapiya bowed, comically low, and introduced us as "just a couple of old friends, good friends, who drop round from time to time, an' we just talk and talk."

Tola immediately invited everyone to sit down and eat. Vicente replied, "No ma'am. Thaaaanks the same, we've already had our lonche. So now it's time for us to set up shop." Dennis shook his head—no, we weren't hungry either—and went back outside.

After wrestling their power shears and gasoline-engine generator out of the pickup bed, the shearers headed down for the ramada to install their electric motors, each with a dentist's drill-like arm. On one side was the corral with the mixed herd of rams, ewes, and hornless lambs. In the fence separating the corral from the adobe pen there was an opening covered by a big tarp, the sheep entrance and exit. Inside the ramada there was just

DENNIS TEDLOCK

room enough for six animals alongside the shearing platform. Ramona and Seff rounded up the rams. Whipping them with leather thongs and pelting them with pebbles, they drove them into the pen, packing them together tightly so that their warm bodies would sweat, making the shearing easier. When they were good and hot, Albert and Kwinsi waded into the bleating flock and separated them by earmarks, owner by owner, and began pushing them, one by one, down the narrow wooden chute. As the first one hit the platform Kwinsi grabbed him and wrestled him onto his back. The older shearer stepped up and rested his spit-polished calfskin boot on the ram's belly while Vicente moved through the curls with his electric shears, everywhere except under the horns, which he clipped by hand.

After the first wool clip rolled off in a soft mat, someone yelled "Uno!" and Hapiya inspected the job then gave the "Bueno!" As each sheep struggled onto its feet Vicente or Ondelace would kick it with contempt, saying, "Just like these foolish animals, these mocosas/*snivelers,* deserve." Then Albert and Kwinsi had to chase the sheep down and grab their legs, one on the front and one on the rear, as Hapiya yelled "Brand!" and Dennis ran over with the O-brand and a pan full of greenish-black paint. He stamped the backside, just in front of the tail, and let it go back, around, and into the corral.

Between brandings Hapiya talked to everyone, and to no one in particular. "I was raised to sheepherding. Got my start when I was just about like these here kids. I've been working on sheep nearly all my life now, since I started up. So I ought to know something 'bout sheep. It's hard work, this sheep business. You keep three or four bunches. Gotta know what you're doing in each bunch. You've gotta train the kids young, to work with the different bunches, because, the older they get, they don't want to be trained; start something else, maybe jewelry, instead of getting to be good shepherds. You might say that *all* Zunis would know how to handle sheep, but that is not the way. Very few are good shepherds, most are just ordinary Indians— Oh no. Damn!"

Vicente had slipped and nicked a ram on the abdomen. Work halted as Kwinsi pushed a clean cloth against the seeping blood vessel. Hapiya grabbed another cloth and wrapped the ram's belly up tight, hoping to stop the flow and prevent fatal hemorrhaging. Then, as he and Kwinsi held the kicking, bleating ram in their arms, he said, "My herd is a hunnerd and eight, if this one, his name is Sandy, lives. That's eight over my permit, but, then, Owen has four hunnerd head and no permit at all. He's as crooked as a dog's hind leg, but he's in tight with them BIA [Bureau of Indian Affairs] boys from Washington."

Dennis had heard him complain about the BIA boys before; how lazy they were, rarely coming round to evaluate an individual stockman to find out if he overgrazed and hurt the range or not. How, when they did come by, they didn't inspect the way they should, just made head counts and ordered any sheep over the permit to be taken off the range. How they didn't understand the Indian, thought they were all just alike. Not only had they tried to trim back his rams last year, but they said they wanted another horse sale. This was bad timing for him, since he'd traded three cows for six quarter horses, including a stud he'd planned to use to sire new workhorses, so Zuni farmers wouldn't be dependent on the Whiteman's tractors.[2] He liked his Massey-Ferguson all right, it was faster than the team, but it was always acting up, needing some part or other, and Albuquerque was a long ways off.

Dennis had also heard about Owen's oversized sheep herd and lack of a permit. But Hapiya never turned him in to the tribal government, since Owen's brother and wife are in his medicine society and, as he put it, "If I get after him, they might quit, and then the rest of my society would get after me." This was a perfect illustration of the sort of thing that holds Zuni together; even in secular politics a medicine society can be an important factor.

The ram's bleeding had slowed down, so Kwinsi wrapped him up in a couple of old towels, picked him up, and nestled him into a cardboard box in the corner of the corral. As the shearers restarted their machine Hapiya remarked, "You know them BIA boys with all the sugar talk 'bout helpin' the Indian progress and all? When they came round this spring I asked one, 'What about people? Sheep are just the same as people. You wouldn't go reduce people, now, would you? So why are you reducing sheep? They have as much right to live here on the reservation as people.' "

■ ■ ■ ■

It's not at all certain that the United States government wouldn't like to reduce people, most especially native people. Over the years numerous government policies have directly blocked Indian enterprise, while simultaneously encouraging "family planning."

The history of the current situation at Zuni began with the American invasion of New Mexico in 1846, when Washington became the official "guardian" of their lands. From that point on, government policies directly interfered with the subsistence base of the pueblo; this was the case even though Zuni warriors fought on the same side as United States troops against the Navajos and the Apaches. Not only did Congress fail to reward these loyal allies, but it allowed homesteading on pueblo lands. By 1877, when the reservation was established by presidential executive order, the land base had dwindled to a fraction of what was used in the past for subsistence. Zuni farmers and shepherds had to ignore the official reservation boundaries in order to provide for their people. At that time they were practicing a system of floodwater irrigation over a large area, cultivating more than ten thousand acres of corn. At this point herders were running nearly sixty thousand head of sheep, many of them off the reservation, but on traditional grazing lands. The government response to this Zuni economic enterprise was to allow more encroachment on their land. During the 1880s logging of millions of board feet of timber for the railroad left Zuni land completely denuded, followed by overgrazing and the construction of destructive dams and reservoirs.

In 1922 the Bursum Bill was introduced in Congress; its purpose was to settle the claims of nearly three thousand non-Indians living and ranching well within Pueblo Indian lands in

New Mexico. The bill proposed to turn all land conflicts between Pueblos and white settlers over to the state courts. It also provided that a survey showing the location of the contested lands would serve as proof that such land belonged to the white claimant, and gave no chance for a legal Indian defense.

Someone in Santa Fe's art colony caught wind of it, and realized that settling these claims might result in leaving the Pueblos destitute, with no land base at all. Indian delegations and women's clubs fought the bill, and won. The Federal Lands Board was established to settle claims. The worst offenders, who had stolen property by moving fences and driving cattle over Pueblo lands, were forcibly put off the land. But innocent intruders, who had paid someone, or whose parents had legally homesteaded on Pueblo lands, were permitted to stay.

Instead of returning any of the seized acreage to the tribe, the BIA, in 1934, built a fence around what was left of the reservation, and prevented Zunis from either farming or herding outside their boundaries. A sheep-reduction program was implemented in 1938; thousands of animals were rounded up by impoundment teams and either hauled to Gallup for sale or slaughtered and dumped in pits dug in the railroad right-of-way, where they were left to rot. At the beginning of the reduction there were just under twenty-six thousand sheep, and by the end there were only slightly more than eighteen thousand sheep. By 1942 some families had no sheep at all, while others retained several hundred. More recently the emphasis has shifted from stock reduction to land management.

The Department of the Interior published, in 1973, a report indicating that Zuni rangeland was overstocked by 23,678 AUMs, or the amount of forage necessary to graze one mature cow, with or without an unweaned calf at her side, for one month. In order to produce more pasture, it was necessary to get rid of the overstory of piñon, juniper, sagebrush, and rabbitbrush. The technique recommended for eradicating the overstory was "chaining." This procedure involves connecting two caterpillar tractors together by a single ship's anchor which is then pulled through the rangeland, wrenching out all trees and shrubs. Such open warfare on what are referred to in sacred songs and prayers as the arms and legs of "ho'naawan awitelin tsitta/*our four-chambered mother*" shocked and saddened many Zuni people.

Although massive chaining and stock reductions were protested by dozens of traditional farmers and religious leaders, including Hapiya, this policy, which bludgeoned both the Zuni psyche and economy, was nevertheless ruthlessly implemented on the reservation.

The initial cause of overgrazing, creating the perceived need for such violent solutions as slaughter and chaining, was land shortage created by government takeover and dispersal of Pueblo floodwater fields and grasslands to white homesteaders, squatters, and land speculators. Since this history is omitted altogether from government documents describing current conditions, readers are left to draw their own conclusions concerning Zuni ignorance or mismanagement of the range, rather than to ponder the possibility of BIA chicanery.[3]

■ ■ ■ ■

As the shearing continued Hapiya reminisced about how, when he was a herder, he grazed his sheep all around Ramah, in the area where the Mormons homesteaded. He saw very little of the village in those days, except during the school year. How he, his brother, and the other herders didn't know anything at all about tribal meetings and ritual doings, and they didn't even care. How they stayed out all summer and grew their hair so long they were embarrassed when they returned to school in the fall. How he was afraid of everything, but he liked being out like that, and how he's still that way.

"One time back in 1917 or 1915, when I was out herding with my brother, we ran out of flour.[4]

"My brother went after the flour and I stay alone with the sheep overnight. It was the first time in the history that I stay by myself.

"When I was having my supper, I heard somebody was crying, just next to where my camp was. Somebody was crying. The dog didn't even bark at all. Probably the dog didn't hear it. But this bone was crying. It was a bone. It was right close.

"So, I finish my supper. Take everything away and make a torch. I've got cedar barks. And I make the gun.

"Then I go round outside the camp to where it was crying. When I got there, it was a little further, the next tree; so, I walk over there. Kept going, kept going, kept going, kept going untiiiil I was about a mile off from the camp. I kept going, it was way late in night, daaark, cloudy that night with no stars, no moon, daaark. I could see where I was going with that torch, you know. I kept going and the crying was just ahead of me, maybe two yards from me.

"That's the way I thought until I got about two miles off from my camp. Then, when I got close to the arroyo, there was something like making a screeching sound, you know.

"When I got to the top of the arroyo, shine my light, a bone was sticking out from the arroyo, about that much [five inches]. Sticking out, you know, this bone, this one [shinbone]. It was oozing a little bit. Bubbles seeping out of a crack.

"I went down and beat that bone. I cussed hell out of that bone. Then I break it and come home.

"Next morning my brother came with flour. The sheep went out grazing around and my grandpa rode from Zuni to check up on us. Came on his burro with a sack of flour, coffee, sugar, cornmeal, from Zuni.

" 'How's the boys going?' he ask.

" 'Well, it's okay.'

" 'That's good.'

"Then he went around and checked the sheep, checked them out good to see how it was. Then I told him.

" 'That's not good, you should not go to the bone.'

" 'I broke that bone, destroyed that bone.'

" 'It's no good; probably your family, or probably my family, in the future, they all pass away.'

"Well, that's the Zuni way. About three years after that, it was really happen, my grandpa's whole family was disappeared. So that was it.

"Then, before this was happening, my grandpa, this same summer, we was herding down below in Number Three. It was around March, before we have lambs, and this thing happened too. My grandpa was with us and we was herding. Me and my brother was sitting on the side of the road, herding one side, you know. Our grandpa was on the other side.

"Back then we had about six or seven hunnerd sheep: well off. It was before them roundups, you know, before government reduced us.

"We got our dinner, cornmeal and paperbread; we were eating when two snakes came toward us, right together, next to each other. I told my brother, 'Look what's coming!'

"Just when he see them, they stand up, start fighting. They was all tangled up, fall down, stand up, tangled up, fall down. We was watching them there; we was interested in watching them.

"Our grandpa came along on the west side and saw snake tracks. Grandpa got mad, he scold us. 'You should have killed them instead of watching,' is what he told us.

"We were just interested on it, you know. We told him we were 'elumawikwa,' we liked to see them, we were delighted to see them, 'eluma,' you know.

" 'But that's danger too, someday your family will disappear,' that's what he told us.

"And it really did too. About four years later, all my folks disappeared. I was the only one that got left. You know, I got no sister, no brother, nothing. I'm the only one I've got left."

The shearers turned off their machines. Vicente untied his tobacco pouch and, fishing in his pocket for a Zigzag paper, joked about how it was "chupin' time," from Spanish chupar/*to suck*. When he had lit up he passed the pouch to Hapiya. After shaking out a bit of tobacco on a paper, squinting up at the hogback, Hapiya said he was keeping an eye on a golden eagle's nest on top, near the rock cairn. He was thinking of ways to get to it when the eaglets were big enough to steal, probably any day now. A couple of adults would climb up there and someone light would have to be lowered by rope onto the rock, probably one of his grandchildren.

Ramona volunteered and Seff gave her a bug-eyed look meaning, "You're crazy; just plain crazy!" Her grandfather examined her face carefully—her jaw was set and she was clearly confident—so he accepted her offer.

He carefully explained to her what her responsibilities were. She and her uncles would have to climb up on the hogback once or twice in order to peek over the ridge at the nest to check out the size of the eaglets. Be sure they were all feathered out, and strong enough to tear up their food. Otherwise, if they were still too dependent on their mother, when Ramona brought them down, they would die. When the two (eagles always hatch twins) were big enough, she would be lowered with a rope onto the rock. She should steal only the smaller eagle, the male, and leave the bigger one, the female, in the nest to carry on her family into the future.

When she brought the hatchling down below, Hapiya would build a chicken-wire cage, and Seff would hunt cottontails and meadowlarks to feed the baby eagle. Later, so Mr. Eagle would not be mean, Hapiya would chew a mixture of blue grama grass and rabbit dung and place it in Eagle's mouth as he prayed. From that time on, whenever anyone approached Mr. Eagle, they would have to greet him as a person, asking politely in Zuni, "How did you pass the night?"

Each year—in midsummer, when he molted—his feathers would be saved for dance masks, medicine wands, and prayer sticks. If they were lucky, he would live many years with them, as one of the family, and when he died, they would send him back to be reborn in Kachina Village, the Land of the Dead.

Ramona, who had listened carefully to everything her grandpa said about eagles, was grinning and skipping. Then, as the shearers reground their blades, Hapiya, Albert, Kwinsi, and Dennis rolled and tied fleeces. Ramona and Seff rounded up the rams.

Every now and then Hapiya threw a fleece to one side, saying, "Can't send any bloody ones back to Boston; they're strict, call me on it."

The good fleeces went into an eight-foot-long sack hung with nails from a wooden frame. Then, since wool is sold by weight, Albert took off his high-sided work boots and climbed down inside the sack, in his red-white-and-blue sweat socks, to stamp the wool down tight. As he stamped he sang about Old Lady Aatoshle, the cannibal ogress with her matted hair and blood-stained knife who hooks little children with a long crooked stick and carries them off in her backpack to eat.

Each time he disappeared down deep inside the long sack, leaving only his spread-open palm behind, he cried in a loud voice trailing off at the end, "Tísshomahháááááá!" Ramona

DENNIS TEDLOCK

shrieked with delighted terror. Seff quipped, "Kyamme, Tsilu, sacred hand. Hapasin lheyaye/*Dead man sticks his hand out,*" then giggled.

Ramona turned and, grabbing hold of my hand, started yelling wildly, "Pecho takit! Pecho takit! Pecho take hand!" Dennis obligingly got out his Minolta SR-T 101 and set a fast shutter speed to freeze the action.

Kwinsi came over to Seff, saying, "Asinn pacchi/*Hand on the face.* It's Elder Brother Anahoho with his bloody right hand.[5] Remember the one with a handprint on the front of the mask? They come together, elder and younger brothers, with the Salimopiya during initiation. They wear raven feathers, warning the people that something bad might happen. These two when they whipped you at initiation took away your bad luck."

Seff and Ramona jumped up and ran off to round up the herd.

Ramona patted each one fondly on the backside as she let them into the pen, calling out his or her name: "Good night, Mickey; good night, Thelma; 'night, Blacky; 'night, Spot; good night, Chief." Seff latched the wooden gate with a piece of rusted barbed wire and walked over hand in hand with Ramona.

As the hogback turned from candy orange to rose carnelian we walked back up to the house. Passing our battered Volvo (whose wrinkled roof was two inches lower than it had been before we'd rolled it in a freak snowstorm near Phoenix, Arizona), Albert noticed a broken tail light and asked, "Is that a bullet hole you two got when you were out witching?" We stared at one another, silently, and, since we didn't know how it happened, failed to respond.

Perhaps we should laugh and say something like, "Are you *kidding*?" But now, since we hadn't immediately responded, I suspected Albert was wondering about us.

I thought, But he couldn't think *that* of us, or could he? After all, we're Anglos and, since Anglos don't even believe that there are any witches, we couldn't actually *be* witches, or could we? Since we're also family in some sense, might we also be witches in some sense? With Albert, I just never knew what he was thinking.

Hapiya and Dennis settled into easy chairs for a chat as Ramona presented me with a platter of pork chops to carry over to the table. Once accepted into the family, a woman was always expected to help out. I walked over to the ancient icebox and got out the worn stainless-steel flatware, the milk-glass dishes and cups. Ramona brought out an overflowing plastic platter of re-warmed Kentucky Fried Chicken. This was followed by glass bowls filled with mutton stew, tamales, noodles, red-chile sauce, and green-chile sauce. Then bunches of scallions and radishes, watermelon, coffee, 7-Up, Orange Crush, Coke, Indian bread, Rainbo bread.

When the table was completely set, Tola called, "Itonaawe/ *Let's eat!*"

First came the mutton-and-bread offering to the dead: "Na-naakwe itonaawe/*Grandparents, let's eat.*" The first prayer a Zuni baby learns. Everyone fell silent. There was only the sound of chewing, followed by swallowing, until Vicente asked in Zuni, "Kulaantu?"

Tola suppressed a giggle as she motioned Ramona toward the kitchen. It sounded so strange to hear him saying the Zuni word rather than the Spanish "cilantro." But this ranch hand was no country bumpkin. He was clever, witty, smooth—a real pícaro who understood his clientele well enough to know that it didn't hurt any to show them a little respect. After all, he was charging a buck twenty-five a head for his services, when there were dozens of Anglo cowboys willing to do the job for ninety-five cents a head. He probably even spoke a few words of Ute at table when he was shearing up in Colorado.

Eating slowly, with his eyes down, Vicente chuckled appreciatively at the family's many little anecdotes. He was slick, his ramrod posture was the picture of Spanish bearing and manners at table, and there was a calculated grace in his every arm and hand motion. His hands were the whitest and softest I had ever seen; no wonder lanolin—wool grease—is used in all those fine soaps and hand creams.

I became so absorbed imagining Vicente's world that, while struggling to open my 7-Up, I spilled most of it on the floor. To save face, I laughed out loud and christened my silly puddle "Ky'ana Uncola/*Uncola Lake.*" Ramona leaned over, slowly up-ending her entire can of Orange Crush into the little lake.

I was sure Ramona would be scolded, but no, Tola and Hapiya were laughing and repeating over and over, "Tsilu an Ky'ana Uncola/*Auntie's Uncola Lake.*" Recovering from this bout with the giggles, the family fell silent until Vicente pronounced the Zuni words "k'ola muwe/*tamale,*" literally *chile bread,* as he bit into a lovely fat one. Tola tittered, and he turned to his partner, gently chiding him for not smiling and barely eating. Then he stood up and, tugging his partner by the arm, thanked the old lady for her fine meal and banged out the screen door, down the hill to their camper-back.

It was a warm evening, so as soon as we women got the remaining food put away and the dishes off the table the entire family wandered outside, around behind the house, where we sat on army-surplus ammunition cases. Old Man talked about the details of house construction utilizing these novel materials. It was simple, really, to build a lean-to: why, the Navvies had even figured out how to make whole grenade-crate hogans!

First, each crate had to have the lid detached from one end, a steel bar yanked out of it, and two strips of wood (the feet on which it rested) removed from one side. This left rectangular blocks to be laid end to end in overlapping courses and nailed

DENNIS TEDLOCK

together. Nelson, who had recently joined the family when he married Hapiya's eldest daughter, Lena, had been there earlier in the week, with his post-hole digger, planting three huge round wooden posts parallel to the back wall of the house. And in another week or two, when the walls were higher, Dennis, with his six feet two inches, would help place the rafters across the tops of the posts.

Tola glanced at me, smiled, and then, in a low voice, pointing with her lips in the direction of the partially constructed lean-to, said, "Your bed can be right over there."

Kwinsi jumped up, climbed into his "cowboy Cadillac," a beat-up metallic-blue Chevy half-ton pickup, and headed back to his family in the village. Moments later, when Hapiya and Dennis went inside to chat, Albert spit on the ground between his square-toed boots, then headed for his cot to finish reading his Wonder Woman comic book. He explained that it was *Revolt of the Wonder Weapons,* narrated by Red Tornado, an emotionless android.

> *Diana Prince has demonstrated the dynamic determination to succeed, the unflagging self-confidence that make her a—Wonder Woman—so imagine her astonishment and bewilderment when she found that determination undermined as one-by-one, she lost control of her amazing Amazon arsenal! First her magic lasso was destroyed, then her robot plane rebelled against her thought-command and fell into the East River. And the man behind it all was the evil astrologer Celestris Ormaon, who had captured her mental determination for his mento-amplifier. . . .*

Tola and her granddaughters were standing there, with me, in the dust-dry darkness when the Owners of the Night arrived: swooping and squealing their evening rounds, dozens of them, with foot-wide wingspans. The giggly little girls moved in close, very close to me. Ramona and Sila were the same age, but Elaine, at four, was only half as old.

I was tired, so I decided to calculate the size of the bat flight, but I kept losing count whenever Ramona reached over and pinched, pulled the hair of, or kicked little Elaine. I didn't know if I should say anything or not and I became anxious, but since Tola was nearby I decided that, if anything had to be said, Grandma would certainly be the most appropriate one to do so.

"You speak Zuni, don't you?" Ramona asked me, sharply.

"Yes, well, some, but I'm still learning," I replied softly, while ducking as a bat divebombed a June beetle.

"Okay, I test you: eshotsi."

"That's easy: bat."

"Halhikwi."

"Witch."

"Wrong. A ghost," piped up little Elaine.

"Tsilu was right," said Ramona, firmly. Then added, after pulling Elaine's ponytail and kicking her shin, hard, "Silly, don't you know hapa is a ghost?"

"Isn't hapa also a skull or skeleton?" I asked, as a bat squeaked, nearly colliding with me.

"Yes, and skinny people are hapa too," Sila replied, ducking.

"Owl," screamed Ramona.

"The horned kind is muhukwi," I replied.

"What's the other one?" called out Elaine.

"A burrowing owl is huuts'uk'i."

"What's the Zuni word for 'window'?" asked Ramona.

" 'Asho'wanne.' "

Sila and Elaine laughed and laughed at my reply, while Ramona sang out, "You said something dirty, Tsilu. Something dirty."

I repeated, "Asho'wanne, asho'wanne, asho'wanne." I was determined to get it right.

They laughed and squealed with delight.

Then slowly and deliberately, with emphasis on the first syllable, I said, "Ash-sho'wanne."

Sila laughed.

But Ramona, who was always straight about such things, said, "No, she got it right that time, 'ash-sho'wanne.' "

I had finally realized my mistake. "Window" had a long, or double, "sh" sound, "ash-sho'wanne," and I had been saying it short, "asho'wanne," which sounds like "vagina."

It was Sila's turn. "What's the boy part?"

"That's easy: 'tu'linne,' " I replied, then ducked.

"Is he your boyfriend?" Ramona whispered, pointing in the direction of the house with her rounded lips.

"No, he's my husband."

"Are you two married?"

"Yes."

"Do you have any children?"

"No."

"Do you have any babies?"

"No."

"Well, do you fuck?"

The girls discussed at length, in Zuni, whether we did or didn't. We had stayed down in the village dozens of times, slept right out in the center of the big room, but there was never a sound, not even with that squeaky fold-out sofa. Perhaps we were very quiet.

Sila and Elaine finally decided we did, while Ramona maintained that we didn't.

Elaine then asked me sharply, "Why don't you live with your mother?"

"Because people like us don't stay with our mothers once we're grown up. We go out and get our own apartments right away."

"Must be real lonesome."

"I don't know. Maybe it is. But I don't remember feeling lonesome."

"Did you have a long white dress when you got married?" inquired Ramona.

"No, when we decided to get married we were down in Guadalajara, Mexico, and I didn't have a long white dress with me. It was summer, you see, and we were traveling, so I wore a short red sun dress."

Ramona unexpectedly thrust out her right fist and slowly opened her palm, revealing, in the dim light from the doorway, a hot-pink button. In the center of the button was a crimson heart proclaiming "P. S. I LOVE YOU!"

I smiled, gave the little girl a big hug, and pinned it on the cotton change pouch dangling from my black leather belt.

Albert leaned out the window. "If you girls don't come in

right away them lice that live on bats will drop all over the place an' crawl all over you, into your ears, into your eyes, into your nose, into your mouth, everywhere."

When we went inside Tola sent the girls off to bed. In the kitchen, they changed into their pajamas and slippers, then scampered across the room. But by the time Tola tucked them in they had removed not only their slippers but also their pajama bottoms, and were tickling each other under the covers.

As Dennis and I were leaving, Ramona leaned out of the big double bed next to the front window, giggling uncontrollably while singing out gleefully after us:

Good night love.

Good night sweet heart.

Good night Tsilu.

Good night darling.

Good night Kyamme.

Good night.

Night.

3

WHITEMAN'S WITCHCRAFT

■ ■ ■ ■

ONE MORNING IN MID-APRIL, setting out together from Ts'u'
Yalanne/*Shell Mountain,* or Santa Fe, heading south and west out
of town, coming down La Bajada hill, we got caught in a dust
devil; around Laguna Pueblo, big-drop rain; from Striped Rocks
to the little Mormon village of Ramah, fog; from there on into
Zuni, the season's final snowstorm.

As we drove rapidly into the headlighted flakes Shawiti
quipped, "Wow! Now, that sure would be something else, something special, if it were all different colors!"

Dennis held on tight to the wheel as we fishtailed into the
center of the village. At Sadie's we were given a much warmer
welcome than usual, probably because we had thought to call
ahead, for a change, warning her of our visit.

We found a house full of visitors, including Sadie's parents,
her sisters with their husbands, and her younger brother Charlie,
who'd come all the way from Los Angeles. Talk centered on the

difficulties of the space mission. Hapiya let it be known right off that he, for one, didn't think much of the project.

"What the heck are they going up there for anyway? Just to help the ones that go up there get rich, or what? And look at all the poor people down here in these United States."

According to television news, Apollo 13 had safely returned the day before (April 17, 1970) after a near-disaster. The mission had been forced to turn back to earth before reaching the moon after an oxygen tank exploded aboard the service module, ripping off one whole side of the spacecraft. But according to Hapiya the astronauts were forced to turn back to earth when the Moon Mother got mad and threw dirt and rocks at them.

Hapiya's logic, as usual, was impeccable. Witches travel in whirlwinds at the center of dust storms.[1] The entire NASA Space Program is white witchcraft; therefore, the Apollo 13 astronauts who turned back toward earth, causing whirlwinds, were also witches. And witches are harbingers of the coming of death to the world, a time when all of our man-made things—hoes, axes, drills, anvils, pliers, hammers, knives, forks, guns, cars, trucks, rockets, wagons, blenders, toasters, lamps, washing machines, radios, televisions, typewriters, and computers—will revolt, the moon and stars will fall, and we'll all be boiled to death in a hot rain.

Ever since the LEM (lunar excursion module) of Apollo 11 went down Space Highway 1, and Neil Armstrong and Buzz Aldrin opened the hatch to begin their extravehicular activity, stepping out onto the surface of the moon, Zunis had been dealing with this new threat to their religious beliefs. If what the television cameras recorded was true and not merely a studio fiction, then the Moon Mother, who together with the Sun Father is the ultimate source of all light and life, had been violated by two crew cuts in a metal space capsule. Not only did these men fail to practice sexual abstinence and make offerings of jeweled cornmeal and prayer feathers before they visited the Moon Mother, but they tramped around on her, planting a TV camera, seismometer, mirror array, solar-wind detector, and a permanently curled plastic American flag in her body. And then, just before departing, they removed nearly fifty pounds of soil and rock, her sacred flesh, without offering her so much as a prayer.

Hapiya pointed out that Buzz, who was described by the television commentators as the religious one, had prayed all right, but it was for the "challenge" and "opportunity" of the moon mission, not for the life of the Moon Mother. Such profane acts could spell the end of the Moon Mother's gifts to humankind; perhaps she, like Salt Woman and Turquoise Man before her, would move farther away, causing serious repercussions.[2] If Old Lady Salt could simply get up and move forty-five miles south of the pueblo, where she is today, what might our Moon Mother do?

Loooong ago, when Turquoise Man came to visit Old Lady Salt, he told her that where he used to live he was of no value. His flesh was simply given out to women for sexual favors. Old Lady Salt said, "I am also too near my people to be of any value. Young women and young men, when they come to gather my salt, befoul my body; it hurts me. I will go far way and then, when they have a difficult time finding me, they will always love me. I've made up my mind; I am going south."

When Turquoise Man asked her if he could go along with her she replied, "Yes, you may come part way with me. But then which way will you go?"

"Toward the east," he said.

"Good, then let us both run away and the people will surely be sorry."

But before she left her sacred home, near the village, she gave the spring to the Frog clan[3] to take care of for all the Zuni people.

The Twin War Gods, when they heard her plans, said, "Mother, if you go far from here, you will be of much greater value, and we will follow you." The next day, together with her friend Turquoise Man, Old Lady Salt left Black Rock. They assumed the forms of golden eagles and soared off together southward. Not long after flying away, Old Lady Salt struck a projecting rock and passed through it all the way to the other side, leaving a large jagged opening known as A'su'wa/*Pierced Rock*. Just beyond this place she dropped a pure white plume which, as it stood upright on the ground, instantly petrified, becoming a sacred shrine.

These beautiful sandstone monuments can be seen today on the reservation, exactly as she created them there so very long ago. Just as Salt Woman and Turquoise Man long ago removed their precious gifts from the reservation, so the Moon Mother, after being robbed of her flesh, would probably move farther away. If so, she could cause extreme cold, droughts, or floods, and women would no longer have babies.

The Apollo 14 and 15 missions would remove even more of the Moon Mother's flesh, and leave two more banks of cylindrical mirrors on her body. These were for the benefit of earthbound scientists who would bounce laser beams off her, in order to measure continental drift and the earth's wobbling axis.

Could Zuni religion, whose most basic obligation is monthly offerings of cornmeal and feathers to the Sun Father and the Moon Mother, survive the unwanted mass-media initiation of the pueblo into the profane cult of the conquest of space?

Perhaps yes.

Perhaps no.

Beginning with Russia's launching of Sputnik I, in October of 1957, the world's first artificial satellite, the Neweekwe Medicine Society clowns had added space burlesque to their repertoire.

DENNIS TEDLOCK

In an early skit a clown with a cardboard box around his waist, shaped and painted to look like a satellite, had gone into orbit and circled the village several times before crashing in the main plaza and rolling over dead before a long line of masked dancers.

Another afternoon, an astronaut clown climbed up on the tallest building in the Old Pueblo and, making a round ball out of himself, was tossed aloft in a blanket by a group of clowns.

When he landed in the plaza below, he was surrounded by clowns bearing a stretcher. They hauled him over near the central kiva[4] to a group of nurses and doctors, who examined him carefully with their stethoscopes, pounded him all over with their rubber hammers, took his blood pressure, made him pee into a paper cup, gave him a series of shots in both arms and buttocks with a giant hypodermic syringe, then asked him what it was like on the moon. He reported that there were people, animals, mountains, volcanoes, lakes, and watermelons—all to howls of laughter.

Over and over again clowns dressed as satellites, rockets, and astronauts ran madly around the village, threw one another into the air, and fell off roofs. Finally, in a wonderfully risqué skit, a clown from Houston Control telephoned the moon to talk with "The Man in the Moon Mother." Audiences laughed and laughed at the absurdity of space exploration: it was a fiction, a silly joke, a lie.

Even so, some Zunis, mostly young men, wondered aloud whether the Moon Mother really was a deity. Perhaps the Whiteman was right after all, and she was only another dead object spinning around in space.

When Hapiya called space exploration "Whiteman's witchcraft," Shawiti jumped up, lit a cigarette, and silently paced the room. After a while he took us into the next room to show us his track ribbons—all neatly framed, glassed, and hung on the wall.

"Do you also participate in kick-stick races?" I asked.

"Oh yeah, but that's different. That's on the side of those two little War Gods. There's a devotion on that side with shrines, prayers, and offerings. Track is just for fun, a sport, you know."

"Looks like you're pretty good at it."

"All us Zuni guys are. I guess it's because we participate on the warriors' side, and our thoughts are on that side, in the right direction—you know, tsemaa k'okshi/*good thoughts,* as we say."

"Have you ever thought about running in a marathon?" Dennis asked.

Taking a long drag and blowing a big circle above his head, Shawiti replied, "Well, maybe, but, you know, I'm smoking now instead of running."

What could I say? "Oh, that's too bad." Or how about, "Have you tried giving it up?"

I rejected both, feeling that they sounded stupid, even offensive, since running, smoking, and the moon are all sacred topics at Zuni. And although I knew enough not to try to chitchat as though I were at a family barbecue in Albuquerque with Dennis' sister's son, I simply didn't know how to talk about such things with my Zuni nephew.

Staring at the new wall assemblage located above the sink, next to the track ribbons, I caught my face in the mirror at the center with two glassed-over pictures on either side of it. On the right, a full-color magazine illustration of a ten-point buck startled by headlights on a dark highway. On the left, an ancient tinted Sacred Heart of Jesus with a small cartooned green monster, her name, "Isabelle," pasted across the top.

My taut face in the mirror with the illustrations on either side formed a triptych held together by a banged-up gilt-wooden frame. A small wooden rack was nailed to the bottom. Below were five brass cup hooks, each with a dangling, individually colored toothbrush.

Tola shouted from her kitchen, "Itonaawe," and I whispered to Dennis, "Thank God it's time to eat."

We sat down at the oval dinette table with Hapiya and Tola on the plastic-covered aluminum chairs, across from our nephew Shawiti and uncle Charlie. Dinner consisted of posole, fresh roast leg of venison, mint jelly, barbecued mutton, boiled summer squash, pinto beans, small conical piles of the body of Old Lady

Salt, scallions, green chiles, yellow jalapeño peppers, Indian sourdough bread, sugary coffee with Carnation evaporated milk, a flatbread of whole wheat and caramelized sugar on a corn husk, watermelon and cantaloupe slices, and Twinkies.

Taking a small chunk of mutton and tossing it into the blazing juniper logs in the adobe fireplace, I said, "Nanaakwe itonaawe/ *Grandparents, let's eat.*" Passing the food around, I was careful not to take too much. A bite of posole, chewing slowly, oh so slowly, deeply, deliberately, keeping my eyes down. Then a chunk of venison: slowly, slowly. Whenever someone wanted something, he or she named it in Zuni, and it was passed on down. A tablespoon of mint jelly, a bite of mutton, a spoonful of pinto beans, one by one, each dish separately, a pause after each one.

Whenever I looked up and caught someone's eyes, I looked away, and slowed down. I was still having trouble properly pacing my eating.

Nearly two hours later the young men stood up, went into the bedroom, and bundled up their masks, moccasins, and feather boxes. In came the second family group, consisting of Ramona, her uncles, Albert and Kwinsi, her aunt Flora, her parents, Sadie and Sabin, her mother's eldest sister, Lena, and Lena's husband, Nelson. The first group retired to the warmth of the potbellied wood stove in the next room. Settling down in the ancient upholstered chairs covered with multicolored Mexican serapes and stuffed toys, they chatted about the upcoming evening of kachina dancing.

Then, as the boys departed to costume themselves for the dance, Charlie spoke to us over his shoulder. "See you guys later. We've got to go play Indian now."

Hapiya, who smiled at hearing one of his own favorite lines from the lips of his son, pulled out his bag of wild tobacco and hand-rolled a cigarette. After taking a deep drag, he blew the smoke out westward toward Kachina Village, the Land of the Dead.

"There'll be lots of dances tonight: Apaches, Hopi Harvest, Old Mixed Animals, clowns, and other masks."

Getting up from his chair, he walked over to his daughter's dresser and, while looking at us over his left shoulder through her vanity mirror, explained that he and Tola had been in the village for ten days now because a woman in his medicine society had died. It had been his job to take apart the mi'le, or personal icon, that she had received at initiation, releasing her pinanne/ *breath* or *spirit,* by making prayer sticks with the macaw, eagle, duck, blue jay, and songbird feathers. She had been depending on him to free her, so that she could travel eastward over to the shrine of Shipaapuli'ma in the Sandia Mountains. There, since she had been practicing for more than twenty years as a sucking doctor, she would be reincarnated as a black bear. Later, if she were accidentally killed as a bear, she would travel back west all the way out to Kachina Village, where she would be reincarnated as a deer, or perhaps an antelope.

Lifting a red-flowered silk scarf out of the top drawer and folding it diagonally into a two-inch-wide band, he tied it around his head with a big bow over his right ear. Reaching into a cardboard box under the bed, he pulled out a long cloth-wrapped bundle, the mi'le he had received at his own initiation many years ago, and said, "Well, see you guys later. It's time for me to go to my society; I'm the one that holds the song string tonight."

He shut the door but then quickly reopened it, saying, "Ulohnan uteya k'ohanna pottiye/*The world is filled with white flowers.* Kyamme/*Uncle,* Tsilu/*Aunt,* it's snowing! Guess my prayers are already working. See you guys later on."

Dennis and I went out to visit some of the dance houses. Next door we were invited by the hosts into their side room and offered rich hot chocolate in glass mugs, with gobs of whipped cream on top.

hissing snow against glass
stomping of muddy boots on linoleum
crackling Juniper blaze
clanking cowbells
rattling deer hooves on turtle shells
bones rasping along wood
pulsing pottery drums
screeching flutes
lightning-gourd rattles
sleigh bells

Listening carefully to the words and failing to recognize a single one of them, I remembered hearing that, although some medicine songs are sung in Zuni, the most powerful and dangerous ones are sung in Keresan. They are memorized verbatim, and neither the performers nor the audience know what the lyrics mean, only that they refer to the curing knowledge of the eastern pueblos, which is respected to the point of fear.[5]

Song upon song overlapped as medicine men summoned in the beast priests and game animals from their six sacred directions: mountain lion and mule deer (north), bear and mountain sheep (west), badger and antelope (south), wolf and white-tailed deer (east), eagle and jackrabbit (zenith), shrew and cottontail (nadir).[6] There were clowns yelling and dashing about, masked dancers pushing words through long leather teeth and lacquer-red tongues, incredibly high-pitched deer calls, car horns, a softly playing transistor radio, laughing, whispering, munching of piñon nuts and corn chips, and plenty of requests for encore after encore.

We left the house where Hapiya's medicine society was supposed to be performing. From outside we heard a flute and looked in the window; there he was, blowing into a yellowed eagle bone, looking right at us. He opened his eyes wide, showing white all around, and tilted his flute up; then, as he raised his little finger off the fourth hole, dozens of Mixed Animal dancers—Mountain Sheep, Deer, Antelope, Bear, Bees, Turkeys, Cows, Yucca Pods, Lizards, Open Sleeves, and Echo Old Man, together with a handful of traders and schoolteachers—entered the house.

It was so crowded we didn't want to try to push our way in. After sloshing around the pueblo in the snow, we decided to return to Sadie's to dry off and warm up.

There, in the second room from the front door, were our nephews, Albert, Joe, and Charlie, together with Ramona and her two-year-old brother, Ray. The men were in full costumes; however, when we saw that they had removed their masks, we hesitated a moment. Perhaps we shouldn't see them like this. But Joe emphatically invited us to enter, saying, "Keshshé/*Helló*. Píkwayí/*Páss on ín*."

I noted that Charlie had a woman's blanket dress draped around him and fastened onto his left shoulder, a string of small sleigh bells around his waist, gobs of streaky orange clay and goose bumps all over his body, fringed leggings, and red buckskin moccasins. On the arm of his chair was the bumpy orange helmet mask of Haatashuku, the Laguna Mudhead clown. Each tiny knob on the mask, filled with clay from the riverbank at Kachina Village, was tied shut with a hand-spun dirty cotton string that ended with a fluffy turkey breast feather.

Albert and Joe had salmon-red body paint with burnt-yellow racing spots, sweet-smelling bandoleers of Rocky Mountain juniper bark and berries, embroidered kilts, woven sashes, black woolen hose covered with hanks of multicolored yarn, and red moccasins. On the floor before them sat Crazy Grandchild helmet masks with topknots of yellow-and-orange parrot feathers tied at the crossroads of four large stiff turkey feathers, each one tipped with a tiny downy eagle breast feather. This is the only mask that has stiff turkey feathers. The reason for it is recorded in a Zuni myth.

Once, long ago, a young Crazy went out hunting turkeys every night while the people slept.[7] He was having fun and just left the turkeys where they fell, never bringing them into the house and properly blessing them. Until, one day, Pawtiwa, the chief of Kachina Village, found out.

"Oh, what a wicked thing you have done. Turkey feathers are our clothing," he said.

Then he punished the boy, telling him, "Since you've hurt the turkeys you'll always wear ugly feathers, stiff turkey feathers that no one else cares for."

Although I had seen Crazy Grandchild masks before and had even painted one from memory, I was impressed by the individuality and sophistication of the artistry. Albert's mask had delicately drawn, beautifully painted bucks, does, and fawns romping in a forest glade, chasing butterflies, and jumping over rainbows. Joe's mask had a field of flowering twigs and meadow flowers with hummingbirds, bumble bees, and butterflies landing, feeding, and taking off. Both masks had dragonflies and tadpoles flying over and swimming up the back.

These particular masks were so extraordinary that I wondered if their artistically talented sister, Flora, hadn't painted their masks for them. But I knew I could never ask her about it, since men are the only ones who officially "know how" to paint kachina masks.[8] But I was sure it was Flora's work, because I had seen an inlaid pin of hers with a Crazy Grandchild mask design closely resembling those on her brothers' masks.[9] In fact, these two masks were among the most complex, colorful, dynamic, exciting examples of Zuni artistry I had ever seen.

The maskers were drinking Yalaa Ky'awe/*Mountain Water,*

Coors, and immediately offered us some. We hesitated, thinking about the possible consequences. Since the reservation was officially dry, we could be fined for drinking here. Also, although we were relatives, of sorts, we were also Melika/*Americans,* and thus not allowed to stand this close to masked dancers, let alone take a beer break with them.

Worst of all, I thought, since little Ray was not yet initiated into the Kachina Society, he wasn't supposed to know that the group of ancestors and nature spirits called kachinas (an Anglicization of the Hopi term "katcina," or "kokko" in Zuni) do not really visit the village, but that his own father, uncles, and brothers impersonate them.[10] If an officer of the Kachina Society were to walk in while they had their masks off, we could be accused of revealing the secret to Ray. And the punishment for this indiscretion is supposed to be having your head cut off by Big Knife.

Looking at each other in that "so now we've really done it" way, Dennis and I slowly examined our nephews. They seemed quite calm, even pleased, and clearly wanted us to be impressed. So, we each grabbed a Coors.

As we popped the tops Albert blurted out, "If any of the dance leaders see you stagger, or smell your breath, they'll wait outside a house and beat the hell out of you. And if they don't catch you, the mask will."

"Yeah," Joe replied. "Did you hear about that old-timer last winter dancing the Hilili? Got muffled up in his mask. Got pasted on. Stuck to his face. They had a hard time taking it off. He died that same night. He was wearing that Heemushiikwe/*Jemez People* mask—you know, the board-on-the-head mask—and when a younger guy tried to dance with it, there was still some skin from that other guy inside.[11] That mask almost got him too."

"You just got to believe in your religion, or the mask takes you," said Charlie, giving Joe a meaningful look. "Did you hear about the guy who was practicing to wear the Huututu mask at Shalako? He told his kiva buddies he thought they were just wasting their prayer sticks. The day after planting his feathered sticks, he went out to his fields and found them still there, showing that the kachinas didn't really come to get the feathers. Then, the following day, when he was out cultivating his corn, he fell into a dream, or something, I guess. A rattlesnake spoke to him, telling him that he would die four days after Shalako.

"He started swelling up all over his body. By opening day he couldn't dance. Late that night he told his society father that he was bitten by a rattlesnake. They called in a lightning-struck doctor, but it was too late. He couldn't be saved. Four days after Shalako he died."

"Those masks cause you to dream all right," replied Joe.

"You know, one thing I've always wondered, when you guys wear your masks, do you *become* the kachina?"

Joe replied immediately, "No, Tsilu. You don't, really, become one. You imitate, impersonate, step into it. You make your mask come alive. You make him into a living, dancing, singing ho"i/*person*, a ky'apin ho"i/*raw person*, you know. Otherwise, a mask is just sitting there, sleeping, till you get in there. The mask doesn't come over to you. No, you have to go in there. Then he'll move. You become part of it, but not *really*, because your body will be the same, but just the head, you know, your thoughts."

"You have to be initiated to wear masks, and when they initiate you, they whip you *hard*, it really hurts," said Charlie.

Albert elaborated this for Ray's benefit. "In a couple of years or so it's initiation time for you. That's when those Salimopiya and Anahoho whip you with their long yucca blades. Blood runs down your back. And blood runs down your legs. You hardly can walk away. I just don't know why it don't break the little kids' backs."

Ray flinched.

Joe called attention to the beauty of his costume, saying, "In every house I was smiling at the women through my mask. And some of them smiled back," he said, winking at me.

I already knew that he was concerned with impressing women—I had heard it all before, from his older brother Kwinsi. For that matter, all kachina dancers seemed to be. And Zuni women do indeed turn their heads for certain young men, whispering to one another about their legs or rears. There was no doubt about it, Joe was a handsome dancer and, even though he was already married, he was getting quite a reputation as a lady's man.

On this occasion it slowly occurred to me, with a certain embarrassment, that Joe was addressing his flirtatious remarks directly to me, as a woman.

Dennis turned to Charlie and asked him, "Are you still playing music in Los Angeles?"

"No, I haven't had a chance to practice since I stopped jamming with the Isleta Thunderbirds. But did you hear, Kyamme, I got myself hitched?"

"No kidding, who to? Anybody I know?"

"No, she works back in Los Angeles and—"

Joe butted in: "Yeah, well, they didn't do it the Zuni way, you know, by moving in together, so they had a lot of trouble getting married."

"What happened?" I asked.

"My Isleta relatives didn't want the marriage, mostly because they're Catholics and she isn't. We talked to a priest back in L.A. But he wouldn't marry us because she wasn't Roman Catholic. Then her rabbi wouldn't marry us because I'm not a Jew."

"So, then, what did you do?"

"We had a Baha'i ceremony."

"What? You're not Baha'i, are you?"

"No. But they don't care what your background—you know,

your religion—is. They believe in the oneness of all mankind. For them all the religions are just the same, you know, and when you get married they don't have priests or nothing like that, just a couple of witnesses. It's more like the Zuni way."

"Now that you're married, how's all the bagels and cream cheese and lox?"

"And matzo balls, herring, and gefilte fish too. Ugh, pure grease."

"Oh yes, I guess there's no tso'ya flavoring, no mint or cilantro to brighten up the taste of those fatty foods."

"Did you hear that I brought my wife out to Shalako last winter? She was so impressed with the masked dancers, she wants to see it again this year."

After a moment, as though on cue, the three maskers rose silently, tossed their empty beer cans basketball-style into the corner trash can, and began wrapping strips of cotton cloth slowly round and round their foreheads, in preparation for remasking.

While struggling into his mask, Joe commented, "Your nose sure gets awfully sore in this kind."

"It's so hot inside this one, you could get smothered," replied Charlie.

The moment the three were remasked they acted as if they were all alone. Speaking not a word, not even looking around, they turned and headed for the front door, tsililing their sleigh bells.

No living, breathing human beings now existed in their world, only the ancestral gods.

4

TROUBLES

■ ■ ■ ■

WE ARRIVED AT THE FARM between two-thirty and three the following Wednesday afternoon. It was cold and cloudy. Just that morning we had found peaches in the market, for the first time in months, and we brought along a bushel-basketful for the family. It was much too early for the local crop, so they must have been from Mexico, or perhaps southern California. Tola's family had always owned peach orchards just outside the village near Corn Mountain. She had been raised on the fruit, and I hoped she would be pleased with our gift.

As we drove up the hill we found her holding a large basin filled with black soil and cabbage sprouts. She was taking them indoors, away from a possible frost that night. At the front door she put down her basin and showed me a willow basket she had been working on; it looked rather crude to me and, although I didn't say anything, she explained that it was the first one she had ever made. Her mother had woven willow baskets each summer when she was young, but she hadn't wanted to learn how, because it would mean having to stay around the house all the time. Instead, she ran away into the fields with her brothers whenever her mother was weaving a basket. Years ago she had bought a willow basket from a Santo Domingo lady, but now it was falling apart and she was figuring out how to make a new one on her own. When I examined the new basket she was making it seemed quite good. I myself had tried to make a willow basket once, as a Girl Scout, but it turned out quite bumpy and lopsided. I had no patience.

Hapiya was down between the barn and the outhouse, cutting cedar logs into pieces for the cookstove and the fireplace. He could easily split a foot-thick log in half after only two blows. He called out, inviting us to visit with him. Putting his sledge-hammer down, he motioned us to follow him up the hill. There, inside a light pole-and-stick fence about four feet high, was a circular stone-and-concrete floor about twenty feet in diameter. He commented that he had built it with a friend in order to thresh wheat with teams of horses—something people have forgotten how to do. "Why, there's hardly anyone up here nowadays but us, and in five or ten years probably, there'll be no one up here at all."

On our way back down the hill he walked us over behind the corral to an antique piece of farm equipment with large wire wheels and a long wooden tray full of rye seeds. He'd be sowing the seed first thing tomorrow morning. Pointing out one of his hay fields, planted two weeks ago, he noted that it had already germinated. He was thinking about where he might store it after the harvest. His barn wasn't big enough; perhaps the Martinez brothers, who lived just off the reservation, on the north side, might help out, in return for some of the hay. He asked if we could drive him over there in a bit, to talk with them.

We agreed, but first I wanted to carry the peaches into the

DENNIS TEDLOCK

house. As I entered the front door Tola smiled appreciatively, handed me a peach, and took one herself. As she bit into it she announced that the family would be going back down to Zuni in a couple of days for the last night dance. We might like to go down to see it, she offered, since Kwinsi would be dancing with his kiva group and Hapiya's medicine society would be providing the music.

Inside, the first thing I noticed was a mechanical corn sheller mounted on a barrel and a heap of dried corn occupying a large

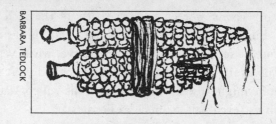

BARBARA TEDLOCK

rectangular space on the floor against the east wall. Noting my interest in the corn, Hapiya commented that when he was a kid corn used to be stored on elevated outdoor racks, but that now the ladies were just too lazy for all that. "Today, it seems, we have to live with this corn—heck, maybe it's going to chase me clear out of here."

Tola gave him a disapproving stare. One ought not ridicule corn, or else this sacred gift of the Corn Mother might get upset and leave. The care and storage of corn has always been women's work, a source of power and prestige, and Hapiya enjoyed kidding his wife about it. Each fall Tola carefully ties together a long pointed ear of yellow corn, full to the tip of perfect kernels, with a short forked ear of white corn that resulted from the intergrowth of two ears within a single husk-fold. The long yellow ear, called a yapoto, is considered male, while the short white ear, called miky'appanne, is considered female. After she ties them together side by side with hand-spun cotton cord, she places them with her stored corn, along with a bunch of unbroken corn soot and a large ear of corn dipped in the waters of Zuni Salt Lake. Soon it magically multiplies, overflowing her storeroom.

There are also sacred songs and ceremonies, including the "dancing" of the corn, that Tola and other ladies perform annually to ensure abundant harvests. Singing softly to baskets of ears while tossing them gently apparently pleases corn as much as it does infants. Each fall, at the end of the week-long Shalako celebration, comes the ceremony known as the Molaawe, in which ten or twenty young women take the parts of the sacred Corn Maidens.[1] But it was hard to talk about such things around Hapiya, since he seemed uneasy, even defensive, whenever I paid any attention at all to female areas of Zuni knowledge. It seemed he thought he might lose his importance if his wife or daughters talked with us, even half as much as he did.

After going back into her kitchen, Tola returned with the bloody head of a freshly slaughtered ram in her left hand and a rusty hacksaw in her right hand. She smiled and handed them over to her husband. Hapiya returned her smile, commenting that bola-tie slides can be made from sheep horn, and then set to work sawing off the horns. I noticed the sheep's liver laid out on the kitchen table.

Albert came in with Ramona and Seff from herding. His rifle was balanced jauntily on his shoulder, and he was grinning. They'd seen a large bobcat, while walking through an area of ridges and hollows, he said, and then he described its height with his hand. It had been facing away from them, waving its short tail. Later he shot a sparrow hawk and Seff got a bluebird. I asked whether the family would eat them or just use the feathers. He looked shocked and said, "Their feathers are what we use." Yesterday he got a jackrabbit and gave the meat to the dogs. When I asked why he did that rather than using it in a stew, he said that maybe Navajos ate jackrabbits but Zunis never have, mainly because these rabbits have too many sores and worms. Cottontails, however, were another matter.

Hapiya said that Legal Aid was back in operation and that he'd been named to its board of directors. "I'm a big shot now." Then he shifted to the weather, saying that with all the rain they'd been having it looked like he might have a pretty good hay crop this year. He would sell some but keep most of it for feed and nesting for the sheep, over the winter. He mentioned again that perhaps he could get the Martinez brothers to come down from their ranch and take some of his hay up to their place for storage. He asked whether we had the time to run up there. We said we had plenty of time.

There was some confusion about who was going to go. Hapiya pointed out that his shoes were muddy and his pants were dirty and suggested, with an irony we didn't catch at the time, that Tola and the kids should go and he would stay at home. But he ended up changing his shoes and pants, while Tola put on a fresh apron and dressed Ramona and Seff. When they all seemed about ready, Hapiya said, "Well, you two go ahead down to the car." Halfway there we heard him back at the house yelling, "GOD-DAMNSONOFA @ # & * + !"

What seemed like a quarter of an hour passed without a sound, except that I thought I heard an angry shout shortly before they appeared. Dennis suspected Hapiya hadn't really wanted Tola and the grandchildren to come along, although he invited them, so he played out a fit of anger. Dennis recalled how Hapiya's daughters, especially Sadie, always seemed to be afraid to tell their father something he wouldn't like; they must have felt he might really yell at them, not just give them a stern talking to. Dennis had seen him get angry before, but he'd never heard him curse members of his own family. To think that Hapiya had managed to hide this side of his character for all these years. At any rate, nothing showed when they came out of the house, except that Hapiya didn't have much to say during the early part of the ride.

Tola, for her part, was more talkative than usual and quite funny. She enjoyed the outing enormously, examining and commenting on everything along the way. As we passed outside the northern reservation boundary and Hapiya got out to open the first gate, a hole showed in the back of his cowboy shirt. Tola remarked that he looked just like a Navajo. When he got back into the car, she repeated her remark directly to him. Farther along and off to the right she spotted a crow walking along with six baby birds in a row behind it, and pointed them out to him. Meanwhile, on the left, Dennis was cautiously making a detour around an enormous bull. When Tola turned to the left she laughed and said, "Oh, I didn't even see him! Why don't you grab his horns? Wrestle him like in the rodeo."

When we arrived we were taken to the side porch and seated there, by Lupe, the younger of the two Martinez brothers. There was a framed cardboard sign on the back wall which read, "Welcome to our home, where Our Lady the Virgin of Guadalupe is Queen. No propaganda of whatever sort of other religions will be allowed or tolerated here in this house." The same message was repeated below, in Spanish, except that the euphemistic "other religions" became "protestante."[2] When Lupe went back inside, Hapiya read the sign aloud to us sotto voce, "This is a Catholic home . . ." and commented loudly, "Let's get the heck out of here. We're not Catholic!"

When Lupe returned, he took us all into the dining room for black coffee and sugar doughnuts, then brought out a stack of old *Boys' Life* magazines and candy for Ramona and Seff. The house was neat and clean, yet rather cluttered. There were linoleum floors, dusty pink plastic curtains, a homemade plywood china cabinet, oak table and bedstead, a Singer treadle sewing machine, an icebox, a wooden wardrobe, a wall niche with a plaster-of-paris St. Francis, framed family portraits, and framed varnished jigsaw puzzles, including one of a World War I Red Cross dog. Lupe and his older brother, Antonio, had lived on this ranch with their parents, without ever marrying, all their lives. Since they were reclusive and rarely went to town this neighborly visit was an unexpected event.

Hapiya told them about wanting his hay hauled and stored; about having lost a part from his tractor; about a prize Sadie had won last year for her jewelry at the Gallup Ceremonial; and about having used a wool sack for some of his wheat, calling it the "old Indian way." Tola traded a twenty-pound sack of dried corn and a small dish of Zuni Salt Lake salt for half of a freshly slaughtered goat. Hapiya wrapped the goat in newspaper, tied it with twine, and placed it in our trunk.

On the drive back, we paused to study a peacock that strolled along beside the road with his gorgeous tail spread wide open. Hapiya jumped out of the car, picked up a feather from the ground, and playfully presented it to Tola. She smiled, waved it around, then handed it to Ramona.

Hapiya remarked on the Martinez brothers' signs of aging; Antonio was especially feeble and rusty. When Dennis asked how old they were, Hapiya said he thought the older one was born in 1904 and therefore was exactly his own age. I suspected him of being older, but when Dennis expressed puzzlement that Antonio seemed so much older, Hapiya replied, "I guess the Indian is tougher."

When we got back home Tola lit the gasoline lanterns, hung one above the table, and carried the other into her kitchen. I followed her, offering to help, but she shook her head no. So I sat down in the big room, next to Dennis, on the double bed. Hapiya sat in one of the upholstered chairs and the kids piled into the other one. Albert sat at the table, connecting a small external speaker to his transistor radio.

Hapiya was feeling talkative and launched into a narrative about his fire-fighting experiences. On a trip to California he saw the ocean at Monterey, together with "big bunches of black ocean birds." Cormorants, probably. On another expedition, when he went to a fire near Globe, Arizona, he was a straw boss in charge of a contingent of fighters. Before they left Zuni he told his crew that they had better wear boots, not oxfords, because on arrival in town they might be sent directly to the fire lines. But he forgot his own instructions and was wearing oxfords. So before going on the lines he fastened his pants to his shoe tops with yucca strips. On the way to the fire, which was reached by walking over rough country, one of the members of his crew didn't want to follow the route he had chosen. He refused to change his instructions and told the man that if he disobeyed he could not be responsible for what might happen to him. The man went his own way but later had to be helped back to camp because he had gotten cramps after drinking a canteen-full of hot water. The crew reached the camp after dark, having felt its way along the route. That night a truck came and took away the tools and the casualty; the rest of the crew had to wait till morning, but they got extra pay for the delay.

Tola rustled together a late-spring dinner consisting of pinto stew with chunks of bacon in it, large wheat-flour tortillas, a mixture of sheep stomach and gizzard called hapnuskinne which is similar to the Scottish pudding known as haggis, and coffee. Hapiya, before sitting down to eat, put a wire grill over the coals in the fireplace and cooked the sheep's liver, turning it with the poker. It was quite black when he finished. During the meal he mentioned that he owned some cornfields down below, near where Tola's house was, "the one she inherited from her mother."

I now understood why he had told us, during my first visit, two years earlier, that the house we were now sitting in was his rather than Tola's. She had already inherited her own country house. Since Zuni is strongly matrilineal, with women passing on the ownership of all important property (including houses and agricultural land) to their sisters or daughters, when both his mother and unmarried sister died the house could no longer remain within their Dogwood clan but had to cross over into his wife's Badger clan. Upon his wife's death it would be inherited by his eldest daughter, Sadie. But the house could also be interpreted as a sheep camp, since Tola owned a house in Zuni and another country place connected specifically to agricultural activities. If it were thought of as primarily a sheep camp it would be interpreted as male territory, so his eldest son, Kwinsi, might possibly inherit it. But why did he want to give it to Albert, rather than Kwinsi? Perhaps it was because Albert was the only one of the children who seemed to want to live up here full-time.[3]

Tola asked Dennis if he wanted some chile and pushed a peanut-butter jar full of red chile powder toward him, warning that it was very hot. Hapiya said that he doesn't like chile very much anymore, since it has made him sick in the past. Once, after eating a chile stew, he fainted and fell off a bridge while out herding; fortunately another herder noticed his untended flock and found him. Last spring, when he stayed up in the country alone and ate chile stew, he woke up so weak that he collapsed back into his bed. Luckily a neighbor's wife came by and found him. She put hot rocks on top of him and later he was taken down to the hospital at Black Rock. He was supposed to have an operation on a lung that had a spot of pus on it, but when the doctor found that the spot had greatly reduced in size, he called it off.

Hapiya abruptly turned toward Dennis, saying, "Pretty soon you're going to be an Indian."

Dennis asked what he meant by that and he replied, "Because you eat with us. They're going to have to initiate you, Kyammc. Are you going to be initiated when I say?" he inquired, in a half-serious, half-joking tone. Dennis smiled and nodded yes.

Somehow or other the subject of Mormon missionaries came up. Tola remarked as to how they always wore neckties, dressed in white shirts, and were clean. Hapiya recalled that once, many years ago, when two of them had come up to the farm, he had been taking corn down off a rack. They came by and said, "We'll help anybody who needs help," so this job was left in their hands.

They were dressed all in white and, since the ground was muddy, by the time they finished they were filthy. "Since that time they never came back, but I guess they learned their lesson," Hapiya said, smiling and breaking into a chuckle.

The conversation turned to the topic of Mormon multiple wives, and then Navajo. Hapiya said that back around 1915, when he was at Albuquerque Indian School, he had a Navajo girlfriend and that he has since been kidded about this. "You should have married that Navajo; then you could have had more than one wife."

Kwinsi was supposed to be initiated last winter into Hapiya's medicine society, but his aunts refused to cook for him, or to wash his hair for his initiation, because of an escapade last summer. Around July he was coming back from Gallup with a man and wife; they stopped near the reservation line so that the man could get out of the car and relieve himself. While he was out of the car his wife said to Kwinsi, "Let's take off, honey!" The two of them did, leaving her husband behind. Kwinsi spent the whole night with that woman, going here and there in her car, and then took her home to Zuni in the morning.

The police were waiting at her house, having been alerted by her husband, who had gotten a ride into the village. "Kwinsi just ran off when he saw the police, and headed up here. He helped Tola with hoeing and other garden chores, and she thought her son was just being nice." Hapiya was down in a field on the other side of the house when a neighbor drove up and told him that the police were looking for his eldest son. Kwinsi left in a great hurry and drove by him without saying goodbye or anything at all.

Hapiya commented, "Well, when a woman has a husband and she wants to go with another man, why, that's theirs." Albert said that Kwinsi "will just have to learn," and that a divorce is bad, "especially when you've got four kids."

Tola added some details. "That lady left her glasses in Kwinsi's car and Sadie took them to her house and planned to get after her when she came to claim them." The woman had been living with her husband in a house near the Malco station, where Kwinsi has been working recently. On one occasion she sent some hotcakes over to him, delivered by her husband, "who didn't even know." Everyone, including the kids, giggled when they heard this.

Hapiya took the floor and launched into a story about a fire years ago in the Albuquerque Indian School gymnasium. Albert, who had heard all this before, started coughing in an exaggerated manner, then made shadow figures on the wall. He created both domestic and wild animals: deer, snake, turkey, dog, cat, and rabbit. His snake was especially good, complete with a flicking tongue. Ramona and Seff, who quickly lost interest in their grandpa's rambling remembrances, were pleased with Albert's animals and began making some themselves.

Hapiya told how the federal government, during the teens, was taking some land from the nearby Mexican villagers, until someone decided to get even. This person somehow got into the basement of the gymnasium, set a fire there, shut off the water to the fire hydrants, and disarmed the fire-alarm system. The fire was not discovered until two or three in the morning. The school bells were rung and someone came to the rooms where the boys were sleeping to get them up. He had to go around four times before he managed to get all the boys up. When they were instructed to evacuate the band instruments from the building, Hapiya carried out a bass drum and a saxophone. To do this he had to run in and out of the building, crouching down under a layer of black smoke, and just as he finished a huge beam he'd been passing under caved in.

Albert stood up, sighed loudly, and coughed, but it didn't sound deliberate this time. Looking out the window, he announced that car headlights had appeared down by the bridge; then he walked over and scraped his dish into the slop bucket in the kitchen, brushed his teeth in the basin by the door, and returned to the table with a tobacco tin. Inside were a pipe, some cigarette papers, and a bundle of loose printed pages. He unfolded some to show to us. They were all torn from wrestling magazines liberally illustrated with photographs of tattooed Japanese women wrestlers, heavy ferocious-looking creatures. He walked over to his cot, in the far corner of the room, carefully removed his shoes, and flopped down on it fully clothed. Tola noticed me studying her son and grinned, then motioned the kids with her lips toward the kitchen. They happily stood up, carried their plates into the kitchen, scraped them, and brushed their teeth. She handed them their pajamas and tucked them in behind us on the big double bed.

Hapiya continued with his anecdotes as the kids alternately listened and whispered under the covers. His parents didn't give him any spending money at all when he was at school, so one year he decided to earn some money himself. He and a friend went all the way up into the Sandia Mountains in a wagon to get sheep manure for Albuquerque lawns. Around one place they went, "everything was twisted; anything you might find up there, a tree or bush or a root, it was twisted." He was passed on to the ninth grade, but his schooling ended at the eighth, because his parents wanted him at home to help herd sheep. Although he loves farming and sheepherding, he greatly regrets his parents' decision not to let him get more education. When his own son Albert said he wanted to stay up on the farm, Hapiya nonetheless encouraged him to finish high school.

Somehow Hapiya got onto the subject of swimming. While he was in Larned, Kansas, working in the beet fields, he went swimming with some other Indians in a deep place above a spillway. One of them wasn't a very good swimmer, panicked, and started drifting toward the spillway; all of them tried to save him, but he was heavy and continued to drift. Finally they took down the wire that supported a swing used for jumping into the water and threw him one end, to pull him out. On another occasion Hapiya dived into a pool that had only five feet of water in it. "I hit that bottom and really saw stars, like Jiggs in the comics." His brother pulled him out, unconscious.

I was bored. All these random anecdotes were starting to get to me. But I decided not to make my discomfort obvious, since perhaps Dennis was actually interested and not merely being polite. But I certainly couldn't tell from his expression. I guess, if I had already done several years of ethnographic fieldwork, the way Dennis had, I'd be more interested in every little detail. Or maybe not. To keep from dozing off, I studied the wall behind Hapiya's head. On the left was a peg with a red medicine-man rattle, a rifle rack holding a .30/30 plus two .22-caliber rifles and three fishing rods. On the right was a miniature deer head mounted at the base of a lifesized antler trophy from which dangled a bright-pink plastic crucifix. A couple of peacock feathers and a straw hat were tucked in between the other antler and the wall. A second crucifix, bright yellow, was hanging from the door frame.

As I tuned back in, Hapiya said that, when he was young, old-timers used to round deer up like cattle and drive them into a corral with the big buck leading. "The leader always got away. Today you can still see such a corral near here, and two more near the road south of Zuni. There were special songs for the deer roundup, and hunters knew how to make a sound something like a crow to attract the deer. Another way to get deer was to trap them. Hunters dig a hole in a deer trail and place a big log across it, inside. Sticks and dirt are put over the top in such a

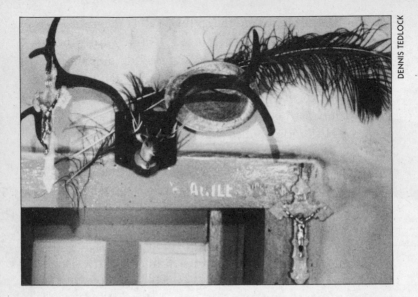

DENNIS TEDLOCK

way that it would cave in when a deer walked on it. The animal fell with his legs on either side of the log and couldn't get out." This kind of trap can be seen today in the draw by the sawmill in a place called "Deer Trap Canyon."

Before Hapiya could launch into yet another anecdote, Dennis stood up and said we were tired. After thanking Tola for the meal, we took our leave. Hapiya and Tola followed us out to the car. Hapiya stood next to my rolled-down car window and whispered in to me, "Tsilu, I'm sending Albert down to the village with you guys, okay? He's got a bad cough, deep. He's been spitting up mucus and blood for a week. It's serious, and I want a medicine man to look into it."

"Sure thing," I replied.

As Tola went back inside to get Albert, Hapiya walked around to the driver's window and said to Dennis in a low voice, "Kyamme, a while ago three cars came down from up near the spring. If you see any of them, or if a fourth one comes, if somebody wants you to stop, just go right on. You're safe that way. Might be somebody drunk or something, or they might ask too many questions. Understand?"

"Yup, we've got you."

"Be real careful if you see a turquoise-colored car. That car's been up this way four times so far this spring. He drives a circular route through the valley, he's got *no land* up here, so he's got no business being here. I saw him a couple of days ago, when I was cleaning the irrigation ditch up at the flume. He drives real slow; pretends he's just going by."

"Is he Zuni?"

"Yes. He's got the biggest ram herd on the reservation, bigger than Owen's. He keeps it over there on the south side. That man's no good, his whole family's no good. Why, they've got *no children* at all."

As Albert slid into the front seat and I felt a rifle butt on my right thigh, I wondered why he was bringing it to the village. It was dark in the car—there was no streetlight, no moon, no illumination at all from anywhere—and Dennis hadn't noticed Albert's rifle. I didn't want to seem nervous in front of family; but, then again, I did want Dennis to know that our nephew was, for some reason, armed.

How to tell him? Since Albert could speak some Spanish, that wouldn't work.

As we pulled away from the house Dennis stuck his head out the window, yelling, "Good night, folks. Don't worry about us, we'll be real careful."

At the foot of the hill, as we crossed the wooden bridge, we noticed that the cars Hapiya mentioned had all disappeared, or had turned their lights off. Albert noiselessly cranked down his window, checked the sight, and cocked his .30/30.

Dennis laughed out loud. "Scared of witches?"

No reply.

We drove through the lower village, past the outhouses, wind-mills, tractor barns, horse sheds, sheep corrals, and out along the dike. We continued along past the willow thickets and clumps of Fremont cottonwood and sweet-smelling Russian ol-ives, past the abandoned grammar school and the cattle tanks, over the long hill, past piñons and junipers, and up into the stand of ponderosa pines, in silence.

No lights and no cars anywhere. And then we saw him; by God, it was Kwinsi! He was limping along the edge of the dirt road into our headlights with his hand covering his right eye. There was no sign of his truck, another vehicle, or anyone else nearby.

As he edged up closer, we could see that blood was trickling down his sleeve. Then, as we pulled up next to him, he shouted in the window, "Got me! Cowboys from Witch Wells, sons of bitches, they got my eye! Four of 'em in a Jeep."

"Where in the devil did they go?" shouted Albert, springing from the car.

"Did you get their license-plate number?" yelled Dennis.

"They ran me off the road, gave me lip, and when I wouldn't take it one of 'em pulled a knife, carved me good. Man, I can't see out of that eye!"

"Climb in here, Kwinsi; we'll take you to Black Rock, get you some stitches," Dennis insisted.

Kwinsi moaned as he scrambled into the back seat, still clutch-ing his eye. Albert climbed in back with his brother and I gave them a clean handkerchief.

Dennis drove like crazy for the pavement; turned right, ac-celerated to eighty mph on the straightaway toward Black Rock subdivision, right again, and up to the emergency entrance. Kwinsi refused to get out and go into the emergency room.

"Man, it's already happened. What good will it do me comin' here now? Doctors will think it's my fault or somethin' for fightin', call the police, make me turn 'em in. Then real trouble begins; them shit-kickers get to talkin', join up together, get some whiskey in 'em and come prowlin' around. Might even find Old Man alone. Maybe jump him. I can take it, but he's gettin' along, pretty old; besides, we can't win the war by tattlin'. Take me to my medicine society."

"Okay, whatever you say, but I still think you need some stitches, and it wouldn't hurt any for somebody to check out that eye," said Dennis with resignation.

Kwinsi shook his head emphatically no, and we headed down the road for the Old Pueblo. Albert directed us to a big stone house up on top of the hill. We were concerned and curious, imagining medicine men and women in bearskin curing gloves dancing along before the fireplace, but knew we weren't welcome.

The next morning, when we called down to Kwinsi's house in the village, his mother-in-law told us that by the time he'd arrived at the society house it was too late. He'd lost his sight from that eye. No, she was sorry, but he couldn't speak with us right now, he was resting. Later today men from his medicine society would be taking him into the Veterans Hospital in Albuquerque for treatment. She guessed they'd be giving him a glass eye.

We stayed away, in Santa Fe, for nearly two months. In the face of this sort of tragedy we felt embarrassed, useless, silly. What could we do? One day, quite unexpectedly, Sadie and Sabin telephoned us, saying that they were in town. They'd tried to find our house but couldn't. Dennis drove to where they were, down by the plaza, and led them back out into the canyon.

When Sabin saw how tucked away our two-room adobe was, he said, "You're hiding back here. Why, you must be hermits." Dennis pointed out that we did have neighbors, but then realized that we certainly weren't in an urban situation, at least by Zuni standards.

Sadie laughed and said, "Why, we would've found you right

away if we'd thought to look behind the brush." Indeed, we were living in what would pass for a rural area with Zunis, since there wasn't any sage, piñon, or juniper right inside their village.

We had a British guest, an old friend of Dennis' from his undergraduate years. When Sabin was introduced to him, he noticed his foreign accent right away and asked, "Are you from England, or London, or Europe, or where?"

Upon learning that he was English, Sadie asked, "Are there a lot of famous people in England?"

When our guest wasn't able to field this question, Sabin jumped in, asking, in mock seriousness, "Are there really those Beatles?"

Dennis quickly changed the subject to our next-door neighbors, the Rodriguez family. He described Maria, the woman of the house, who always has a stew bubbling away on top of her stove, and her husband, Urbano, who always wears overalls and rubber boots, and never seems to go anywhere, not even to church. Sabin said, with a sarcastic tone, "He's full of sin," and everyone laughed.

They were in town to pick up Shawiti. He wanted to leave school right away and never return, because of the strange Anglo guy he'd been boarding with. Why, the man has no wife, no daughters, no family at all. He lives in a big house with several other young Indian boys, most of whom are studying art. Sadie doesn't want to say anything bad about the guy—after all, he *did* give her son almost two years of free room and board and he even commissioned Tola to make him a large beaded doll worth sixty dollars. However, when he heard that Shawiti would be leaving early and not returning to Santa Fe next year, he decided not to pay for it. To think that he would try to steal from a boy and his grandmother! Shawiti would just have to get a job this summer and pay Tola for her doll; in the fall he could go back to school in Zuni. They probably shouldn't have let him go away to school so young, but he did want to study art, and there simply weren't any good art teachers at the school in Zuni.

I pulled some beers out of our refrigerator, passed them around, and started warming up my pinto stew. Our Zuni friends were clearly a bit much for this shy Londoner, who had never met a "real Indian" before. Who knows what sort of feather-bedecked, children-of-nature Indians he had somewhere in his mind, but one thing was for sure: Sadie and Sabin's aggressively humorous ice-breaking was certainly not what he had expected.

Even so, by the time dinner was ready our guest was entranced by our Zuni friends, who had proved to be very pleasant company. Sadie had as much to say about everything as Sabin. When we sat down to eat bean stew, chiles rellenos, and Indian sourdough bread, our British friend was famished and gobbled down three bowls of stew in the same time that our Zuni guests politely got through a little bit from each dish.

As Sadie and Sabin left, they made us promise to come by Zuni soon and visit with Hapiya. Sadie said her dad was lonely and missed talking to us.

OLD LADY SALT

■ ■ ■ ■

When we arrived, Hapiya was talkative, saying that he and Kwinsi had visited Zuni Salt Lake last March, but found the water so high that there was no salt at all for sale. Apparently the mine had changed hands and the new company hadn't yet been able to remove any salt. He'd heard rumors that the old group sold out when they tried to bring in a big "boat" of salt that dissolved before they could get it to shore. Now the huge pile of mined salt, more than fifteen feet high when he went over there just last year, was completely gone.

A friend who had visited the salt lake recently told him that he saw two dirty little boys with long stringy hair wading out of the lake, heading westward. Because of where they were and the way they looked he figured they must have been the twin war gods, the Ahayuuta, sons of the Sun Father, and guardians of Old Lady Salt. Their home has long been deep within a black volcanic cinder cone that rises out of the shimmering white salt lake.

These boys accompanied Old Lady Salt long ago, on her migration nearly forty-five miles due south, to her present location. Perhaps she was angered once again as young salt gatherers started bringing their women friends with them on their expeditions. Some men and women surely lacked respect and just played around there, had their "picnics" on her sacred body. Afterward they went home leaving their Kleenex and toilet paper all over her.

"Well, I guess you've been seeing how the younger generation goes to McDonald's?" asked Hapiya. "You know, buys the hamburgers, the French fries, and Cokes, then tosses wax paper and Styrofoams all over? These young guys probably took Old Lady Salt home, played with her sacred flesh, threw handfuls at one another, wasted her; they made trip after trip and trampled her. Women should not be visiting over there at all, and just lately they're going in pickups, without even making prayer sticks. Perhaps she was offended and ran off someplace."

Tola needed a new ear of salt-dipped corn for her upcoming harvest rituals, the family was almost out of Salt Lake salt, and since no one liked store salt, Hapiya hinted to us that he wanted to go see "Old Lady Salt, you know, to kind of check up on things." Dennis immediately offered to drive him and asked if I could go along too. Hapiya smiled broadly. "Sure, it's *Zuni* ladies who aren't supposed to go; she's a different tribe." He promptly changed from his dirty work boots into oxfords, then gathered up a bag of cornmeal, prayer sticks, sourdough-bread scraps, a gunny sack, a perfectly kerneled long corn ear, and a large cardboard carton.

Early in the drive, when we approached the place where Old Lady Salt lost her downy eagle feather, Hapiya insisted that we pause long enough to get out of the car and admire the white

DENNIS TEDLOCK

sandstone butte known as U'ky'ahayan El'a/*Where Downy Feather Stands*. This white feather-shaped rock stands before a row of pink-and-white-striped sandstone mesas with good nesting places for Cooper's hawk, red-tailed hawk, and golden eagles. Since no one lives nearby, the silence here is pierced only by an occasional cack-cack-cack-cack, or kee-kee-kee, and shrill descending screams of soaring birds of prey. As we climbed back into the car Hapiya remarked in a low, tense voice that his son Joe had left ten days ago for Vietnam.

Throughout the long drive Hapiya looked around, noticing each and every detail of the passing scene, even on the dullest stretches. I sat in the back seat jotting rough notes, then compiled the following more detailed trip log.[1]

AUGUST 11, 1970: TRIP TO ZUNI SALT LAKE

▪ Kw'alashi/*raven* flew up off the road where it had been picking a road kill clean, a jackrabbit. The metallic sheen of its plumage and hoarse, low-pitched croaking seemed somehow ominous. Dennis asked if a raven might also be called kokko kw'inna/*black kachina*. Hapiya said yes but he would only be called that in prayers and songs. The feathers of this bird are not used in the making of prayer sticks, because it eats dead things. They are, however, used for making ruffs worn by some of the more dangerous kachina masks such as Salimopiya. Ravens are considered attanni/*dangerous*.

▪ A pair of niishapak'o/*mourning doves* flew up and Hapiya commented, "There goes those little Navajo girls, the ones killed by the Ahayuuta. I guess there's a lot of them around here because of all the haasuski/*coyote leaf*."

"Are they good to eat?"

"Sure, when I was growing up we had a lot of dove chile stew, but it's not eaten so much these days."

Coyote leaf (*Croton texensis L.*), which is named in Zuni for the characteristic foul odor of the plant, is a purgative used by medicine men and women. A tea made by boiling the entire plant is also a common remedy for stomach ache, gonorrhea, and syphilis. The root is chewed by medicine people before sucking on a rattlesnake bite and then applied to the wound.[2]

▪ "Look, a yashi crossed the road," Dennis called out.

Hapiya corrected him: "No, it's an ohchi. The yashi lives

in pine trees and the ohchi lives in rocks. Ohchi is very good to eat. Too bad we didn't bring Albert along, with his rifle."

The squirrel looked about the same size and color as the common Eastern gray squirrel (*Sciurus carolinensis*), but it was not. Since the ohchi lives only in rocky terrain, it was the rock squirrel (*Spermophilus variegatus*), whereas the yashi must be the tassel-eared squirrel (*Sciurus aberti*), also gray, but with prominent black ear tufts and fluffy white tail. The yashi subsists chiefly by chiseling seeds out of ponderosa-pine cones.

- An abandoned sheepherder's tent way off to the left.

- On both sides of the road dozens of wild zinnias, tuna ikyapokya/*put it into eyes*, with showy yellow flowers.

Zinnias (*Zinnia grandiflora*) are in the thistle family. These bright-yellow blossoms are gathered by Zuni healers and crushed in cold water to make an eyewash. The remainder of the plant is ground into a powder, which is heated on hot stones and inhaled to reduce fever. Both leaves and flowers may also be chewed, and then applied topically to reduce bruises.[3]

- Red-and-white plastic tourist flags mark a ruin known as Heshota Ullha/*Close-Up-to-the-Mountain*, but there were no tourists in sight.

- Turning left from Route 53 onto Route 32, "Ooo, a lot of dust," Hapiya said, looking in the direction of the gravel pit.

- Along Highway 32 Hapiya recalled that his first trip to Salt Lake was by horse and wagon back in 1923. He commented that the old road was more direct and pointed out sections of it, abandoned since the paving, saying that he had helped build the new road when he worked for the ECW (Emergency Construction Works), one of Franklin Delano Roosevelt's New Deal enterprises.

▪ Continuing south on Route 32 past Tsitutukkya Ky'ana/*Place-Where-the Spaniard-Drank*, on the left. It's a sandstone outcropping with numerous small depressions in its horizontal surface. The only Spanish soldier to survive a massacre in the church at Zuni, long ago, passed this way on his flight. "He was lucky enough to find water in a hollow place in these rocks."

▪ Achiya Teky'appowa/*Knife Hill*, a rocky outcrop toward the east, where that same Spanish soldier apparently dropped his knife. Further on is the Place-Where-the-Spaniard-Lost-His-Shoes and was killed by pursuing Zunis during the Pueblo Revolt in the 1680s.

▪ Hokti tasha an kwiminne/*mountain lion's herb*, flannel mullein. Dennis commented that Hopis gather the leaves, dry them as tobacco, and smoke them before dancing.

Hapiya did not reply for a mile or two and then said, "In my group, we use that hokti tasha an kwiminne to clean out sores and rashes. I've never heard of smoking it; those Hopis probably have another way over there in Arizona, but as for me, I don't think it would taste too good."

Several different Zuni names for flannel mullein (*Verbascum thapsus*) have been reported in ethnobotanical studies at the pueblo.[4] The name "anna lhanna/*big tobacco*" seems to indicate that at least some Zunis gather, dry, and smoke the large, soft, white, woolly leaves as tobacco. The plant is also used to cure various rashes and skin infections, including athlete's foot. At

Hopi, where flannel mullein is called "wupaviva/*tall tobacco*," it is used in the same manner as regular wild tobacco. It is also smoked in combination with *Onosmodium thurberi* in order to cure people who have experienced "fits," or are not considered to be in their right minds. It is steeped as a medicinal tea by several Southwestern groups, including the Navajos, and long ago the Romans collected and dried the long yellow flower stalks to use as lamp wicks.

- Heavy equipment, including graders and dump trucks. The road is being graveled and retarred.

- A sign saying **Valencia County,** then the reservation marker.

- **Crockett's Bar** on the right. "How about a drink?" Dennis joked.

No reply at first, then, "That's where the muumaakwe/*Mormons* drink.[5] A couple of years ago a bunch of them got into a fight with some Zuni guys; the people were just piled up there."

Last year he stopped there, with Kwinsi, on his way home. "He told me he needed some oil and I believed him, but he got beer. He needed 'oil' for his lips! When we got back late, I told his wife that we stopped at Crockett's for oil for Kwinsi's lips. Boy, she sure cussed him out!"

- A roadrunner on the edge of the highway. My first sighting of the New Mexico state bird! Enormous, as big as a raven with bright-yellow eyes, long legs, long gray-brown tail, silly-looking bushy crest. It ran alongside the car clucking, cooing, and whining like a dog while jerking its tail wildly: first from side to side, then up and down.

Hapiya explained that roadrunners are "hish tewusu/*very sacred*," and therefore must never be eaten.

The Zuni name for the roadrunner is "poyyi." The use of its feathers is esoteric, reserved for the six sacred Rain Priesthoods. There is a Roadrunner clan at the pueblo.

- Once we were past the abandoned Hispanic village of Atarque, there were rectangular clearings in the woodland filled with brown grass and weeds. The remains of the Texan homesteaders' fields. As we went by Hapiya kept making a bilingual pun, "Noowe (a Zuni word for "beans"), noooo more bean farms."

A late frost killed these farmers' plantings one spring; then another frost killed their second plantings that same spring. Now the people that are left are mostly cattlemen.

- The community of Fence Lake, a dismal collection of collapsing buildings: houses, a school, post office, store, garage, and Baptist church.

At the edge of the village we saw a small child. "Is that a Mexican?" asked Hapiya. But when he saw the parents in the doorway of a shack he exclaimed, "Navajo!"

Strange—I'd read somewhere that the inhabitants of Fence Lake were one hundred percent Anglo Texans.

- "Noooo more bean farms." Hapiya could see the traces of the former pinto-bean fields stretched out in all directions but we couldn't.

- We drove over to the lake of Fence Lake: a patch of green grass in a low place. Hapiya said that in olden days the wagon

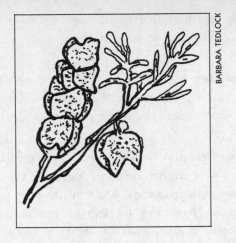

BARBARA TEDLOCK

route passed right by this lake and the horses were watered here.

- STOCK ON HIGHWAY

- Gray-green shrubs, nearly four feet tall, with burrlike seeds and transparent papery winglike bracts line the road on both sides for the next several miles.

"That's the one we call ke'maawe/*salt weed*. We use that one to fix bee stings and ant bites. We grind it up good, make a paste of it, and then cover the bite. It makes the bump shrink and relieves the redness from the poison that animal left in there."

Four-wing saltbush (*Atriplex canescens*) is widespread and can grow to a height of eight feet. The female bushes bear the fruits, which, together with the root, are gathered and dried by healers.[6]

BARBARA TEDLOCK

- Sagebrush, rabbitbrush, and snakeweed, all dried up. "Guess there's nothing much left for the antelope to eat here."

- On an electric pole insulator, a hawk. Wrong, an owl!

- WATCH FOR CATTLE

- The only plant on the shoulder now is atoowe/*Rocky Mountain beeplant*, hundreds of beautiful lavender flowers, clustered together on a large central stalk.

"Old Lady looks for this one. The leaves are good cooked with shelled corn and ground chile, it's good for stomach ache, and she makes a black paint from it too, for her owls and other potteries."

"Should we gather up a bunch to take back to her?" I asked.

"No, Tsilu, there's no need to take any back with us, there's plenty of it scattered all around the village."

Rocky Mountain beeplant (*Cleome serrulata*), sometimes called "skunkweed" because of the strong odor of its leaves when crushed, is boiled together with chile and dried corn on the cob as a traditional winter food for everyone except members of the Shiwanaakwe/*Priestly People Society,* for whom it is taboo. The plant is also boiled down and used in the preparation of black paint for ceramics. At Hopi it is used in the manufacture of prayer sticks for the Powamu ceremony, and at Hano it is named in prayers, together with the three most important cultivated plants: corn, pumpkin, and cotton.[7]

- An abandoned cabin built of log slices set on edge in mortar so that the exterior wall surfaces were masses of circles.
  "Still standing after all this time."

- NO PIÑON PICKING

- In this case the sign was right, and the next eight miles were lined with large piñon trees, covered with masses of cones.

- On the left, far away, a volcano called Sitting Mountain.

- Crossing along a treeless, grassless, flat stretch, Hapiya commented, "Hish tewuuli lhana!"/*What an enormous empty space!*

- A lone cow with ribs showing.

- An escarpment below which you can see a mile-wide crater that hides the Zuni Salt Lake. If you know where to look, that is. From the top there was a wonderful unobstructed view of miles and miles of woodlands and grasslands far to the south.

- A tangle of roads from Zuni, St. Johns, Springerville, and Quemado cross here, but there's no traffic.

DENNIS TEDLOCK

- Two black volcanic cinder cones rise from the brilliant white water, remarkable. Hapiya pointed out that the western cone has a crater in its top, but the eastern one is pointed. Rain Priests visit the western cone and Bow Priests the eastern one.

In 1598, when Juan de Oñate colonized New Mexico, he sent Marcos Farfán to explore Zuni Salt Lake.[8] He reported that the lake was a marvelous thing; the entire surface was encrusted with salt, except for a place in the center where waters bubbled up; a person could easily walk on it without breaking through, and to obtain a sample it had been necessary to use a pickax. He declared it the finest saline in the world and said that not even the Spanish king enjoyed salt of such excellent grain.

- On the north side of the lake are various buildings and pieces of equipment having to do with past and present salt-mining activities.

- Coming in closer, the water seemed low, and there were only a few white patches along the shore. We talked with workers who pump fresh water into the lake in order to dissolve the crystallized salt, then pump out the salty water.

- The Anglo foreman showed us the solar evaporation pans along the shoreline and told us that his workers were able to harvest more than sixty tons of salt per day.

- On the western shore we found a lot of tracks where Zunis had been wading into the lake to make offerings.

- The owners of the mine did not disturb these salt gatherers, since their own mineral rights were only temporarily leased from the State of New Mexico.

In 1978 the tribe purchased all lease rights to the area for $250,000, but the title to the land remained with the State of New Mexico. It would be ten more years of litigation before the Secretary of the Interior was directed to purchase and hold in trust, for the Zuni people, the six hundred acres of land surrounding and containing the salt lake.[9]

- Hapiya stood at the end of a wooden plank someone had abandoned between the salt mine and cinder cones. He stooped down, made a hole at his feet, and then straightened up, facing east, to begin a long prayer.

- Near the end of the prayer he bent to plant his prayer sticks in the hole, sprinkled the crumbled bread on top, and stood to finish praying. Then he rolled up his pant legs and waded

DENNIS TEDLOCK

into the shimmering lake to wash Tola's corn ear and sprinkle cornmeal.

▪ The corn particles formed a fluffy cloud that settled gently on the water and vanished into the overall whiteness.

▪ When he walked out, not only his corn ear but also his leg hairs and toenails were coated with salt. He said that he'd have to wash it all off when he got home, or the salt would make cuts and cause swelling.

▪ He put us both to work filling the cardboard box with tso'ya ma'uteyaawe/*beautiful salt flowers*, tumbleweeds encrusted with salt crystals, which he said we should take back with us for the family as "souvenirs."

- Returning to the north shore, we bought fifty pounds of salt, for seventy cents, from a Hispanic worker.

- Near the top of the road, out of the crater, Hapiya instructed Dennis to take the right fork and park the car near Tsililik'o/ *Sparrow Hawk* Shrine.

"There's supposed to be another pile of salt over at that cedar tree," he said, and walked over to a flat stone while we waited in the car.

- Facing east, holding a lump of salt in his left hand, he began a long prayer; at the end he whirled the salt four times in a wide circle above his head and cast it on the shrine. Then he bent over and carefully studied how it had landed.

- Climbing back in the car, he said, "Hish tewusu/*very sacred*."

- As we crossed the flats south of the escarpment he remarked on the poor condition of the range, noting the predominance of sagebrush and rabbitbrush now, and saying that in former times the grass here was so good that ranchers could cut it for hay with their mowing machines.

- Along the escarpment there were hundreds of Datil and Navajo yucca plants, which he studied intently for several miles. It turned out that he was looking for sweet black cylindrical pods, called "tsupiyaawe," which Tola had asked him to gather for fruit conserve, but there weren't any yet. He guessed they'd appear later in the season.

In ancient times, before the introduction of sugar, yucca-pod conserves were made each fall.[10] The bananalike pods were boiled, then left to cool until the skin could be loosened with a knife and pulled off. The fruit was bitten off, close to the core containing the seeds, and chewed. Then the fruit was ejected from the mouth into a bowl, covered with a stone slab, and placed on the roof overnight. In the morning, the bowl was emptied into a large cooking vessel and stirred over hot coals. After it was sufficiently cooked, it was cooled, then made into thick pats, about four inches in diameter, which were placed on polished stone slabs and sun-dried for four days. When they were sufficiently dried, they were taken and squeezed together into twelve-inch-long-by-four-inch-wide rolls, and carried to the roof again, where they remained for about ten days, until they were perfectly firm. Later, when they were needed, a piece the width of four fingers was cut crosswise, broken into a bowl of water, and manipulated until it was dissolved, delicious.

▪ At Atarque we took a side trip into the village. Although the church was in good repair, there didn't seem to be a single resident. Hapiya was edgy and said, "Maybe some Tsipoloowa/ *Mexicans* might get after us."

▪ He spent the remainder of the drive reminiscing. There was a second, nonsalt lake in the crater, which was good for swimming. He once placed rocks in his shirt in order to discover how deep this lake was, but never reached the bottom. Another time, when he had finished swimming and collecting salt, two Hopis, dressed in white cotton kilts and yucca bandoleers, arrived and ran around the salt lake four times, calling out to Old Lady Salt. Then they drank some of the briny water and washed themselves before gathering her sacred body.

▪ Near the house Hapiya commented that when you've been to visit the Salt Woman your kuku/*father's sister* must wash your hair and you must give her some of your salt. Then he held out his salt-whitened hands and corn ear, remarking that they would prove to his family that he really had been over to the lake.

■ ■ ■ ■

Tola greeted her husband at the front door with a prayer, hooked fingers with him briefly, and withdrew, breathing from her hands. Hapiya presented her with the salt-caked corn ear, which she immediately hung from a beam for good luck, health, and protection. Later that fall, she would gently place it, together with a bunch of corn soot, in the center of the harvest as the bed for Mother and Father Corn.

Albert, along with the grandchildren, had seen us pull up and came in from herding. They had had some luck hunting and were carrying a flicker, a piñon jay, and a cottontail. Reverently sprinkling them with sacred cornmeal, Albert breathed from them, then placed them on the hearth.

Although it was only three o'clock in the afternoon, Tola set out our dinner: venison jerky fried in a lot of fat, onions, cilantro, tortillas made of whole-wheat flour, and coffee. She said she had ground the flour herself, "with mano and metate," using their own wheat. We sprinkled salt on the table and dipped our jerky in it (it was eaten with the fingers, though removed from the serving bowl with spoons). Hapiya told me, "You're used to eating the Indian way now, at all different times. You've got spoiled."

Ramona jumped up, grabbed the dead cottontail off the hearth, and brought it over to the table. Its intestines were dangling out. No one scolded her, but Hapiya gently pushed her away from the table as he began narrating the story of his trip. In minute detail he described the condition of Salt Woman's hair and skirt, saying that, although she was greatly diminished, she was still pure. Then he brought out the salt flowers and passed them around for all to admire.

Tola repeated, over and over again, "Hish ayyuchi'an ho"i/ *Very marvelous* or *amazing being!* Hish pikwayin ho"i/*Surpassing* or *superior being!*"

As Hapiya stood up to go to the house down below, in order to have his hair ceremonially washed and combed, we took our leave. We explained that Dennis had a new teaching job back east, at Brooklyn College, and that I'd be enrolling at the Art Students League in New York City. We promised to keep in touch.

Hapiya took Dennis down to the garden, where he picked two zucchini squashes, four ears of green corn, and bunches of onions and coriander. Back at the house Tola offered me that wonderful sourdough oven bread called mu'le, a hunk of freshly roasted mutton, and a beaded velveteen pincushion in the form of a traditionally dressed Navajo woman. Then, softly grasping my hand, she breathed from it. Instinctively I copied her gesture and she smiled.

Outside, by the front door, Hapiya jumped up on the masonry bench, which placed his head level with Dennis' head. He shook Dennis' hand, softly, looking him squarely in the eye saying, "Goodbye, Kyamme."

"Goodbye, Ky'asse/*Sister's Child,*" Dennis replied gently.

"I'll try to make the chicken scratches."

"Good, and I will too."

"Be sure to come around and see us, if you're around here ever again, and if we're still living yet. . . ." Hapiya trailed off.

"You *will* be," Dennis asserted firmly; then we climbed into the car and waved as we drove away.

6

THE MEASURE OF LIFE

■ ■ ■ ■

WHEN I RETURNED A YEAR LATER I was more enthusiastic and felt somehow more prepared to understand my feelings and experiences than I had been earlier. A month before we left Dennis accepted a teaching position at Wesleyan University, so we moved to Connecticut and, although it was only a two-hour train ride from Middletown to New York City, I suspected that my painting career would devolve into nothing more than a hobby. But by then I'd read nearly all the books we owned on the native peoples of the Southwest and decided to enroll in the anthropology graduate program at Wesleyan. Perhaps my growing curiosity about the peoples of the Southwest might take the place of painting. I wasn't absolutely sure, but thought it might be worth considering anthropology as a career rather than art. Or perhaps I could somehow combine anthropology with art.

Clutching oranges and T-bone steaks, we entered Tola's house in the village without knocking. She was sitting in her Naugahyde recliner, wearing her blanket dress and a needlepoint squash-blossom necklace, covering a Pima basket with beadwork while staring straight out the side window, unseeing. Approaching, delicately, I handed her our gifts while greeting her in the special ceremonial way: "Hom tsitta, hom cha'le, ko'na to' te-wanan teyaye?/*My mother, my child, how have you been passing the days?*"

"K'ettsanisshe, Tsilu/*Happily, Mother's Younger Sister,*" she muttered deliberately while rising slowly, sending the basket and glass beads slithering and tinkling onto the linoleum-covered plank floor. Stepping clear, the old lady walked stiffly into her kitchen with the presents.

I was dumbfounded. We *had* been invited to visit, hadn't we? It's true that we'd been away, but we'd kept in touch. We'd called just last week and announced our arrival. What was going on?

Dennis slipped out the screen door and drove over to Lena's, looking for Hapiya.

I became uneasy, since I'd never before been left alone in the pueblo. It was ominously silent, especially if you considered that this was a day when there were supposed to be big doings. I was sure that Sadie had mentioned a dance or something. And where was she? It wasn't a school day, so where were the kids? I would have to figure out how to interact with Tola, whom I instinctively liked, although I could hardly communicate with her. Over the course of the past four years, I had managed to acquire a vocabulary of a few hundred Zuni words, a bit of grammar, plus an accumulation of memorized greetings, songs, and short prayers. Though Tola's grasp of English was considerably better than my own grasp of Zuni, she definitely preferred speaking in Zuni.

I had to socialize with her somehow—and quick—or else I would find myself sitting silently alone for hours. Entering the kitchen, I caught sight of a troop of silly-looking, soaking-wet, half-naked men trotting by the window in single file. Holding on to one another by the waist, they sang, over and over, their vocable song, "Tumichimchi, tumichimichi, tumichimchi, tumichimchi."

Tola, who was busy filling a large aluminum bucket with water, saw the men and shouted at me, "Quick, Tsilu, it's Muddyheads. Run, get, grab cornmeal."

I dashed over to the bedroom dresser and returned with a cloud-stepped prayer-meal bowl, approaching her gingerly. She turned away from the sink with tears slipping down her cheeks and shoved the bucket toward me, whispering, "Here, sprinkle good thoughts for our dead."

Breathing into my left hand, grabbing a fistful of cornmeal flour from the center of the bowl, turning over and over the prayer Sadie had taught me last year, opening my hand above the center of the bucket, slowly letting go—four narrow powder paths of flowing cornmeal, paths of breath, paths of heart, from the living for the dead—grabbing the bucket of water and cornmeal, swirling it until it formed in galaxies, open and globular cornmeal clusters on the surface of the water, we raced out the side door, climbed up the wooden ladder, and hurled the icy water over the clowns.

All around us, women with pots and buckets, smiling and sobbing their remembrances, pelted water and cornmeal over the passing clowns. And, although my own dead were flipping past me like slides in a timed carousel—my father, aunt, grandfather, grandmother, other grandmother, other grandfather, great-aunt—somehow I just couldn't cry.

Back inside, Tola blotted her eyes on her apron, tucked a long gray strand back behind her right ear, wrinkled up her eyebrows, and looked out from under her puckered epicanthic folds: evaluating my ignorance, my callousness. She knew that I had my own dead—didn't everyone? And she noticed that I hadn't cried. Not a single tear.

SMITHSONIAN INSTITUTION

Why should she talk about sacred things, special things, with a person who, although adopted, could never be truly Zuni? No, she would never tell me why dousing these clowns, known as Koyemshi or Mudheads, made women cry. And I shouldn't have expected her to, after all; she was Badger clan and really tight: kept her money rolled up in the bottom of her apron and her knowledge locked up inside her heart.

I wanted so badly to know, but luckily I had sense enough to keep quiet.

"Tsilu, don't you know those Muddyheads are attanni/*dangerous*? You must show respect, obey them. They're the grandparents of all the kokko/*kachinas*. As rain bringers, they're the most powerful masks of all. If you hold back, deny them anything— water, food, gifts—even in your mind, you get hurt. Maybe you hurt yourself; maybe you hurt your family. Last year Sadie keep back a bushel of apples at Muddyhead Payoff. Pretty soon Shawiti fall off his mountain bike, break his arm. So, if you think to take part in our doings, you must learn to respect Muddyheads, to fear them."

Grabbing my hand, she walked me into the side room, where Sadie had just arrived in order to help out. Around my waist she tied a checkered apron with an appliqué of masked dancers along the hemline, then ordered me to wash and powder my hands with cornstarch. Passing me a chipped cream-colored enamel basin, she set me to work kneading dough.

It was hard work, but just right for contemplating. Though I had helped Tola splash the clowns with water, I had also denied them my tears; I had tried to cry, just couldn't; but maybe next time. If today was Mudhead dunking, I thought, then the men must have left yesterday on their pilgrimage to Kachina Village, the Land of the Dead.

Tola plunked down a small pottery jar which overflowed with fresh blood and a large speckled blue-enameled bowl filled with sheep's liver and stomach, plus yards and yards of grayish-yellow intestine. Smiling at me, oh so broadly, as my mother used to do whenever she gave me a hateful task, Tola said, "Here, when you're done with the sourdough, stuff these."

Negative thoughts coursed through my head. How can this disgusting stinky stuff become the delicacy known as "blood pudding"? Why am I always nearby when revolting work comes up? What is Dennis off doing anyway? Probably just talking and talking with Hapiya, or helping out with something or other, whatever. Surely men's work is less disturbing.

Noticing the look I gave when her mother pushed the sheep gut at me, Sadie smiled and remarked, "You'll get used to it. I'll help you, this time." As we rolled up our sleeves together I noticed, for the first time, Sadie's tattoos. I had never thought much about them before, since the subject of tattooing had never been mentioned by any of that famous flock of ethnographers who, over the past one hundred years, had found themselves at Zuni Pueblo. Actually, I'd noticed quite a lot of tattooing on other ladies: arabesques and letters of the alphabet stretched from wrists past elbows—each one a friendship pledge, a man or woman not to be forgotten—and that was about all I knew of it thus far. Someday, perhaps, I would ask Sadie all about tattooing: how, when, and why it was done. Should I do it? Should Dennis do it? Did Zuni men ever tattoo themselves? I'd never noticed.

Sadie helped me empty the undigested food from the sheep stomach, turn it inside out, and wash it till the water ran cream-colored. Together we cleaned and washed the intestines, mixed four cups of cornmeal and about a tablespoon of salt into the blood, diced six potatoes, six chiles, about a quarter-pound of fat, and mixed it all together. Grabbing gobs of multicolored gunk, we started ramming it into the long, limp intestines.

Sadie told me that one time, a while back, she had found two mice in her washing machine, so she put a cat in there with them; but that tabby just stared straight ahead and refused to do anything to the mice. Finally, when they ran into the outlet pipe, Sadie pulled them out with a pair of jewelry tweezers. Then there was the time a mouse got into her toaster, inside the crumb tray; there was a strange smell in the kitchen, but she couldn't find it, just kept using that toaster until, one day when she was cleaning it from the top, the cloth caught on something way down inside, the claws of a dead mouse. She removed them and cleaned the inside of the toaster with Lysol, over and over. Sabin wanted her to throw the thing out. He still refuses to eat toast made in that toaster.

I countered with a mouse story of my own. One morning Dennis, on arising, put his feet down and a mouse ran out from under the bed between them. It scampered across the room and into the closet. We looked inside and, in the corner under a mound of dirty laundry, we found a nest. Since we didn't want to kill the mouse we couldn't use a spring trap, so we looked all around and found a sturdy cardboard box with the lid still attached at one end. Placing the lid on the floor, Dennis held the box open with one hand while flushing the mouse out of the corner with a coat hanger. Mr. Mouse ran right at him and he dropped the box. When he lifted the box and peeked in, the mouse was not inside, but smashed flat on the floor beneath the lid.

We continued to stuff the sheep gut in silence; my hands stank, clotted blood caught under each nail. I wondered why in the devil was I sitting there making blood pudding and telling inane domestic stories?

Sadie stood up, washed and patted dry her hands, and carried over a VM reel-to-reel tape player. While cuing a tape, she explained that she had captured the songs last fall. She had set up her machine in a house next to the kiva on the main dance plaza, with the full knowledge of all those inside (people entering were motioned to be quiet), but without the knowledge of the performers. She remarked that the Muddyheads were barefoot with black leggings, the Zuni-Hopi kachinas were hish tso'ya/ *very beautiful,* there were lots of colors, and the female kachinas, impersonated by men, wore tablitas/*wooden headdresses.* She suggested that I copy the tape, so that we would have some "good music" to listen to back east. While I dutifully copied the recording, Sadie brought out others, dozens and dozens of tapes.

Maybe Sadie would let me copy all her tapes, I contemplated; then perhaps I could study music with Sabin and Kwinsi. I already knew that Zuni music had not been well described, because songs had always been collected from men who performed alone for strangers and their machines. The inadequacies of the recordings did not bother these collectors in the least, since their goal was to study Indian music as a cultural survival rather than as a contemporary "art" form. Early descriptions of Zuni dance as "a monotonous movement of the body," and Zuni song as "more or less monotonous, but said to have been composed for the occasion," were echoed by generations of later scholars. Not only were such people uninterested in the artistry of the music they collected, but they placed it in the junkyard of the "primitive," asserting that Indians have no musical system, no rules of composition, few musical composers, no teachers, and no concerts. Apparently Indian music was somehow natural, like birdsong.[1]

It was clear to me that the Zuni musical repertory included distinct ceremonial genres. Corn-grinding songs, for example, which are sung in a soft, relaxed manner, have a range of an octave or more, and their texts shape rhythmic units arranged in single or double stanzas. Medicine-society songs have simple texts and diatonic melodies without semitones which are composed strophically, in a chain pattern, with each section containing a short repeated phrase. Kachina songs, with their complex allegorical texts, are sung fortissimo with strong glottal tension, tonal pulsation on longer notes, and glissando between tones. Each song has as many as three distinct diatonic melodies embroidered with short chromatic sequences of semitones.

I had met David McAllester, an expert on Navajo music at Wesleyan, and thought that perhaps Sadie's live-performance tapes might prove useful in studying such topics as melodic contour, vocal register and embellishment, cuing, evaluation, and audience response. I grew excited about the prospect, but upon reflection I became concerned and asked Sadie if anyone ever commented on taping kachina music. "No one looks at me," she replied, but then admitted that on one occasion a dancer wearing a Salimopiya warrior mask, but with the "clothespin eyes" of a Haatashuku (a Laguna clown), stared at her and another lady who was making a recording. "He was acting as if he were trying to make himself big."

Nervously shifting the topic, I mentioned a Hopi kachina dance in which twenty Badger-clan ladies were dressed as traditional maidens, with pinwheel hairdos, shell necklaces, black blanket dresses, multicolored petticoats, red-and-white ceremonial mantles, and silk shawls. The leader and two others were dressed as warriors in short masculine dance kilts, with small copper bells tied behind their right knees and fox pelts attached to their wrists. They carried bows and arrows, which they shot into a bundle of rushes as they sang kachina songs, and danced with the same steps the men used. At the end they threw food to the all-male audience.

Sadie responded that dressing like men, shooting arrows, and singing kachina songs would be too embarrassing for Zuni ladies to do, right here in the pueblo.

"But those ladies, although they don't dress like men, do sing kachina songs," I countered.

"Daisy Hooce started up our group a while back and she's Hopi; they have another way over there in Arizona. Besides, that dance isn't valuable and ladies aren't allowed to sing it in the village, except during Tribal Fair. They mostly dance it around at powwows and Gallup Ceremonial, where the men really kid them, imitate their high voices."

I asked why tape recording was taking place so much lately while picture taking wasn't, at least not openly. Sadie suggested that it might be because there was no ordinance against taping and there was against taking pictures. But recently a Blackfoot policeman, working for the tribe, stopped a lady on her way home from a dance, after she had been seen with a stereo machine peeping out from under her shawl. He asked her, "What are you planning to do with that tape?" When she said it wasn't commercial, "just for herself," he let her go.

Every Saturday now, since Sadie got her machine, her brothers, and other men too, have been dropping by to drink beer and listen to her tapes. Whenever they hear recordings of their own kiva's dances, especially fast ones like Hilili, they get up and start dancing.

Two years ago she went to a Nahalisho/*Crazy Grandchild* dance at Acoma Pueblo, where men and women from the audience got up and danced alongside masked kachinas. Last fall, at a Zuni Crazy Grandchild dance, a Laguna lady started dancing in the audience. "Then she acted like she just couldn't help it, joined the kachinas, and they had to take her out of it. I guess she forgot where she was."

"She should have noticed that she was alone."

"Everyone was looking at her, it was embarrassing.

"Last year, after Shawiti's initiation, he danced only two days and then quit; he was ashamed, felt that everyone knew who he was. We were given instructions as to how to prepare him for dancing. He should wear short pants and a scarf with something valuable, a piece of jewelry, tied around his waist, so that the performance wouldn't just be for nothing.

"You know that old long-hair, living over there near the Gallup Road?"

I nodded. (I'd met him two years earlier at a rain dance.)

"His grandson borrowed some beads for a dance but afterwards didn't return a string. When he brought the bundle back, the owner wasn't there, so he left the bundle. Next day, when the man discovered one strand was missing, he went to the boy's home and accused him of stealing. The child lied, saying, 'It might have been one of your own family.' I just don't know what's happening to our young people today. It must be something going on in the schools.

"Then there's the alcohol problem. You've heard about that boy over there on the south side who shot himself?"

"Yes, I heard. Why do you suppose he did it?"

"He was liquored up, arguing with his father, shouting at him about something. His father broke down, started sobbing, started crying, and when he wasn't looking the boy, his only son, shot himself through the head.

"Kwinsi was there right after it happened and had the job of notifying the suicide's relatives. There was blood and brains splattered on ceiling and walls, and two piles on the floor. The rifle was a really big one, a .30/30. Most of his head was gone, blasted out, but he was left with one red eyeball, just dangling."

After a silence, Sadie added, "Have you heard about Kwinsi's new wife? She's a priest's daughter and doesn't even know how to cook."

"No, but how do you suppose he gets his meals?"

"Maybe her mother does all that for them. Her family's mean, you know, tight in that religious way; they have important masks in their house, and you have to be real quiet when visiting over there. I wonder if they know how wild Kwinsi is. Guess they like him 'cause he's religious— not many are initiated by *two* medicine societies. He paints the masks for his dance group."

"Where is Kwinsi?"

"Over there in Arizona, on that pilgrimage."

"What do you suppose he's thinking about?"

"He's a Coyote man and that group always sings deer-hunting songs, so he must be thinking *deer,* and when he thinks deer he thinks *woman.* You know, if he didn't like the ladies so much he could *do* something in his life, but he's a real hanitu! What is it you call the type?"

"Lady's man, womanizer, Don Juan."

"He's always been like that. Poor Linda, his first wife, she stayed in the house all the time, making her jewelries and crying. I don't know why she didn't go out there into the plaza and fight off those other ladies: she's strong enough all right. His kids still really love him—when he bothers to come around, that is. Korea must have done that to him. You've seen what the army does to our men?"

"Yes, I've seen them return with lots of psychological problems: irritability, touchiness, anger, depression, women problems, work problems, alcohol and drug dependency, insomnia. . . ."

"When Kwinsi left Zuni he didn't have problems; now he's back, and especially now that he's lost his eye, he hardly sleeps. Comes over to Mom's each afternoon and dozes off during the soaps on TV when he should be out tending sheep, working at the Malco station, or some other line of work. I don't think this new wife has got him figured yet. At least he's got no drug or drinking problems, the way other guys did when they returned from fighting overseas. But for some reason, unlike the rest of us, he don't much like making jewelries. Maybe that's why he started having problems with Linda; she was one of the best with channel-inlay turquoise, jet, coral, abalone, and mother-of-pearl kachina masks set in silver watchbands. Almost every year she won prizes at Ceremonial. All Kwinsi seems to like is staying up there on the farm catching eagles, shooting deer, feeding turkeys, watering horses. Of course, there's no money in any of that, but women like him, and since they're the ones to look after a man, he's fine.

"We're done, so all we need do is cook 'em. Now you know how to make blood pudding—so Dennis will never go hungry."

"Should I start up a kettle?"

"No. Old Man wants to roast them outside, probably to-morrow."

The door opened and Hapiya walked in with his son-in-law Nelson and Dennis, who had struggled all afternoon with the transmission in Lena's pickup. Their hands and clothes were filthy and Dennis had big smudges over his left eye and on his chin.

After washing up in Sadie's bathroom, Hapiya walked back into the kitchen proclaiming loudly, "Where's Shawiti? It's time to make the prayer sticks."

"I'm not sure, probably listening to records in his room," Sadie replied.

"Always listening to that rock-and-roll when he should be learning something serious," Hapiya said with disgust, disappearing into his grandson's bedroom.

Although we were both bushed, we perked up at the thought of prayer sticks. Hapiya had suggested, more than once over the years, that he might teach Dennis how to make prayer sticks.

We left the pueblo, heading out for the country. As we drove past the abandoned day school, Hapiya demanded the car be stopped; everybody jumped out and he instructed Shawiti to run down to the creek and harvest red-willow shoots. He was to pick straight ones, from the center of each rootstock, so they would stay together in families, in clans.

He must apologize to the willow, not the one he cuts but the one right next to her. Offer her a bit of jeweled cornmeal and a prayer, then cut softly, only what he needs and no more, bundle her up, and take her home. Since he had just recently been initiated he would have only three sticks to make. But one day, after he joined a medicine society, he would have five.

Up at the country house, Shawiti measured out each stick, one by one against his right hand, and cut it with his penknife. Hapiya cut four sticks for the ancestors, two from the tip to the base of his right center finger, one to the center of his palm, and the other to his wrist. The fifth stick, for Sun Father, he measured from the tip of his center right-hand finger to inside his elbow. Leaving the big room, he walked back into the kitchen, where he found Tola dozing at her work table in the corner. Upon his approach she awoke from her dream.

It had been snowing. The men were out hunting and she was sitting by the fire, in her black blanket dress and flowered petticoat, with her white doeskin leggings and moccasins stretched out straight in front of her, waiting for them to return to camp. Gazing up at the fine snow slipping through long thin pine needles, she sensed something, someone, a person perhaps, nearby. Upon turning around, she found it was a large buck! Looking right at her, he said, "Tie me up, Mother." She jumped up and hit him over the head with her cast-iron frying pan. It was all she had. But then, because she lacked a corn ear and jeweled cornmeal, she could not properly send him over there to the deer remake at Kachina Village. She was worrying and worrying, because she didn't want to offend him, to kill him outright, once and for all. Maybe his road had not yet come to its end. Maybe he wasn't really a deer.[2]

Hapiya took her arm and measured four sticks: three for the ancestors, tip of her right center finger to the base of the finger, tip of this same finger to inside base of palm, and tip to wrist. Her Moon Mother stick, like his Sun Father stick, was measured from the tip of her center finger to her inside elbow.

Opening a cedar box, he laid out his feathers one by one: turkey, downy eagle, Canada goose, warbler, robin, bluebird, and mallard. After getting out hand-spun cotton twine, he crushed a turkey quill between his teeth, wrapped it tightly with cord, attached it to the top of the stick, then wound the cord down, feather by feather, with four wraps between each quill.

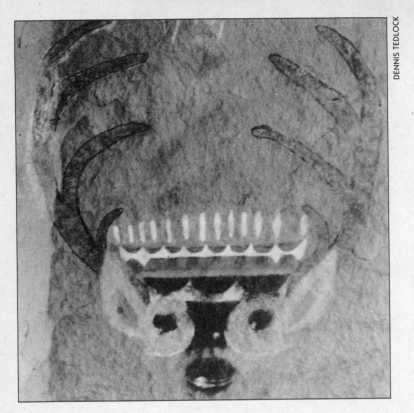

Next came the pendant series, with tiny coral beads and smaller feathers from all the same birds except the first, which was a downy-turkey feather.

He peeled each stick, cut flat surfaces for feet, and carved a face with turquoise eyes and coral mouth. Then he got out his paints, black for ancestors, yellow for Moon Mother, and turquoise for Sun Father. When he finished cutting, feathering, peeling, and painting, he taught Shawiti a prayer.[3]

> *Thus many are the days since the middle time*
> *for those who are our fathers*

BARBARA TEDLOCK

sacred bundles
rain bundles
corn bundles
when four days were made.

From all wooded places
we break young shoots
male willow
female willow.

In our hands we hold them fast
give them human form.

With striped cloud wing
who is our father
male turkey
we give our wands human form.

With the flesh of our mothers
Black Paint Woman
Clay Woman
Cotton Woman
even a poorly made cotton thread

Four times encircling

> *tying their bodies*
> *we finish our sticks*
> *our Sacred Younger Sisters.*

Wrapping the sticks in corn husks and placing them in a basket, Hapiya cautioned his grandson, "Remember these things are tehya, kind of precious, not to be thrown away on just anyone."

It was time for us to leave. Since we wanted to be back before dawn, we drove to the trailer park on the eastern edge of the reservation and spent the night crumpled up in the car.

At dawn, when we arrived in the lower fields, Tola and Hapiya were sprinkling cornmeal while talking in Zuni to the corn plants: "You, our children, hurry along now." Hapiya dug a shallow east-west trench the length of his right arm, sprinkled cornmeal mixed with bits of turquoise, coral, and shell into it, and unwrapped the prayer sticks, handing them out to the people he had measured them by.

He stood at one end of the ditch, facing east, with Tola at the other end, also facing east, and they deposited their sticks at the same time. Shawiti planted his in a straight line between theirs. They each took a bit of cornmeal and, holding it to their lips, prayed for health, long life, clouds, rain, food, clothing, then sprinkled the feathers. Now they would return home to begin a four-day sacred time, known as Teshkwi/*Fasting,* when there could be no commercial transactions, arguments, or sex; a time when no one used salt or consumed greasy foods—meat, avocados, or coffee.

As for us, well, we could participate in the fasting if we really wanted to. Hapiya might make us a pair of prayer sticks next full moon, next Shalako, next winter solstice, next summer solstice, next whatever, and take us along the cornmeal path with him, but not now, not this summer solstice—Itiwana/*Middle Place, Middle Time,* where everything that happens, happens here.

Coyotes walking the line together
watching
waiting for the invite in
a scrap of food or a cornmeal blessing
some other day
some other time
some other place
perhaps.

7

THE GLEAM IN THE BUTCHER'S EYE

■ ■ ■ ■

IT WAS RUTTING SEASON and the does, with their hugely swollen vulvas, were pacing back and forth along the rim of the woods, waiting impatiently. A six-point buck, with bulging neck and peeling velvet dangling from his antlers, arrived and dashed around the herd, sniffing hocks and genitals. Finding a doe in estrus, he licked her vulva, slowly. Stimulating her. She urinated. He licked her urine, then curled his upper lip up and raised his head, flehmening—breathing in her odors deeply. He licked her head and body with his tongue. She returned his caresses and he tried to mount, but, rather than stand for him, she paced. He flicked his tongue in and out, rolled it round and round his lips, licked her all over, again and again. This time she allowed him to mount her. The flexible tip of his penis sought out her vagina, he thrust once and plunged into her—ejaculating, then withdrawing. She squatted as though to urinate, pushed down hard with her tail upraised over her body, and ran off into the woods.

We had only been back in Zuni a couple of weeks when we went out behind the hogback to hunt for bones and feathers for some mixed-media sculpture I had started working on. Dennis was first to reappear, cradling a jumbled load: four deer vertebrae, a horse jaw, a cow skull, and a coccyx. Mockingbird and flicker feathers were stuck, like pens, behind both ears.

Tola burst out laughing and improvised the opening line of a song to commemorate the occasion: "Ho'naawan kyamme saw lhat allukkya/*Our uncle went out hunting for bones.*" Then she asked me if I planned to reconstruct a deer, a horse, a cow, or something like that. When I failed to respond she volunteered that back in the 1940s or '30s there were Zunis who decorated cow skulls for sale to tourists: smoothing, filling in gaps around teeth and hairline skull cracks, painting with gesso, gluing on bits of buckskin, dripping on rainbows, glass beads. But they don't do this anymore; only a handful of Apaches, over on the White Mountain Reservation, are still making them.

Back at the farmhouse I timidly passed around photos of my boneworks and featherworks. Sadie took a quick look and asked seriously, perhaps, if feathered skulls could be traded back east for groceries.

What could I say? That there were no real trading posts back east? That I made these strange sculptures with no thought of actually selling them? That I mixed feathery painted bones together with flowering potted plants in my living- and dining-room window boxes back east as a reminder of the constant presence of death within life?

No, this gap between us was just too big to fill in with a quip, a joke, or an anecdote.

My silence invited Sadie to suggest that pottery might be a

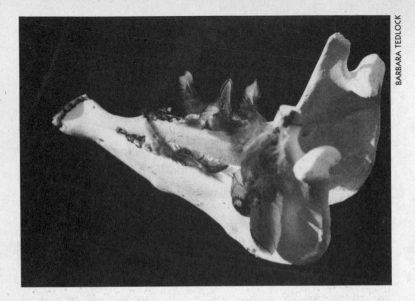

better craft with which to support Dennis, and she offered to teach me. I accepted and was sent down to the barn for paintbrushes, dried bee plant, kaolin, and red clay.

The huge hand-hewn barn was filled with the heavy odor of aging hay. Finding a row of narrow-leaf yucca brushes spread out neatly on a wooden shelf, I picked one up and examined it. Someone had chewed the blade separating fibers; there were ten bristles in all. I picked up one brush after another, counting bristles: some had but one fiber left, while others had as many as twelve. Chunks of powdery-white kaolin, for slip, were lined up next to the brushes, and dangling above them was a mass of brown leaves dotted with lavender flowers: Rocky Mountain beeplant, for making black paint. I had trouble finding clay until I realized that it was kept under an empty pinto-bean sack, inside a big white-enameled bowl. After gathering up a fistful of brushes and chunks of kaolin, I pulled out my Swiss Army knife and cut off two bunches of beeplant. With all these things tucked under

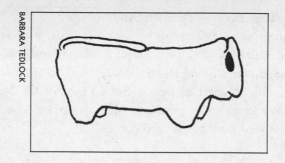

BARBARA TEDLOCK

the sack on top of the bowl of clay, I had just one load to carry up to the house.

While walking back to the house, I contemplated asking about the religious significance of beeplant and yucca leaves. Yuccas had attracted me since my first visit. Not only were the spiny leaves and long spike topped with creamy bell-like flowers handsome, but I knew that a wonderful shampoo could be made from the thick fibrous roots. I wondered if I should ask Sadie how to prepare the shampoo, but decided not to: if she had wanted to tell me, she would have, long ago. Likewise for kaolin and red clay, the body of Our Mother Earth. After all, not only was humankind born from within her body, but the precise location of any individual potter's clay bed, whether up on Corn Mountain or here in the valley, was a secret. So, even though I was curious, very curious, I kept my mouth shut tight. Once I had set the bowl down in the stone sink, I helped Flora clear breakfast dishes off the table and wipe the wood clean.

When I carried over the damp clay, mixed with powdered potsherds,[1] and mounded it in the center of the table, Sadie's daughter, Ramona, realized that she would be expected to help out. She slammed out the screen door and dashed down the hill into the cornfields, searching for her brother. Tola smiled patiently, and sat down as her other granddaughters, Elaine and Sila, scooted up to the table next to Flora and began hand-building. Together they rolled out thin ropes of red clay, coiling them, squeezing, scraping, and smoothing owls, ashtrays, and bowls, breathing in the sweet, sweet smell of Mother Earth. I built, sanded, and slipped Hoktitasha/*Longtail,* Hunter of Deer, Hunter of Elk, Hunter of Bison, Beast Priest of the North—seven inches long, small pert ears, short stout legs, and thick tail laid forward from rump to shoulders.

Lonely lovely cat of as many latitudes as names—puma, panther, painter, cougar, coj, catamount, onça-parda, galaxmu, suasuarana, hoktitasha, mixtli, nashdúitso, mountain lion, American lion, Mexican lion, león—I've loved you ever since that summer day in the Canadian Rockies when we saw you, or thought we did, my father, now long gone, and I. You there at the mouth of the river with your muscular buckskin-brown coat, white nose, dark lips, yellow eyes with black slit pupils, bits of black both sides of muzzle, hissing, then rippling belly, slack skin swaying, black blurs behind both ears and on far tip of disappearing tail—

Tola noticed me whispering while I shoved watermelon seeds into my mountain lion's eye sockets, and poked me gently with an elbow. "Tsilu, you have to make little balls for eyes. Those won't work when he bakes."

Sadie looked up, chuckled, and said, "Our aunt makes Longtail, but no one else does."

Everybody giggled and Tola suggested, "Why don't you polish and paint him? Then we fire him and take him along with the others to the traders. If we tell them he's a Beast Priest, they probably think a Zuni built him. Then they maybe like him. Buy him. Sure would be a good one on them." They tittered

BARBARA TEDLOCK

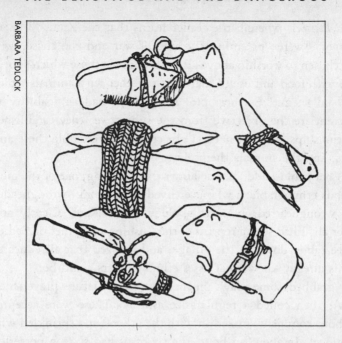

while passing my first figurine from hand to hand, pulling on his short ears, tugging on his long tail.

Why don't the women like him? Because they don't build ceramic prey animals today, and perhaps they never did.[2] After all, it's men's tiny limestone, azurite, and alabaster wolves, bears, coyotes, and mountain lions that slip from buckskin pouches locked away at the Smithsonian Institution; fetishes brought back east during the 1880s by soldiers and ethnographers.[3] But why don't women build these power animals?

Perhaps because prey animals are hunters, warriors, and curers. Zuni religion, and most especially that magical topic "fetishism" (uttered in hushed tones by collectors as tiny stone animals pass from hand to hand at ever-spiraling prices), had been steadily mined since 1883, when Frank Hamilton Cushing published his

Zuñi Fetishes, wherein the reader learns that the Zuni, "like all savages," were "preeminently men of war and the chase, who had chosen to worship above all other animals those which supply him with food and useful materials together with animals which prey on them." Furthermore, since they "had an inability to differentiate the objective from the subjective, they established relationships between natural objects which resemble these animals, and the animals themselves."[4]

What could I add? A disclaimer that Cushing, one of the most famous ethnographers who ever lived, was wrong, wrongheaded and wronghearted? No. An apology to the Zuni? Clearly not. After all, I had seen a reprint of the Cushing pamphlet on Sadie's coffee table, down in the village, and realized that all educated Zunis already knew what asses ethnographers could be.

I grabbed some clay, pinched out a miniature prayer-meal bowl, then coiled a regular-size ashtray. These were accepted without comment, mixed in with the others, and sprinkled with cornmeal. In about an hour, the six of us had sixteen potteries, which, after setting, painting, and firing, would bring a carton of Pampers for baby, a bushel of peaches for grandma, and some comic books for the herders. Not bad, but . . .

Dennis suddenly shouted from the corral, "Cooome. Bring the truck. They've got a deer."

Jumping up, I headed for the cornfield. Sure enough, Ramona's brother Seff had shot a doe with his father's gun, a Winchester single-shot bolt-action .22-caliber rifle.

There she was, green-eyed and lovely in her russet coat. Hapiya was kneeling down beside her, saying softly in the Zuni language, "May you visit us often. Be happy." He lit a hand-rolled cigarette, took a deep drag, and blew strong wild-tobacco smoke into her hair. As he gently sucked the remaining breath from her nostrils, her eyes seemed to turn from pale blue-green into dark jade-green.

Kwinsi unbuckled his hunting knife from his belt as Hapiya flipped the doe over on her back. Grasping a hank of hair about five inches above her vulva, Kwinsi pulled the hide and muscle away from her viscera, and inserted his four-inch blade. He then firmly sliced through flesh and layers of meaty muscle into the inner cavity, thrust his left hand inside the carcass, sawed upward till he hit ribs, and pushed hard with both hands, cracking through bone, wiggling the knife toward her throat. Pausing a moment before attacking her windpipe, he said, "Well, Tsilu, as you can see, it takes some skill for this."

I nodded, trying hard to be nonchalant, as he wiped his knife on his dirty khakis. But when he took a deep breath and plunged his blade in at the top of the doe's windpipe, I jumped. He drove it through her hide, up to the hilt, and cut up and out in a single stroke. As Hapiya grasped the windpipe and yanked, loosening her heart and lungs, I started feeling weak.

Now, at her crotch, where the hind legs joined, Kwinsi sliced straight down till he hit the pelvis. Wiggling his knife around, he found a longitudinal hairline crack, stabbed hard, then hammered the handle with the heel of his left hand. Levering the blade downward, he finished the break, exposing the small intestine, and cut out her anus with a single stroke. He reached into her chest and cut the diaphragm loose from the body cavity, then, grasping her windpipe with both hands, pulled till heart, lungs, and viscera came out in a rush, all together.

Kwinsi instructed Ramona and Seff to dig a small hole about a foot from where the doe fell, and bury her lungs and bladder together with "strong cornmeal," that special mix with white shell and turquoise that he carried in a tiny buckskin pouch tied to his belt, next to his hunting knife. On top they placed her liver, kidneys, stomach, and intestines, an offering to "raw persons": mountain lion, coyote, bobcat, and wolf.

Respectfully they lifted the doe into the truck in order to bring

DENNIS TEDLOCK

her up the long hill to their grandparents' house. As they approached the front door, Tola emerged and leaned over the flatbed, sprinkling cornmeal on the doe from her throat down to where her heart once was. Addressing both the hunter and doe —"Kesh to'n aawiya?/*Are you coming now?*"—she led the way into the house with a cornmeal trail. The grandchildren grabbed front and rear legs and strained to lift their doe. She was bulky and heavy, heavier than either of them, but they managed somehow to carry her up and over the threshold.

After leading them into the center of the room along the narrow cornmeal path she sprinkled as she walked, Tola showed them how to lay out the doe on the floor, gently, with her head toward the east. Together they would help her travel the paths of raw people out west of Zuni, all the way to Kachina Village, Land of the Dead. If she had always been a deer, then year after year they might hunt her, and send her back over there to be reborn as a deer. But if she had once been a human, akna ho"i/*cooked person,* living off cooked food, then she could be reborn as a deer, ky'apin ho"i/*raw person,* living off raw food, but three times.[5]

After a total of four deer lives she would be transformed into a stinkbug, living on tall grasses beside streams and ponds until one day, squashed under someone's foot, she would let go her perfume, odor of electrical fire, and slide backward into the black hole of emergence. But nobody was quite sure which kind of deer she really was.

As blood trickled from her muzzle and streamed out toward an enormous crack in the linoleum, where it would seep into the earthen floor beneath, Tola placed a speckled, forked corn ear, the female kind, against Doe's breast, where her heart once was. Gathering around the doe, everyone took up a handful of corn-meal, and Hapiya started singing her home. Between stanzas we dusted her with jeweled cornmeal till head, neck, and shoulders were coated, fluffy white, and she was on her way.

Kwinsi sat on the edge of a big bumpy bed under a clothesline, from which hung hunks of jerked mutton, quarter-inch strips of jerked venison, and a drying box turtle. A black horse-tail braid was tied round Turtle's neck and a river-smooth pebble was tied to his tail. In a couple of days he would cut his turtle down, remove him from his shell, and bury the flesh with a prayer to carry him back to Kachina Village to be reborn, a turtle. Then he would scrape the inside of the shell with a rasp, wedge in a stick to expand it, and leave it outside in the sun to dry. Later he'd drill a hole, thread it with buckskin, tie on a bunch of dewclaws: a new leg rattle.

Everyone had gone outside except for me, Flora, and the little girls, who stayed behind watching Kwinsi sharpen his hunting knife. He ran the blade over and over his whetstone, added water, then pulled the edge over the circular razor strop eight times in each direction, while explaining how breathing the final breath from a dying game animal improves a hunter's relationship with all animals. It gives him both success in hunting and the knowl-edge of which ones to kill and which ones to let go.

DENNIS TEDLOCK

He grinned as he ground the gleaming edge of his blade on the stone, while explaining that it was important not to slip and cut into the musk bag, or tarsal glands, on the inside hocks of the hind legs. Just one stab in any of these places and a willing sacrifice became spoiled meat. She had been willing, all right: looked straight up with her huge moist eyes, without a cough, a snort, or even a twitch. Still, as Seff took aim, fired—"It was just exactly like Grandpa told us," Ramona announced. "She saw us there and stopped. Didn't sneeze, cough, bleat, stomp, flap her ears, wiggle her nose, tail, or nothing. But that loud towowo sound, that ruined it for us."

"Yes, it would have been much better if you had walked right up to her, sure of yourselves, and smothered her in cornmeal and white shell with your bare hands; for then, and only then, would she truly be yours," Kwinsi replied.

"Could you please explain to me why it's better to smother a deer than shoot it?" I asked.

Back and forth ground Kwinsi's knife on the whetstone. Elaine and Ramona giggled, but Flora looked away, embarrassed. I realized that I had asked a direct question. The only sound was that of the sharpening knife. After what was only a few seconds but seemed to me like ten minutes, Kwinsi began singing a song whose words translate:

> *Dawn Boy goes along singing*
> *with rainbow arc and lightning arrows.*
>
> *"Yellow flowers sprout from my ears*
> *blue flowers from my nose*
> *red flowers between my eyes*
> *white flowers from my mouth.*
>
> *Each knee has flowers*
> *each elbow has flowers*
> *navel flowers*
> *heart flowers.*
>
> *Come deer*
> *come to my flowers*
> *come to my all-colored flowers."*[6]

I was relieved that he was acting as if I simply weren't there. He was a Coyote Society member and this was a hunter's song, a religious song, and by then I knew enough not to attempt to ask him anything about it.[7] But I had heard that Coyote men were trained to cure "deer sickness," a form of nymphomania caused when a hunter is startled, witched by an antelope or a deer. The grandchildren were clearly surprised by this doe, so it was crucial to ask her forgiveness, that she not transmit to them her feral sexuality.

Kwinsi prayed rapidly in a hushed voice with half-closed eyes, then, opening them wide, gazed at the lifeless doe. Beginning at her head, he separated the skull from the atlas joint by cutting all around her neck, through to the first vertebra, and twisting. Carefully lifting her head off, he placed it on the floor before the corner fireplace, facing east. While still praying rapidly, he sprinkled the top of her head and big ears with cornmeal.

I felt suddenly compelled to take photos of the skinning-and-butchering process. I could just see it: my grad-school friends lounging on floor pillows and Navajo rugs dreaming away during one of our exotic Southwestern slide shows, vision-questing an ancient, pristine, melancholy, lost America, then—these gory slides. The dull eye of the dead deer and the gleam in the butcher's eye.

"Mind if I shoot up a bunch of film? Or use a flash?" I blurted out.

"Since when do I mind photos, I'm k'okshi/*handsome,* no? Seriously, look here, Tsilu, see these larvae in her nostrils? Old Man says that when larvae come out of a deer's nose they turn into napulakkya/*deer-butterflies,* and it's the butterflies that witch you, craze you."

"When you're stalking a deer, singing about flowers blooming all over your body, I suppose the butterflies slither down the deer's long nostrils, and flutter over to your body flowers?"

"You might say that."

"Then the deer's curiosity about deer-butterflies brings her over to you?"

"Deer do like to eat flowers, you know."

"Oh, it's the flowers, then, not the butterflies?"

"Well, you might say that. But remember, Tsilu, it's the *hunter* that gets the deer."

Kwinsi explained that, if Seff hadn't blasted the doe, he'd have a perfect hide for women's doeskin leggings and moccasins, but with that black hole, the hide was worthless. Another time, when Seff was a bit older, and understood what he was about, he'd come up softly, singing and talking to her, a young man ready to marry. Like old-timers, he'd smother her in cornmeal, slit her viscera, and stab through her diaphragm. Reaching all the way to her four-chambered heart, he would grab a handful of fresh hot blood for his stone mountain lion to drink, then tear out her liver and eat it raw, ottsi/*like a man!*

Later on, perhaps, when he had two perfect skins from two perfect kills, he'd ask for a woman in marriage.

Ramona shouted, "But I saw her first. She should have been mine."

"Yes, you probably did, and in the future you'll bring your husband many deer by your dreams."

"But I want to hunt too. Just the same as Seff."

"You can, while you're still small. I'll take you along with me next time I go," Kwinsi promised, then chuckled as he flipped Miss Doe over onto her back and began peeling her. Starting at her neck, he slit the skin down to the slot where he had gutted her, then made another cut on the side of each hind leg, starting at her crotch and running down to her musk sacs.

I stood on the threshold, evaluating the subject brightness, the contrast rendered by incident light bouncing off her hide. Then the subject reflectivity range, the quality of light bouncing off her matte hair and urine-soaked tarsal glands. Wanting images that were simultaneously documentary and interpretive, in order to learn about the butchering process and to evoke the dismemberment of this lovely once-living being, I decided to bounce my electronic flash gun off the whitewashed ceiling at the classic $f5.6$.

My shutter clicked and the gun flashed.

Straddling the doe, Kwinsi loosened her hide around the gut opening and placed his hands inside, working them around her hips toward her back. When he was halfway round, he separated

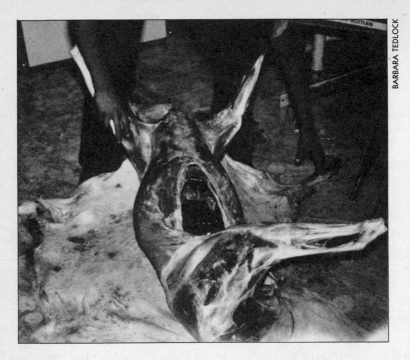

the skin on the outside of her legs, then peeled it off, musk sacs and all, exposing her purple-red flanks, green-violet veins, and gray-white tendons. Click-flash. He looked up at me, grinned, and yanked the skin down over the rump and off her tail. Then he slit her from neck to gut and slipped the skin slowly off her forelegs, like unzipping a kid from a snowsuit.

Click-flash.

"Have you ever noticed how deer flesh looks human?"

"No."

"Her hair is thin, smooth, soft, straight, just like human hair, like women's hair. She smells just like a woman too."

"No, I've never noticed, but I've heard deer musk is an important ingredient in perfume."

"Yes indeed, but it sure can spoil meat."

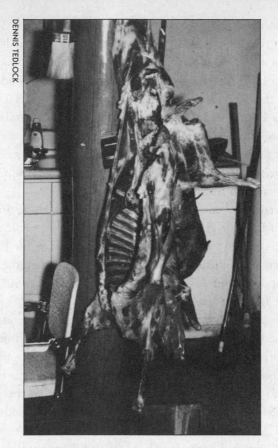

DENNIS TEDLOCK

"But venison is sweet. At least compared with beef, that is."

Shaking his head and smiling broadly while hoisting the carcass onto his shoulder, he replied, "No, Tsilu, not sweeter, just better. More delicate—tender, you know, like the ladies. Especially Zuni ladies, those two-legged *dears* who love corn so much their flesh has that corn-loving fat in it."

Hanging the dead doe from the huge steel hook to drain her blood, he smiled knowingly at his sister Flora and me. We looked away quickly from both him and his dripping doe. I kicked open the screen door and walked down the hill, to where Tola was toasting green onions and chile peppers in the hot coals.

Hapiya asked me if anyone had brought along ummo ky'awe/ *foam water* from the village, so I went back up the hill and inside to check the Styrofoam cooler. Yes indeed, there was Tuush an Hepikkya Ky'awe/*Horse Piss,* and Yalaa Ky'awe/*Mountain Water.* Both brands named in Zuni for their key advertising symbols: *Horse Piss* for the giant Clydesdale horses pulling covered wagons on Budweiser ads, and *Mountain Water* for the idyllic Colorado mountain stream featured in Coors ads.

Flora reminded me that her father preferred Horse Piss, so I grabbed a Bud for Hapiya and two Coors, one for Tola and one for Dennis. Sadie, who came up to grab a 7-Up for her drive back down to the village, called out to her elder brother, "Hey there, handsome guy. What do you say? What have you got for your ever lovvvely sisters?"

Kwinsi pulled down the doe, placed her on the wooden work table, hacked off her hind- and forequarters, split her midsection in half, separated her flanks from her ribs, and cut through to her backbone. Then, getting out a long role of white freezer paper, and a black marker, he wrapped and labeled the venison: flank for Sadie, short loin for her elder sister, Lena, and the ribs for Flora. After wrestling these huge hunks of meat into the back seat of the emerald-green Buick, Sadie and Flora climbed in and, without starting up the motor, coasted down the hill, waving goodbye.

When he returned to his butchering he said to me, "I've got to save these little bones. We plant them in the cornfield to improve our harvest." Afraid to ask any more stupid questions, I silently nodded.

After all of the steaks were prepared, I carried them down to the open fire. Hapiya placed them on his grill, a warped refrigerator-shelf balanced on four stones, and I went back up to the house.

Standing in the blood stench of Tola's country kitchen that late summer evening, I stared at the weathered windowsill that held a weasel skull, a red bandanna, an empty potato-chip can covered with a constellation map, a headless rubber doll, rusted screws, bolts, nails. In one corner was an aluminum bucket with miscellaneous bloody sheep parts, a charred head with empty eye sockets on top; in another corner, a pink plastic bucket bulging with vegetables: red and white radishes, carrots, cabbage, jalapeño peppers, spinach, and Bibb lettuce. In the center of the room, on the work table, surrounding what remained of the carved-up carcass, were fistfuls of fragrant spearmint and cilantro, mixed with pungent garlic and scallions.

Kwinsi nudged me gently with his forearm as he wiped his hands off on his mother's checkered apron. "Hey, Kachinmana/ *Mother of the Kachinas* [my Hopi name], did you know that twin unborn fawns stuffed with corn, carrots, radishes, onions, oregano, chinchweed, and cilantro, roasted all night in an outdoor oven, are the most tender, the best of all meats?"

"No. But one thing I know for damn sure is that Asheewe/ *Zunis* sure do love their shee/*meat*."

Giggling together, we grabbed a couple of Mountain Waters, popped the tops, and headed down for the fire. Fresh venison on piñon coals, scorched chiles in our nostrils, and cold Coors: the ultimate Zuni barbecue.

This time our goodbyes were not as traumatic as before; I guess that Hapiya and Tola had figured that we would keep coming around, whenever we could. Tola gave me two loaves of fresh oven bread and a bagful of jerky for a road picnic on our way back.

Down in the pueblo Sadie and Sabin told us of an encounter they'd recently had in Gallup with Puushi, an infamous Zuni witch. He left a small container of salt on their restaurant table after talking to them. "He must have wanted us to use that stuff," but they knew better and didn't use it (for fear it might be poisoned). He also gave them some pork chops, which they later gave back to him. He wanted a ride back to Zuni, which they reluctantly agreed to, but on their way out of town, when they saw him standing outside a bar, they speeded up to get past. Sabin said, "Everybody around here is really afraid of that guy."

Sadie mentioned that she was worried about her younger brother Joe, who was in Vietnam. He'd joined the service because he'd been having a drinking problem and had split up with his wife. She'd heard that some of the younger soldiers had gotten into drugs and she wondered if he was okay.

After a brief pause, she added that she'd been staying at home nearly all the time these days and hadn't even been inside the new tribal office building. Sabin invited her to a PTA pot-luck supper, but she didn't go; her kids would like her to attend the basketball games they're playing in, but she doesn't. She noted disapprovingly that kachina dolls are being sold over the counter in the Zuni Craftsmen Cooperative and added that many older Zunis object to this.

Sabin complained that ever since last year, when the tribe took over local BIA functions and the tribal council was presented the Interior Department's Indian Leadership Award, "those guys have been bragging all over the village." They had made important decisions without even bothering to call a general meeting, including paving the major streets and putting in storm drains. Sadie's dad is furious about this, since he always attended and nearly always used the occasion for fancy oratory. Sadie is pleased, though, because her dad, without these public meetings to attend, won't be so visible, won't be so vulnerable to witch attacks.

"The governor seems to be scared of the people and prefers to communicate with the 'Zuni Tribal Newsletter.' But this just isn't right," Sabin said. "Besides, there's still a lot of old-timers who don't read English, and how are they to keep themselves notified on all the important changes? We can't just throw our old people away. They've got a lot of knowledge. As Old Man says, 'The world must be getting too old,' yes, the world must be getting too old." Sabin went on to remind us of what the old-timers had said about how one day there would be black water (coffee) and other new things to drink. Since these things had come true, it might also come true that the world would get too old and we'd be boiled in a hot rain.

He asked if we'd noticed that all the water in Black Rock Lake was gone. We hadn't. It seems that the irrigation gate had been opened to send water down to the Zuni Redi-Mix (the latest tribal enterprise). The usual procedure was to open the floodgate first in order to wash out some of the silt, and then open the irrigation gate. But somehow, by mistake, they opened both gates at once, with the result that silting caused the irrigation ditch to overflow. Then, when they went to close the gates, they bent the shaft in turning the wheel for the floodgate and couldn't get it shut. "Perhaps a rock had washed under it and the gate just stopped there; then they tried to force it and bent the shaft." As a result, all the water in the lake went out the floodgate.

"And that's the end of my story. All the water in Black Rock Lake is gone, and all the little fishes were just left there to die."

On this note we said our goodbyes, promising to return again next summer, when school was out.

MOON SONG

■ ■ ■ ■

Arriving in Gallup the following summer, we quickly found a comfortable furnished apartment and phoned Sadie in order to let the family know we were in town. Then I phoned Kwinsi, at his mother-in-law's place down at Zuni, and after asking about everyone's health I asked him if he would consider doing an interview with me sometime. He jumped at the opportunity, suggesting that he and his wife would be in town the next morning to do some shopping.

I planned to ask him about kachina songs, maybe play him a tape from his kiva group, the one that I'd copied from his sister Sadie. But since Sadie had mentioned on the phone that he had recently been initiated by the Neweekwe Medicine Society, my thoughts turned to clowning. Neweekwe clowns were even more ill-tempered and fearless than Mudheads, but they were also the wisest people in the pueblo. Membership came when a person with a stomach ailment sought help from the society. Neweekwe knowledge not only cures stomach aches but also enables clowns to eat any kind, or amount, of food or garbage, including human excrement, and to engage in outrageous public behavior without feeling shame.

During a Neweekwe performance I attended back in 1970, one particularly funny skit opened with a roly-poly clown in a skull cap and black-and-white-striped face paint marching into the plaza carrying a sign that read "Oklahoma Indians" on the front and "Zuni Ceremonial" on the back.[1] The word "ceremonial" was an allusion to the infamous Gallup Inter-Tribal Indian Ceremonial. When the clown got to the center of the plaza he turned his back to the kiva and said, "We from Oklahoma, that's a long ways from here." The audience laughed at his use of English in a sacred context, where only Zuni should be spoken.

In trotted six other clowns, sporting the fringed breechclouts and beaded vests of Plains Indian powwow performers. The lead man, dressed in a Day-Glo feathered war bonnet and wraparound sunglasses, ran up to a clown in a baggy J. C. Penney suit, wing-tip shoes, and with a sign reading "BIA AGENT," and said with a sharp tone, "When we gonna get the money from the Whiteman?"

Then the drummer, in a buffalo-fur cap and half-moon glasses, ambled over, saying, "We gonna put the Whiteman in jail." A perfect reversal of the usual situation during Gallup Ceremonial.

A man dressed as a woman, in a fringed white buckskin jacket and skirt, beaded collar and headband, and a necklace of luminous plastic beads (looking more like Christmas-tree ornaments than silver jewelry), with a single eagle feather jutting out ridiculously from the back of "her" head, waltzed in. Holding a feather fan in her left hand and clutching a huge mock microphone in her right hand, she sang "Indian Love Call" in cracking falsetto.

Four clowns, wearing huge half-circles of dyed pink and yellow feathers attached in back at their waists, danced to Plains Indian music provided by a Victrola in the window of a house on the plaza. During one song the dancers assumed a push-up posture and wiggled their hips in time to the music. At the point where they were supposed to leap to their feet and pivot around 360 degrees, with one hand on the ground, a clown fell down instead and did the entire pivot flat on the ground, to howls of laughter.

Two clowns collided heavily with each other and responded with a comic-book "OOOF!" And another clown asked, with great urgency, "Where's the Zuni rest room?" When no one responded he went over to the kiva and thrust his hand beneath his breech-clout, relieving himself on the wall of that sacred edifice. When he began to belt out "Ooooklahoma," another clown interrupted him with a classic country song, "You're in the Jailhouse Now."

The lead clown, calling attention to his star-shaped badge, announced himself at the top of his lungs as "governor of this pueblo." Then he laid out a large piece of canvas and two Navajo rugs over the bench outside the main kiva, and proceeded to seat the seven newly elected members of the Zuni Tribal Council. Seven clowns shook hands with the seven governmental officials, and gave each of them a sacred ear of corn (one with every kernel perfect and in place, even at the tip). To the top-ranking councilmen—governor, lieutenant governor, and first teniente —they gave an eagle feather as well. The female impersonator, who was wiggling her hips and batting her false eyelashes in imitation of an Anglo transvestite, sang again, breaking into a piercing screech that caused the first teniente to shrink back, holding one hand before his face in shame.

At the end, they stood in an east-west arc along the northern edge of the plaza together with the councilmen and prayed. During their prayers the vocalist fanned herself, causing the head feather of the clown next to her to wiggle in the draft.

The governor and his council thanked the clowns by powdering them with cornmeal; as the "woman" was dusted, she said, in an insipidly sweet English falsetto, "Oh, thank you!" Then, as the councilmen gave the clowns coins for their raucous performance, she said sharply, "I want some money, paper money." When the officials left the plaza, the clowns broke ranks and, with shouts and war whoops, danced wildly.

Neweekwe clowning, because it revolves around a continuing discovery, or rediscovery, of religious and secular boundaries, provides an anticreed for a religion that lacks any formal creed, or codified body of doctrine. Beyond creeds and anticreeds, the clowns, by their ability not only to conceive but to carry out their burlesques, display their ultimate detachment from the particulars of religious beliefs of all kinds.

Even Zuni sacred beliefs and practices come under direct inspection; thus, when the woman from Oklahoma said, "Oh, thank you," to a sprinkling of cornmeal, the humor cut both ways. In their gluttony the clowns even violate the boundaries of their biological being: not satisfied with saying the unsayable, they eat the inedible.

Their path is finally that of the Milky Way, arching clear across the night sky. From this perspective, they see boundaries, of whatever sort, as easy hurdles rather than as walls. Which is why they never laugh at their own jokes but, by causing others to laugh at the leaping of a boundary, share a moment of shamanic detachment with the uninitiated.

Breaking my reverie, I realized that it was past one o'clock and became anxious: perhaps Kwinsi had forgotten our appointment. But it wasn't like him to stand a person up, especially since he said he had a song. What kind of song could he be bringing? Must be on the kachina side, for he would never sing a medicine-society song into my tape recorder. At least I hoped he wouldn't, since I didn't want to get into any serious religious trouble at Zuni; with Kwinsi, one could never tell what he might do.

The door opened and in he waltzed, with a huge watermelon

under his left arm. "Well, Kachinmana, how are you? Brought you some sandía/*watermelon.*

"Elahkwa/*Thanks,* please be seated and eat," I said, taking the watermelon into the kitchen. He followed me, opened the refrigerator door, and started twisting off lids, tasting things. I said, stiffly, "If you're interested, I've got some fried chicken, pinto beans, turkey, green-chile stew . . ."

"Got any beer or whiskey?"

"Sure, but aren't you driving?"

"No, my wife will drive. She's over there at Piggly Wiggly, grocery shopping."

The minute he sat down he began behaving like an outrageous clown: cramming his mouth with food as fast as he could, drinking down a beer in a single gulp, then farting loudly. Moments later he jumped up, grabbed another beer, drained it. Heading for the Jack Daniel's bottle, he said, "Now, tell me, Tsilu, why do you eat so slow? We've got *work* to do."

Since I had lost my appetite, I put the food away and sat down across from him on the sofa. He was humming to himself, then suddenly demanded, "Hop tom maakina?/*Where's your machine?*"

I brought out our four-speed Sony and put on a fresh tape, and he broke into song. When he was done he smiled mischievously. "Now, what do you think, Kachinmana? Hopi way that means you're the mother of the kachinas, don't it?"

"Yes, a Hopi friend gave me that name a couple of years ago, when we were living in Santa Fe and I went to the airport to meet a British friend. The Hopi guy got off the same plane. He was too drunk to get home safely by himself, so I took him back to our place to sleep it off. Next morning we covered for him, lied for him, said he'd just arrived, so his wife wouldn't get angry and get after him."

"Good name for you, Tsilu. You're real interested in kachinas, so you can be their mother. Now, Kachinmana, I'm going to test you, what did my song say?"

"Something about a trip to the Moon Mother on a dragonfly."

"Yes, yes, what else?"

"I couldn't really catch it all."

"Okay, this is a good one, we'll work it out together."

I got out a pencil and notepad, and he dictated the Zuni words to me, phrase by phrase. Then we translated it together, section by section, into English. First came the vocable introduction, which Kwinsi labeled "penan kwayinanne/*talk coming out*."

> *ho-ho-ho he-he-he*
> *ho-ho-ho he-he-he*

"So now what do you know?"

"That it is an Upik'ayap'ona/*Downy Feather on a String* song. Or else, perhaps, it might be Hupon Shilowa/*Red Beard*."

"Ex-cel-lent, Kachinmana. Now for the kwayinanne. How do you call it?"

"Let's see. I guess I'd translate it 'coming out.' At least that's what it literally means in English. But since it functions just as verses do in English songs, maybe 'verse' would be better."

"Fine, then verse it is."

> *"Rejoice! Holy bundles, sacred bundles.*
> *By means of your wise thoughts*
> *there in the east your Moon Mother spoke*
> *gave her word*
> *when we went up there with the dragonfly*
> *entered her road.*
> *Rejoice! You will be granted many blessings*
> *flowing silt."*

> *Two stars say this to all the sacred bundles*
> *here now, mmmmmmm.*

"The second time you sing the kwayinanne, the last line changes a little bit: 'The lying star says this to all the sacred bundles here now, mmmmmmm.' Okay, ready? Now the shilh-nanne/*naming*. Guess that part's called 'chorus' in English?"

"Sure, if kwayinanne is translated 'verse,' then shilhnanne could be translated 'chorus,' if you like."

> *"By the Moon Mother's word*
> *from the Middle Place*
> *aaaall the way to Dawn Lake*
> *your paths will be complete."*

> *I the masker say this to you the people*
> *here now, mmmmmmm.*

"When you sing it the second time, instead of saying 'your paths will be complete,' you say 'you will reach old age.' That's the only difference."

"I get you."

"There are five parts in this type of song: two kwayinanne with two parts each, then two shilhnanne with two parts each, then one more kwayinanne. Now for the i'ts'umme/*strong part*. It goes at the end of each of the five sections. So, what would you call that?"

"The 'refrain,' I guess."

> *Maskers rainmakers soaking the earth with rain*
> *making lightning, thundering, coming, coming*
> *stretching, stretching, streeeetching.*

"Then you repeat this, but it's the same both times."

"Well, Kwinsi, a 'chorus' is actually a type of 'refrain' in

English. It looks like we have only the one word, 'verse,' for two Zuni words, kwayinanne and shilhnanne."

"Kachinmana, those two languages got a different path; they don't fit exactly. But no problem, you might say that Zuni shilhnanne and kwayinanne are two different 'verses' in English.

"Now, there it is, that's all you need to know in order to sing it. It's tso'ya, kind of pretty, you know. It's a new Upik'ayap'ona/*Downy Feather on a String* song, and when I sang it to my group they all kind of chuckled, you know, like they really liked it, enjoyed it. We're going to use it later on this summer for our rain dance. Do you know what it says?"

"It's a summer rain song and . . ."

"And what? Come on, now, I'm testing you, Tsilu."

"I like that stretching, streeeetching, streeeetching part."

"What does it mean?"

"I don't know."

"Corn plants are streeeetching to get rain, the rocket is streeeetching for the moon, and all mankind is streeeetching to reach old age."

"Oh, I see, it's an allegory." Kwinsi ignored this comment and went on.

"The two stars are the morning star, the red one you know, and the lying star."

"The red star would be Mars. But what is the lying star?"

"It's a bright star that comes out where you would expect the morning star, but it's nowhere near morning."

"That could be Jupiter, when it's not the morning star, or else Aldebaran."

"Whatever you say. Now, do you remember what decorations the astronauts had on their helmets?"

"No."

"Two stars, one on each side. Also, there were two astronauts on the moon. And what's the Whiteman's dragonfly?"

"A rocket."

"Good. They report back to their bosses, those people down here on the surface of the earth who have their special sacred bundle."

"Houston Control."

"Fine. And they'll be blessed with silt. Do you remember when NASA reported there might be water up on the moon?"

"Sure, they thought they saw alluvial deposits, like the kind we have out here after every heavy rain."

"There, Kachinmana, you have it."

"When will it be performed?"

"Probably next week, or maybe the week after. You should come down and see my group; we're just about the best."

At the sound of a pickup beep, he jumped up and jerked open the venetian blinds, peering out the window. Staring up and down the street, he suddenly spotted his truck. "Got to run now. Old Lady's waiting on me."

"I should pay you. Let's see, you've been here with me now about two hours, so how about ten bucks?"

"Too little. That song is special, it's exciting, tso'ya, you know, kind of new and colorful."

"Twenty?"

"Fine. Where's Kyamme?"

"He had an appointment downtown interviewing the mayor about the alcohol problems here in Gallup."

"Tell him I'll see him round town sometime, probably in a bar," he said, without even cracking a smile.

Barely suppressing a laugh I replied, "Okay, well, thanks for stopping by, and tell your wife to drop in and visit with me, next time you two are in town. See you around again real soon?"

"Sure, the pay's not too bad, for a one-eyed bandit," he said, chuckling as he eased the door shut behind him.

■ ■ ■ ■

I mused about the results of my first formal ethnographic interview. It looked as if I would be able to get together enough materials to write my master's thesis on Zuni music. In fact, the situation had progressed beyond anything I had ever thought possible; not only had I proved to myself that I could work with Kwinsi, but it was fun, even outrageous. And, still more wonderful, I learned much more than I had ever dared hope to about the specifics of song structure.

There was one thing I now felt more sure of than ever, and that was that Zuni songs could never again be dismissed as "monotonous." That was what the songs sounded like to people who didn't perceive the structure, or understand the multileveled complexity of meaning within the lyrics. It was also clear, from my initial interview, that Zunis *do* have a musical system, rules of composition, composers, and teachers. And I decided to take it upon myself to learn as much about this artistic-religious system as Kwinsi was willing to share with me.

There were also, undoubtedly, other native musical terms besides the three I had learned so far. But, even more important, I had learned that kachina songs could operate simultaneously on two levels, creating an ironic doubling in which one message might be read through another. Such allegorical texts might help to heal the gap between the present and the disappearing past by simultaneously valuing the traditional Zuni world and allowing for the existence of the intrusive American technological world.[2] Zunis are indeed dancing, as they always have been, in order to bring rain and fertility, but they are also dancing the modern world into place: giving it meaning, order, perhaps even a sacred existence.

AURORA BOREALIS

■ ■ ■ ■

We could see Tola stoking an outdoor oven late the next afternoon when we drove up. It was the middle-sized one, which meant she would be baking bread. It was exciting to see the gold-and-crimson flames surging through the door and leaping and twisting through the vent on top. When the blaze died down a bit, Tola swept the hot coals into a iron bucket and then, with a couple of long cedar boughs, sprinkled water on the earthen floor to cool it.[1] Next she sprinkled cornmeal lightly over the entire floor. The meal immediately turned dark, which meant the temperature was too high for bread baking. She again used water and the meal test, then both twice more; in between times she swept out the darkened meal. Finally, when just one spot turned black, she carefully wetted only that.

Looking up from her work, she nodded in my direction, then dashed into the house and returned with six loaves of bread neatly arranged on a plank. She placed them on the floor of the oven, one by one, with a log-handled paddle. Smiling at me, she motioned with her elbow toward the house and handed me her plank. I went inside and found more unbaked loaves spread out neatly on the dining-room table. After placing them on the plank, I brought them to Tola, who carefully positioned them one by one, close but not touching. As soon as the oven was full, she plugged the vent hole on top, then sealed the doorway with a large stone slab, pieces of sackcloth, and wet adobe. The baking took about thirty-five minutes.

As I helped Tola carry the lightly browned loaves into the house, Dennis drove Hapiya down to cultivate one of his wheat fields. While they worked together, Hapiya said that just last week Owen, the mean one married to a Navajo, chased his herd clear out of the valley. He must have been drunk, since he was not acting within the law. Then he gave the herders—Albert and Kwinsi's eldest son, Harry—a bawling out, and they both came running home "just crying." Subsequently a ram became sick and died, no doubt partly as a result of the driving of the herd. He had wanted to go to court about it, but Tola told him to be calm, to be patient, to wait until other people got mad too and then, with all the others, take him to court. Hapiya didn't want to wait.

It was starting to get dark and the men could barely see the milkweed they were chopping, so they quit and came up to the house, where Tola and I were busy preparing supper. They sat in the two worn easy chairs chatting about the situation at St. Anthony's Mission. It seems that the mission had been getting free clothes, from somewhere back east, and was selling them to Zunis for around five, ten, and fifty cents apiece. Also, they had recently sent out letters all over the world asking for contributions and more clothes, saying how poor the Zunis were—the children run around in ragged clothes with bare feet. Hapiya was very indignant about this: "If they say the Zunis are barefoot, why, then, they can just get the heck out of Zuni!"

He recalled that back in the twenties, about the time he left

Albuquerque Indian School, there had been a big controversy over readmitting the Catholic mission, which had been away from Zuni for a century.[2] When they were finally permitted to build a church and school, they had to sign an agreement that they would never again interfere with Zuni religious ceremonies. "But they *do* interfere," Hapiya said. "Last winter, during one of the night ceremonies, they held a big dance party at the mission, with door prizes, a live band, and everything. They were trying to get the young kids to go over there. That's got to be stopped."

The other day, when Hapiya left the government offices, down in the village, and went by Halona Plaza, one of the councilmen was there. The trader talked about giving him a cow (he had none). Hapiya said, "That's just like the Whiteman, to go and give a person a present when he becomes a councilman, just in order to get on his good side."

The traders call Hapiya a name that means *cedar stick*. He got the name when he was in California fire-fighting. He saw a Zuni

DENNIS TEDLOCK

guy he hadn't seen for a long time, who had gotten really thin, and told him, "You're just a stick—haven't you been eating anything?" But that man gave the name right back to Hapiya, who, although he has never been very thin, is incredibly honest, straight as a stick. The name stuck.[3]

I carried into the main room a big bowl of pinto beans, mixed with bits of venison jerky; three-quarters of a rewarmed Pizza Hut deep-dish special; fistfuls of scallions, cilantro, and carrots; Cokes, Sprites, and a pitcher of iced coffee; and four loaves of hot bread from the outdoor oven. Albert asked Dennis if he had any of Sadie's dance tapes, or any other Zuni music with him; he replied that indeed he did, and brought the tape recorder in from the car.

The family enjoyed the music, especially Albert and Harry, though they kept up a running conversation, complete with Little Moron and other jokes, throughout it. As the kids were clearing the table, Hapiya suddenly blurted out, "Tell me when you get to some empty tape. I'm going to tell a story."

I hit the pause button and fast-forwarded. The suggestion that he might tell a telapnanne/*tale* during summer was scandalous, since fictional stories are forbidden between the spring and autumn equinoxes, lest the narrator be bitten by a rattlesnake.[4] Rattlers are unusually sensitive to, and intolerant of, false behavior. In all the time we had known Hapiya, he had never broken this rule.

There was plenty of fresh tape, luckily, so on signal Hapiya settled back in an overstuffed chair, cleared his throat, and launched into a narrative. He told it first in Zuni, then elaborated on it in English.[5]

SONTI INOOOOTE.
NOW IT BEGINS TO BE MADE LOOOONG AGO.

■
It seems
the children—
when the hunting opened—
it seems their fathers left them and went out hunting in different
    directions
when these two (points to his grandsons Shawiti and Harry)
let their sheep out, they let their sheep out and
the two of them

went out herding.
And their fathers had gone out elsewhere.
They went around, all day they went around.
And their grandfather
was working in the fields until late afternoon and
he came up and
their grandmother told him
"Our grandsons
killed a deer." "Where?"
"Over there someplace around back."
"I see.
What happened?" "ONE of them came after a KNIFE.
He got the knife and I
told him to castrate it, maybe they castrated it."
"I see."
"Oh dear, my poor grandsons
maybe you'll do it right."
That's what their grandmother had told them.
And now their grandfather came and, "It looks like I'll have to go
  and get it,"
he said, and he
went to his wagon
and got it READY.
He headed out and went around to Tree Crescent, he got there and
that's where the sheep were spread out, he got there. "Where?
  Where is it?"
"At the far side of that clearing, by a grove of trees, that's where."
■
"Why don't you get in and we'll go."
Those two
just left their sheep. (softly) Both of them were all covered with
  blood.
Their grandfather took them along, they went on over there.

"Where?" "Right over there by that grove of trees."
They went over to the trees. "Right over there.
On the north side."
(softly) They got to the far end of the trees, (louder) to a clearing,
"HOW did this HAPPEN?"
"Oh, there were three of them.
One of them
was crippled, and there was a doe, and her—
we just let her be.
When they came up
the other two stopped
with this one in front—
pow!
I dropped him.
(softly) I dropped him
but then I didn't have a knife."
So, "Well
well now—"
he said to the other boy, "Listen:
you go get a knife and I'll look after the sheep."
So then this
other boy
went to get the knife
he went to their grandmother's.
(softly) He went to their grandmother's and
(louder) ran all the way.
"Oh dear, grandson
why is it you're
running like this?"
"Well we've killed a deer," he said. "WHERE?" she said. "Over
    there.
It's a great big buck." "Oh dear, my grandsons, so you've
ended someone's ROAD.

Perhaps
one of your fathers might end someone's road too."
That's what their grandmother said.
"When your grandfather comes I'll tell him."
Sure enough, when their grandfather came she told him, so now all
of them were going along together, together
the two boys with their grandfather, and when they got to where the
deer was, it was s o o o b i i g.
"What are we going to DO?"
"LISTEN:
why don't we put him in the wagon antlers first
then we'll all lift up on the other end."
So then
they put him in the wagon antlers first and they all got together and
lifted him up
and finally they managed to get him in. "Now that he's in, let's go
back."
"Where are the lungs and the heart?"
(sheepishly) "Well, lying over there."
"Hey, they're big ones, a lot of fat around the lungs."
"Yes indeed there's a lot of fat, but it's got sand on it, let's go."
Then their grandfather turned around and they came along
■
came along until they got to where the road was too rough for the
wagon
and the BOLTS got LOOSE on the tongue.
Then the two boys
got left behind there and their grandfather went on
and when he looked back his
wagon was way back there.
"Why didn't you SPEAK UP when that happened?"
They laughed and

he backed up, their grandfather fixed it for them.
They came along, came along until

■

they

got to their yard. "How are we going to get it down?"
There were two old ladies, their grandmother and
and
Mayku's mother. "With those two women, we can probably get it
down."
They laid a plank from the wagon to the door and pulled it down.
They put it down inside.
Now the sun was about to go down
it was halfway behind the horizon when their fathers came home.
When their fathers came home their deer was lying inside.
It had thirteen points.
"Oh, who killed it?"
"Well these two killed it."
"Thanks be."
After a while
others came in.
Everyone breathed life from their deer and went back outside.
They went outside, went outside, and their
grandfather
said a prayer, (softly) he said a prayer and they all came back in
to sprinkle cornmeal, and in this way they completed it.
Then the father of the boy who killed the deer said, "NOW
this was a day
when something terrible happened to me." "What?"
"Well now
I thought there was a bear in the canyon, that's what I thought.
It was lhelelekya. 'Where could it be?' "
This was the father of the little boy who killed the deer.
"Where? Where was it?" "It was right there by that gap, he was
lhelelekya.

I thought it was a BEAR, *so I went up very quietly.*
I went up very quietly and when I got CLOSE *to it*
right up close
it kept on lhelelekya.
So I got my gun in a good position.
(softly) 'Well, when I see him I'll blast him.' "
When he looked over the hill
he wasn't LHE-le-le-kya, *he was* LHE-lo-lo-kya, ASLEEP.
It was a HUNTER.
"Aaaaw, it sounded just like a bear."
Then he went on down there.
*"*HOW COME *you're sleeping so hard, you're lhe-le-le-kya like a*
bear,"
he told him.
This was the father
of the little boy who killed the deer
that's who was talking.
"Well I just lay down there and I must've slept for a long time, I
was so tired."
That's what he said. "I see.
But that shouldn't happen."
That's what he told him.
"Anyway let's go now, the sun's going down."
Both of them went on down.
When their father got home he told them about it.
"How could this happen? A person out hunting isn't supposed to go
to sleep,"
he told their grandfather.

■

"Well then

■

well then, what can I DO *about it?"*
"Why not make up a story?"
"Why not?" he asked the boys' grandmother.

"It's up to you." "Let's go ahead and make one up.
We'll tell it as if it happened long ago."
So their grandfather talked about what had happened.
A STORY was MADE.
He talked about what had happened
and when it was all straightened out
it was about the father whose boy had killed a deer, and that
hunter who had gone to sleep
and was lhe-lo-lo-kya and wasn't a bear lhe-le-le-kya it wasn't a
*   bear but a sleeping hunter.*
This happened long ago, enough, the word is short.

Everyone laughed. Hapiya lit a cigarette and went on. He was done with his tale, but not done telling about what happened that day.

"It was Kwinsi. He was out in this Spring Canyon. He was looking for deer and he heard the sounds, making noise, *snoring.* Sounded just like the bear. He was making a noise, you know. Kwinsi got scared, thought it was a *bear.*"

Albert added, "The hunters have, like, a nest over there, you know."

"So, he was expecting that it was a bear. It was snoring hard in the canyon; the echoes make more and more, like there was really a bear, but Sabin was snoring. He wasn't a *bear.* Sabin was sleeping and snoring. It's a little valley in the draw and there's a little gap over here, and that's where Kwinsi looooked over, and that's where Sabin was making the noise.

"So Kwinsi got his gun ready, ready to aim it, and he peeeeeeked over. His brother-in-law Sabin was right on the sunny side, sunny side of the slope, laying down. He was *snoring.* Kwinsi went over and woke him up.

"I decided to make a story of it myself, and I said 'inoooote.'

That is just the old-time word, but then it *actually* happened. I made it inoooote."

"Lhelele?" asked Dennis.

"Yes, lhelelekya," replied Hapiya.

"Lhelolo?"

"Lhelolokya means *sleeping* when you're *snoring*. Bears lhelelekya. Means making the noise of the bear, you know, *growling!* Lhelelekya means growling."

"So, Kwinsi thought he heard the lhelele, but it was lhelolo?" I asked.

"Yes, it's got two words to it. Kwinsi got scared because he thought it was a *bear*."

"There's lots of black bear back in that canyon, you know," added Albert.

"When you're in a canyon there are echoes, and they make you hear a lot a things. Get scared, maybe. He was just ready to shoot him—"

Albert interrupted: "The first time we went hunting, Sabin didn't know how to skin a deer."

"He never did kill a deer that time but, well, he was like a young kid, he'd get up the things, like plastic bags, so he could put the liver in there. Before he went out he'd get everything rigged up, empty out the skillet, get it ready at his wife's house. Gonna put this in there. Gonna put that in there."

"He was gonna take the whole guts, you know, and take them home to Sadie," added Albert.

"Sabin, well, this is how he was acting, and this is the one that was sleeping instead of hunting," concluded Hapiya.

"What was that about a sixteen-pointer?" asked Dennis.

"Thirteen-pointer," corrected Albert.

"The horns are up on the roof and—"

"Want to see?" Albert asked, standing up.

Dennis nodded and Albert went out, climbed the ladder onto

the flat roof, retrieved the antlers, and presented them to us. Carefully examining the tines, Dennis counted five on one side and eight on the other.

"Who got that one?" he asked.

"Harry, Kwinsi's eldest, he's the one that killed the deer."

"When was it?"

"This past fall," said Hapiya. "Next day, Kwinsi went up there and he saw a big one. He shot his buck *ten times,* ten bullets. He didn't fall down right away when he was shot. There's an arroyo up there, steeper than this one. The buck was running down from the hill and jumped, missed. Thought he was gonna make it up on the other side of the bank, fall down in that steep arroyo. Kwinsi chased him down there. He was already dead then. And there's no way to pull him up. So they got a rope, got a pole, put the pole above, and tied it up on top. Pull him up on the pole, and hang him up there. They were coming down from this hogback. I was plowing down here when Harry and Shawiti came running.

" '*Let's go over there.* The deer's in the arroyo, we couldn't pull him out,' Shawiti shouted.

" 'We've got chains and we've got a rope,' Harry said.

" 'But the only thing we need is a tractor, so we can pull him out,' said Shawiti.

"So I quit plowing."

Dennis turned to me, showing me the rack. "They put the antlers on the roof. Every farmhouse around here has some of these antlers stuck up on the roof."

"It was around March, or February."

The kids took the antlers back outside. But then one of them suddenly burst in the door, proclaiming excitedly, "Hish attanni/ *Very dangerous!* Run outside, Kyamme, Tsilu, and you'll see something AMAZING!"

A pale-greenish airglow hung in the center of the northern

horizon as white rays, tinged magenta and lime green, flashed across the black sky, broke up, and re-formed into undulating luminous sheets. Phantomlike translucent light flickered across the celestial arch, melted into a choppy river of fire, and was extinguished. Tiny greenish points of light were all that was left behind, glimmering along the edge of the horizon.

"Kwap uhsi?/*What's that?*" asked Hapiya.

"Aurora borealis, the northern lights. You never see them this far south," Dennis said. "They're caused by solar radiation. . . ." Neither of us could think of the whole explanation, and it didn't seem to explain anything anyway.

"That's strange," Hapiya said, only it sounded like "Tat's strainch." He was imitating a Navajo accent. "What time of the night is it? Almost ten?" he asked.

Dennis said, "I can check it in the car. Ten-forty. Time for people who get up at five o'clock to go to bed."

"I wake up about four-thirty. Time to go," Albert said matter-of-factly, going back inside.

Tola said, "See you Saturday, down in the village, when the pilgrims return," then turned toward her husband and stepped inside, leaving us alone on the doorstep.

It had been a bizarre evening. First, the narrative Hapiya insisted on telling us was unusual in many ways. He left off the beginning of the introductory formula, "sonahchi," retaining only the second half, "sonti inoooote." The grandparents in the story were not from some long-ago mythic time, but were Hapiya himself and his wife, Tola; the two boys were their grandsons Harry and Shawiti; the father of the boy who killed the deer was their eldest son, Kwinsi; and the sleeping hunter was their son-in-law Sabin. At the end of the tale Hapiya described the making of the story itself.

So, instead of the usual etiological tale telling why things are the way they are now in the world, Hapiya inverted the process and narrated recent events that accounted for his story. Then the universe answered with the wonderful, dangerous luminescence of aurora borealis.

The wonder and terror of it all is expressed in stories and proverbs of Inuit peoples, who frequently observe this phenomenon. For them, the multicolored display reflects gigantic fires lit along the shores of the Arctic Ocean by the giant Oulahankigi, and whoever looks too long on these lights becomes mad.

For Tola and Hapiya these strange northern lights were so anomalous they did not immediately associate them with anything meaningful within the Zuni world. Some months later Hapiya suggested, half-jokingly, that since we were living so far north we must have brought the aurora borealis south with us.

10

PILGRIMAGE

■ ■ ■ ■

UNDER A SWOLLEN LAVENDER SKY a crowd of men in black blankets and white headbands appeared along the western horizon. As they approached I could make out the leader of the masked dancing society, his warrior priest, and the leader of the Coyote Society; behind trailed forty Good Kachinas, the ten Koyemshi or Mudhead clowns, and dozens of pilgrims.

Scrambling off my rooftop perch, I raced across the street and jerked open the front door—momentarily arresting Tola's corn grinding. Seeing that the old lady had been crying, I decided not to blurt out my news just then. I was confused by finding her this way and didn't know if I should enter or not; if so, should I, or should I not, offer her comfort?

I slipped back outside and leaned against the cool stone wall, tensely at ease. I gazed at the ten silly-looking, but nonetheless sacred, serious, even dangerous, Mudhead clowns. Adobe-colored beings in tight-fitting cotton masks with inside-out eyes and doughnut-shaped mouths, simultaneously expressing eternal amazement and voracious hunger. Ears, antennae, and genitals (stuffed with hand-spun cotton, garden seeds, and the dust of human footprints) protruded knoblike from their heads. Without noses or hair, they were naked except for lumpy orange-brown body paint, feathered ear ornaments, black neck scarves, men's woolen kilts, and women's blanket dresses, concealing their tied-down penises.

Loooong ago, these clowns were created when a priest sent his son and daughter to locate a village.[1] The children ascended a mountain, where the girl became drowsy and lay down under a cottonwood to rest. Her brother went on looking all around the countryside, then returned at midday to find her sleeping soundly. A delicate breeze lifted her skirt; he became enchanted, lay down beside her, touched her, slept with her there.

When she awoke and realized what had happened she became enraged, tore out her hair, and beat her face and head till lumps appeared. Screamed till her lips turned inside out. Wept till her eyelids became unsightly puckered swollen rings. Babbled unintelligibly until her brother, unexpectedly, began to understand her and they changed their language there.

And when they changed their language, the boy said to his sister, "It is not good for us to be all alone. We must prepare a place for others." He descended the mountain and drew his foot through the sand, creating the Zuni and Little Colorado rivers. Where they converged a lake was formed, and in the depth of that lake the village of Kolhuwalaawe/*Kachina Village*, the Land of the Dead, came into being.

That night the girl bore ten sons; all but the first were infertile and, like her, deformed. Each had a distinguishing personality trait and a sacred gift for humankind.

Molanhakto, with a miniature rabbit snare dangling from his

BARBARA TEDLOCK

right earlobe, brought native squash. The Speaker, a daydreamer who rarely spoke, and then only irreverently, carried yellow corn. Great Warrior Priest, a coward, brought blue corn. Bat, in his black blanket dress, who feared the dark but saw marvelously well in daylight, red corn. Small Horn, who thought he was invisible, white corn. Small Mouth the glum, gabbling and cackling constantly, offered sweet corn. Old Buck, frisky and giggly as a young girl, black corn. Gamekeeper, in his woman's dress, speckled corn. Water Drinker, always thirsty, toted his water gourd. And Old Youth, the self-centered, thoughtless adviser of the team, brought the clairvoyance locked tightly within the tiny cracks in parched corn.

I hear a muffled shuffling of mud-red bare feet, goat hooves rattling against turtle shells, and jingling abalone on shell-bead necklaces, announcing the arrival of Kokk'okshi/*Good Kachinas*. Kachina chief and spokesman, dangling netted gourd jars filled with sacred water, lead the dance troupe—in their turquoise-painted wooden masks with slit eyes and long black horsehair beards, zigzag lightning streaks across their clay-pink shoulders—into the earthen plaza.

Clustered behind the masks come dozens of pilgrims with white pants, white shirts, white headbands, and white face paint meandering across noses and dripping down cheeks. Their bulging knapsacks wriggle with turtles. Fistfuls of cattails jammed into black leather belts. Hidden among the masks is Sadie's eldest son, thirteen-year-old Shawiti, this year's Fire God, carrying a juniper-bark torch in his right hand.

Pounding bare feet, cracking of dewclaws on turtle shells, trembling painted gourds, whining growling bullroarers, followed by song:

Aa-ha ee-he aa-ha ee-he
hiya elu [joy] *naya elu* [joy] *it's our day*
"Oh, this is our happy day
Come out with your rain,"
the North Priest says to his younger sisters.
Hiya [surprise] *hiya* [surprise] *lii-lhamm* [here-mm]

"Oh, this is our happy day
Come out with your rain,"
the North Priest says to his younger sisters.
Hiya hiya lii-lhamm [here-mm]
ohoho elu [joy] *ohoho elu* [joy] *he'ahi*
ohoho elu [joy] *ohoho elu* [joy] *he'ahi*
ahahaha i-i-i-hihi hiya [surprise] *hiya* [surprise]

▪

Aa-ha ee-he aa-ha ee-he
hiya elu [joy] *naya elu* [joy] *it's our day*
"Oh, this is our happy day
Come out with your rain,"

the North Priest says to his younger sisters.
Hiya [surprise] *hiya* [surprise] *lii-lhamm* [here-mm]

"Oh, this is our happy day
Come out with your rain,"
the North Priest says to his younger sisters.
Hiya hiya [surprise surprise] *lii-lhamm* [here-mm]
ohoho elu [joy] *ohoho elu* [joy] *he'ahi*
ohoho elu [joy] *ohoho elu* [joy] *he'ahi*
ahahaha i-i-i-hihi [surprise] *hiya* [surprise]²

A chorus of half-turns and sharp pauses follows, the shaking of long black horse-tail wigs over a medley of gray and red fox furs, with dangling fluffy tails, and skinny hind legs inches from the ground.³ Yellow parrot feathers bounce on the crown of each dancer's head; long black rain beards sway across each male kachina's chest. Six female kachinas, all but one danced by a male, dressed in their single-shouldered black wool blankets and double-pinwheel maiden hairdos, hurl piercing falsettos through rain words as they spin the lead dancers, twelve future Shalako maskers each marked by a two-foot-long glimmering military macaw tail feather.

Hapii-me hapii-me
Rainmakers come to our sacred water bundles hiya lii-lhamm
	[surprise here-mm].
Rainmakers come to our sacred corn bundles hiya lii-lham
	[surprise here-mm].

ohoho elu [joy] *ohoho elu* [joy] *he'ahi*
ohoho elu [joy] *ohoho elu* [joy] *he'ahi*
ahahaha i-i-i-hihi hiya [surprise] *hiya* [surprise]

■

Hapii-me hapii-me
Rainmakers come to our sacred water bundles *hiya lii-lhamm*
    [surprise here-mm].
Rainmakers come to our sacred corn bundles *hiya lii-lham*
    [surprise here-mm].

ohoho elu [joy] *ohoho elu* [joy] *he'ahi*
ohoho elu [joy] *ohoho elu* [joy] *he'ahi*
ahahaha i-i-i-hihi hiya [surprise] *hiya* [surprise]

■

Aa-ha ee-he aa-ha ee-he
hiya elu [joy] *naya elu* [joy] it's our day
"Oh, this is our happy day
Come out with your rain,"
the North Priest says to his younger sisters.
Hiya [surprise] *hiya* [surprise] *lii-lhamm* [here-mm]

"Oh, this is our happy day
Come out with your rain,"
the North Priest says to his younger sisters.
hiya hiya [surprise surprise] *lii-lhamm* [here-mm]
ohoho elu [joy] *ohoho elu* [joy] *he'ahi*
ohoho elu [joy] *ohoho elu* [joy] *he'ahi*
ahahaha i-i-i-hihi hiya [surprise] *hiya* [surprise]

The Mudhead song gently filters through, whenever the Kachina Society song is soft, like something seen through the windows of a passing train:

We emerge from fourth inner world.
Carrying our grandchildren
we emerge.

On my back
staring in six sacred directions
sits my poor grandchild.

Hurry
call for rain
poor grandchild
I carry.[4]

The singleness of purpose of the dancers, pilgrims, and clowns marks them off from the surging crowd. With four sets repeated in the four plazas, their danced prayer opens the Flour Cloud Season.

Off Torn Place Plaza, House Chief sits within the northern kiva
all alone, in total darkness on the cool earthen floor, chewing his
sacred root, talking silently with songbirds. Maskers and clowns
dance his heart along jeweled cornmeal, rainbow, and star trails,
carrying him back to that time, long ago, when the earth was so

soft that water was gathered simply by pulling up grass. Arriving at the beginning, he dreams life-giving thunderheads, lightning, and big-drop rain into a gemstone sky.

■ ■ ■ ■

That evening we drove Tola over to the north side of the village to visit Sadie in her subdivision home. The cramped stucco frame house, painted canary yellow in order to distinguish it from the row of nearly identical Housing and Urban Development (HUD) houses, was unbearably hot, although all the windows were wide open. The kids, trying to cool off, were alternately running to the kitchen sink to splash themselves with cold water and panting like Siwolo/*Buffalo,* their shaggy black dog.

Sadie apologized for the intolerable heat, explaining that she had never really moved in. They didn't much like the place; it had plumbing but, unlike the older Zuni stone homes, it was divided into many tiny rooms, making it a scary place to sleep. So they used it primarily as a bathhouse.

She and her mother had decided to tear down the big stone house in the center of the Old Pueblo and build a new house on the same spot. In late fall, after the Shalako house-blessing ceremony, she would move into the new house with her mother and leave the subdivision house to her younger sister, Flora, or else to whichever of her kids married first.

The door opened soundlessly, revealing her barefoot husband in his pilgrim's pure-white clothes and headband. He held out his right hand toward his mother-in-law, with his fingers curled downward, and said something.

Gently meeting his down-turned right hand with her up-turned left, Tola replied, "Le'happa/*The same.*" After hooking fingers lightly, for just a moment, they withdrew to breathe from their hands.

He turned to Sadie, then Ramona and Seff, greeting them each in the same manner. Removing his cornmeal pouch from his right shoulder and looping it over a forked tine on the rack of his first buck, he lowered himself stiffly into his favorite easy chair. Tola and Sadie returned to their butchering, and the kids to their games.

Homecomings are often approached gingerly, which leaves the returning male, if at all talkative (and most are), disconsolate. On this occasion Sabin solved his problem as his father-in-law had many times before, by talking with us. Actually he didn't exactly talk with us so much as he talked aloud to the room.

He spoke slowly, with many pauses, while staring straight ahead, with a glazed look, at nothing.

We went all the way over there to Kachina Village Lake.

Saw some of them
what do you call 'em with white marks?

Antelope.

You can't drink water on the way there or on the way back if there's
*   no rain.*

Lucky for us
there was rain
on the way back.

Shawiti
is Shulaawitsi
Fire God this year
so he couldn't drink anything the whole time
until it rained.

When it rained
it rained hard

DENNIS TEDLOCK

really hard
and that rain smothered out his fire,

We called him
Ky'a Shulaawitsi

Water Fire God.

I used to ride a horse
when I was a kid but
I stopped when I was in high school.
I'm not used to it.

When it rained we had to force the horses to come in.
I got sore.
I didn't take any warm clothes.
I got cold.
You walk and walk and walk and walk
then you ride a horse and someone walks in your place.

If the bosses run you run
so you've got to be in shape.

On and on you go until
you come up on a high place and
just see more country streeetching out.

Then you go on until you come to a high place again and you see
   more country.

There were a lot of new barb-wire fences we had to cross
and lots of windmills out there.

One of them wasn't working so good
it didn't look like there would be enough water for a cow.

That's a bad sign for next year.

We went way up on Fire God's mountain and
left our feathers there.

Shawiti had to make fire with his drill.
He did it right off
so as you know his kuku/father's sister loves him.

I went down into that cold muddy water and
got some of them drown children
you know
turtles.

There were lots of
cattails—

Guess you saw them in the dance?
We went way inside the cave into that fourth inner chamber
and it was dry.
Dry.
Bone dry.

Guess we'll have another bad year.

On the first day we got aaaall the way over to someplace on the other
*   side of St. Johns Highway.*
We spent the next night over there.

Then we woke up
way early in the morning
and walked all the way to Ojo Caliente.

It rained really good with good lightning and good thunder.

When we got to Ojo Caliente
Mother came to feed us
and we spent the night there.

When you go over there
it's like going to Zuni heaven.

He went on to explain that tonight would be something like
Shalako. The dancing would start late, at midnight or so, and
last until dawn. Tomorrow, in late morning, they would dance
in each of the four plazas.

"Where's Kwinsi, and Shawiti?" Dennis asked.

"Don't worry 'bout them. They had to spend some time in that Longhorn house. Kwinsi will be back in a couple of hours, but Shawiti won't be home for a couple of days—not until they wash his sacred paint off. Poor little fellow wasn't allowed to ride a horse, and even though I massaged his feet about an hour, each night, boy, they are sure swollen!"

Standing up awkwardly, he walked across the room and stood at the kitchen door, where his wife and mother-in-law were butchering a sheep. Sadie had her arm way up inside the carcass and was working away on the ribs with a small hacksaw. Her porcelain tabletop rippled red with spread-out mutton.

I suggested that we might take a picture of Sabin—for history and all—maybe with Sadie and Tola, sitting around the kitchen table. Sabin smiled and nodded but Tola said sternly, "No, out there in the front room."

With an audible sigh Sabin stood up, putting his white head-band and cornmeal pouch back on, and walked over to the vanity mirror. While adjusting his headband, he explained that he couldn't wash his muddy feet or remove his face paint till it was all over, tomorrow evening. He stood next to his favorite deer-head trophy for two full-length portraits.

In the first photo, a gleaming-white electronic blur bounced back from his glasses. The second, without glasses, revealed a blank red-eyed stare. Pictures no one loved, liked, or even wanted. Technological failures revealing the insistent documentary urge to freeze, store, and retrieve the authenticity of an encounter with a returned pilgrim. Examples of ethnographic bad faith.

BACK FROM VIETNAM

■ ■ ■ ■

JOE GREETED US in his Tony Lama ostrich-skin boots. With his smooth oval face, aquiline nose, large brown eyes with thick black lashes, burnished bronze complexion, and tall slender build, he was certainly the handsomest of all of Hapiya's boys, and knew it. His four-year-old son, Joe Junior, looked just like him, and already seemed to have something of his character—a certain sweetness mixed with sadness that bordered on the effeminate.

Back before Joe volunteered for the army he had split with his wife, Rose, or, more precisely, she left him. As his sister Flora explained it, "My brother was picking up girls all the time, and I guess his wife didn't much like it, so she threw him out."

During his training at Fort Polk, Louisiana, he wrote his mom just one letter, on stationery decorated with an infantryman in action. "They're making me work my ass off down here, like a robot. Be sure and put my insurance papers in a safe place, or you won't be able to collect my insurance, if something happens to me. Now I'm not saying that something is going to happen to me."

Just before he got shipped to Vietnam, he sent home a booklet describing basic training, a package of discarded clothes for the herders, and several issues of *Sex to Sexty,* a raunchy magazine filled with dirty cartoons and jokes for Albert. Once he was in Vietnam they heard nothing more. When he returned Rose felt sorry for him and for her son, who clearly needed a daddy, so she took him back.

At dinner that evening, Sadie said that Ramona had been getting stung by spiders a lot recently, ever since she had started hanging around the Shalako house site. When Dennis inquired about the progress on the house, Sadie said that the foundation was in and they were just now beginning to lay the cinder-block walls. It was going pretty slow, but she wasn't worried, because as soon as fall came Kwinsi's kiva group would get serious about finishing it in time for the blessing.

The spider bites were all over Ramona's right leg, and there was a large, mean-looking red lump on her left arm. Sadie was planning to take her over to Sabin's sister's right after dinner, since a person's father's sister takes care of spider bites. She makes a poultice with burnt bluebird feathers, herbs, and cornmeal, which she plasters on the bites, then covers them with a towel or blanket. Usually they're healed within a day.

If you're lucky, though, and see a spider before it bites anyone, then there's a charm you must say:

*Lhaayaluk'o
tom lhaaluk' tsam k'okshi
to' aynakka
uhsona tunaa kusk'atu!*

Bluebird
that handsome fellow bluebird
he's the one who killed you
shrivel up his eyes!

If you kill a spider and fail to say this, you will go blind. You only get sores when a spider bites you and you fail to see him. "That's our Indian way," Sadie said, then chuckled at hearing herself using one of her father's favorite expressions.

At dinner Joe discussed his stay in Nam. When Hapiya asked him what Vietnamese people were like, he responded with stories of thefts. He, of course, had never lost anything, but he knew "lots of people" who had expensive cameras and tape machines taken right off their backs in public: the thieves just cut the straps. He told about a friend of his who, while on guard duty, "burned" some dope peddlers. The dealers threw the stuff over the fence, but his friend never threw any money back. When the dealers opened fire it was returned by several guards with machine guns.

They kept giving him medals—CIBs (Combat Infantry Badges)—for this and that. "But they're too heavy to wear. So now I never use anything but the ribbons."

After dinner Sabin drove his wife, Flora, and Ramona to his mom's, where his sister was living, and Hapiya left for his kiva. We sat around the scuffed ranch-style coffee table with Joe, Tola, and Joe Junior, nibbling parched corn and piñon nuts.

Joe explained that it was hard around Zuni, with all the returned vets and not many jobs. Jewelry was bad: the prices of silver and turquoise were high, but the market was down. Crazy archeologists, hired by the BIA, were digging around in the graveyard, scattering human bone dust all over the place: "Why, you can hear the dead screaming, even in broad daylight!"

Junior got fidgety during all this worry talk and begged to

look at pictures. Tola went over to the bookcase, but instead of an illustrated book about warplanes, she brought over Matilda Coxe Stevenson's enormous Zuni monograph. Dennis had found this copy in a used-book store and had given it to the family.

"Tims Okya an ts'inaawe/*Stevenson Woman's writing*," Tola said, opening it gently.

It was a heavy musky tome, 634 pages plus 139 full-page plates, covered in military olive with a gold-turbaned and be-feathered Indian in bear-claw choker pressed into the center of the front cover. Oh, how that woman struggled to get it all down for science, before the Zunis either died off or forgot their old ways.

One summer day, in 1879, she set off in her wagon for the shrine of Payatamu, God of Music. When she arrived at the foot of the mesa, east of the village, a twelve-foot rock wall blocked her ascent, until she hit on the plan of making two Indians serve as her ladder, one standing on the shoulders of the other, so that she could reach the shrine. Once on top, finding it too shady to photograph the sacred icons in the cave, she decided to remove them; but, as she herself reported it:

The aged officer was horrified on discovering the writer's intention and begged that the images of Pa'yatämu be not taken from the place where they had rested undisturbed for centuries of moons. But it had to be done, and the curious figures were placed in line on a ledge below the shrine just as they stood in the cave (see plate XLIb). Had the people in general known of the temporary removal of the images of Pa'yatämu their wrath would have known no bounds; but these children of nature are like civilized beings of tender years, and can be controlled through kindness or firmness, as occasion requires, by those for whom they entertain profound respect.[1]

MATILDA COXE STEVENSON: SMITHSONIAN INSTITUTION

Later that winter she gained admission to magical curing and rain-bringing performances, pretending to furnish lightning for the sacred ceremonies. She made photos with her flash powder.

ALTAR AND FETISHES OF RAIN PRIEST OF THE NADIR

RATTLESNAKE SHRINE

SWORD SWALLOWERS' DRY PAINTING, AND FETISHES

SHALAKO GODS

MASK OF LONGHORN: FRONT AND SIDE VIEWS

Tola pointed to the top of Longhorn's mask. "See, the feathers point straight ahead, giving the people a long road. You remember back when Longhorn and Huututu had them on backwards, cutting our lives short?"

"Yeah. There was the war and a lot of Zuni guys went over there to Nam that never came back," remarked Joe.

"A lot of old people and babies died here too, and a couple of young guys suicided themselves. Then, right after that Shalako, Old Man took this book down below," Tola said, pointing with her puckered lips to the house at the foot of the hill.

"You know, Tsilu, the one with the plaque outside with the Longhorn mask on it?" said Joe.

"Umm-hummm."

"They must have showed them this old picture right here," said Tola, thumping the tinted photograph. "So I guess, by now, they've got it right."

BOXES OF SWORD SWALLOWER FRATERNITY

MASK OF MUDHEAD CLOWN: FRONT AND REAR VIEWS

ALTAR OF NE'WEKWE CLOWN FRATERNITY

ALTAR OF LITTLE FIRE FRATERNITY

ALTAR OF U'HUHUKWE MEDICINE FRATERNITY

"Wait a minute," Dennis said, as Tola started to turn the page. "This medicine-society altar doesn't look quite right to me."

"You're right on about that," said Joe. "Old Man told me that altar's not from his group, 'cause they never even let that Stevenson woman in the door. Besides, his group doesn't carve rattlesnakes, and Knife Wing is only brought out during initiations. Some people say it's a picture of the Shumaakwe altar, but I don't believe it. She just made that one up."

FLAYING A BEEF

CHILD WITH BROKEN LEG IN SPLINTS

IDOL OF ELDER GOD OF WAR

SCALP POLE

Tapping the image of the scalp pole, Joe said, "Did you know that way back in the 1880s, when that Whiteman called Kuushi [Frank Hamilton Cushing] got initiated as a Bow Priest, he went out across Oak Wash to a Navajo hogan and took a scalp?"

"What? No. We've heard lots of stories about Kuushi, how he spoke good Zuni, was adopted into the tribe and given a name. But we've never heard about him scalping a Navajo. Are you sure about that, Joe?" asked Dennis, incredulously.

"Do you know any other details about how Kuushi got that Navajo scalp?" I inquired.

"No, I've never heard anything about that, but I *do* know he had to have the scalp for his initiation.

"A while back, Old Man told me how on initiation day Kuushi got himself all painted up just like the others, with black stripes on his white body, and while the others said their prayers from their hearts, he read his from a piece of paper. Even though he was a Whiteman and all, and could hardly remember anything without his paper, he learned a lot and was second in command among the Bow Priests, until the first one died, and then he was first. When he served as Bow Priest he led lots of raids against Apache and Navajo sheep rustlers. But then he went and made the Scalp Dance known back east, and all the secret things that go with the War Gods.

I. W. TABER: MUSEUM OF NEW MEXICO

"Some people even say he stole War Gods and sold them to museums. I've heard that one of them is in Germany! That's kind of scary to think about, you know—some guys say that Germany's where World War III will get started. So our War Gods, without us even knowing, knowing in time how to stop it, might have a role in that one.

"Because Kuushi publicized the Bow Priesthood, and those War God carvings, people came out to the village and stole them from the shrines. They're all over the place and it's pretty dangerous now, because those white people who keep War Gods don't know the right prayers and all. They don't understand how to treat them, you know, how to talk with them, what to feed them and all. It's sure to cause serious trouble in the future."[2]

■ ■ ■ ■

In a letter to his boss, Major Powell, dated January 13, 1881, Cushing told of his discovery of caches of miniature bows, arrows, and war clubs, along with prayer sticks and carvings of the War Gods. They were in caves, cinder cones, and rock shelters scattered all along the pilgrimage route from Zuni to Kachina Village. His intention was to send them all back east to the Smithsonian Institution. Though he did manage to send one War God back to Major Powell, by way of a Mr. Kirchner, his larger shipment was lost in transit and never arrived. A second carving found its way to a German museum, the Museum für Völkerkunde in Berlin, for which Cushing wrote a special catalogue concerning the cultural importance and use of this fetish at Zuni Pueblo.[3]

For the Zunis themselves, Cushing did everything he could to produce an acceptable scalp, together with an exciting narrative about his valor in obtaining it. This is revealed in a section of the draft of a letter he wrote in October of 1881, shortly after his initiation into the Bow Priesthood, to a reporter for the Boston *Herald* by the name of Sylvester Baxter.[4]

Do you remember mention made of the Masonry of the Zunis, of the prayers, unwritten bible and ancient songs, obsolete language, etc., reposed in the order of *A-pithlan Shi-wa-ni*, "Priesthood of the Bow"? And of my desire—

through securing a scalp—to get into this wonderful organization?

The scalps secured for me by my father and officers of the Army were insufficient in themselves for this purpose; but the timely outbreak of the Apaches enabled me to acquire another and far more genuine article with right and title to possession; for I passed through country constantly raided by these boys for four days, and nights, saw very effectively a fight between them and some rancheros. Moreover, grand old rain poured down over New Mexico—the valley of Zuni in particular—and washed away the foundation of the scalp house, destroying all save one of the trophies of centuries of Zuni valor.

My Zuni brethren were therefore ready for the story I had to tell them, made me bury my insignia, guarded me all day, took me under the cover of night to the chamber of warriors, convened a council, smoked me, listened to my tale of blood, refused absolutely my entrance into the order, consented to listen to a strong speech from me in which I mentioned former allusions tending to my initiation, my service to the god (*Kia-pin-a-hoi*),[5] my love for my people (*A-shi-wi*), the sadness to think that as a *Pithlan Shiwani* my heart would be always Zuni, as a baffled warrior I should return forever, ere two moons passed, to Washington—

Here it was broken. Fifteen minutes after the discussion as to which clans should adopt me—the Parrots for my gens, the Eagles for my fathers, [it was] decided—the vows of eternal fidelity to the Zunis and obedience of rules [were] administered. Then I was hustled off, without warning, guarded by four warriors and two priests until morning, taken out to the burial place of the scalps, where a sham fight with prayer, song, and ceremony ensued. A pole was then prepared, and the scalps being tied to it, I was directed to shoulder it, and at the head of my little party I was marched to the vicinity of the western gardens, where, the pole planted, I was perched, bare-headed, on a sandhill filled with ants, compelled to sit motionless in the hot sun watching my scalps until evening, when the prayers and initiation into the clans took place—the pandemoniac march round the pueblo, the killing of twenty-five or thirty dogs, and ere I knew it, I was hustled off to be baptized as son of the Eagles and child of the Parrots, locked up in the chamber of the warriors, tabooed from exit, fire, salt, meat, tobacco, the touching of outsiders, the looking at women, and what not for four days. How fearful, these four slow days, with their motionless sittings, their nights of only five hours sleep, their emetics, sacrifices, etc. etc.

But I must stop here. I cannot describe the multitudes of prayers, songs, ceremonials, which the following twelve days brought forth. I can only say that fresh in my memory as they are, they seem to me the grandest, most interesting, weird and terrible experiences and days my life has ever seen, and open up the sublimest depths of meaning to my researches in Zuni. And it is not an American who writes you now. It is a *Zuni* by right of his "clanship with the Parrots," his "sonship of the Eagles," his "birth from the Sun" and *Kia-pin-a-hoi,* his membership in the "Order of the Bow," and his sacred position as "Junior Priest of the Bow," and secular status as "Commander of the *A-shi-wi.*"

Surely the gods have favored me. Eighteen days have changed the possibilities of my life and labors, and opened up a new significance to the study of Indian ethnology. It may be that when I see you I can tell you more about this, or at some leisure time write more. But I can only add now that I have told you only the beginning and most uninteresting part of my new experience[s], that these have revealed to me the fact that all my previous work amounts to nothing as compared to that which is at hand, for the Indians have already compelled me to learn by heart five long ancient prayers and commit to paper for memorization as many more, with songs and rules of the order—all [of] which, you remember, I was using every means to record and had about despaired of during your visit.

Since no Navajos are mentioned, this letter does not substantiate Joe's claim that Cushing scalped a Navajo. But did he perhaps scalp an Apache? At the very least, he was close enough to combat that the scalp sent to him by his father seems to have been accepted at Zuni as the genuine article.[6]

And here we were, nearly one hundred years later, sitting in the very house where the chief Navajo scalp, Pa'ettonne, lives within an ancient water jar in a corner of the back bedroom. Inside the bundle is the original, the most powerful, rainbringing fetish of all times, a Navajo woman's scalp.

Tola feeds Pa'ettonne cornmeal every day and, together with her daughter Flora and several other Badger-clan ladies, honors her with special food, prayer, and song at each full moon. But every now and then, when Pa'ettonne gets restless, late at night, and her doeskin moccasins shuffle out of the back room and across the linoleum floor, the householders get down deep into their blankets.

■ ■ ■ ■

"There's one thing I don't understand," said Junior. "Why did those old-time Zunis make that Whiteman into a Bow Priest?"

"Don't know, maybe 'cause he knew some strong Whiteman ways of killing," Joe replied, then stood up and went looking for something. Tola took the opportunity and said good night.

When Joe reappeared he was carrying an old boot box full of curled and faded color snapshots, mostly from Vietnam.

JOE AND A SIOUX IN ARMY FATIGUES WITH WALKIE-TALKIES

PARATROOPER WHO LOST HIS LEG IN A MORTAR BLAST

JOE WITH A PRETTY TEENAGED VIETNAMESE GIRL

THE SIOUX AND JOE ZONKED ON ACID

"What was it like over there?" I asked.

"Hot, and it rained all the time. The bush was nice, real green. I made a tape of insect sounds. I'll play it for you sometime, when I find it. There's a bug over there that sounds like he's saying 'Fuuuck!' all the time.

"The girls were kind of pretty, more like Navvies than Zunis, though, always asking for money and things.

"The best part was the drugs. I tried everything they could give me: grass, hash, heroin, opium, orange sunshine, purple haze. The grass in Nam is out of sight—not like the shit they sell here—and cheap too. Bought it by the shopping-bag-full, only smoked the flowers, threw the rest away.

"Got busted for grass, but my CO restored my rank: I was a RTO, a radio man, Specialist Fourth Class. It's pretty dangerous backpacking radios, you know. Got hit by snipers couple times; the battery stopped the bullet. You know, sometimes you put a radio back together and there are some parts left over? You throw them away and tell 'em they'll just have to order a new one, this one can't be fixed.

"Man, but opium is really weird; me and my Sioux buddy here went to a place that had a fifty-buck entrance fee, it was pretty strange, all kinds of weird food and drinks, and masks, and all. Everything was alive in that room, rugs, cushions, chairs, tables, plates, forks, and all that stuff floating around. My body got real light too, you know, like I lost the gravity."

"How was the food?" asked Dennis.

"C-rations are horrible—ham and lima beans and more ham and more lima beans. But whenever we got off we'd find great food: lots of different kinds of mushrooms and seafood. Didn't much like all the rice, though.

"Me and my buddy went to the beach a lot and swam on acid. Boy was that something, with rainbow colors and criss-cross waves coming at us. We sat in the sand, built forts and houses, and he talked Lakota. You know, it was strange, I really understood him, and when I talked Zuni, he really understood me. I know those languages aren't alike. Guess it was just a miracle or something, since now I can't understand a single word."

"Did your company lose anyone?"

"Yeah, a patrol was sent out without a radio. When I tried to raise them on the radio and they didn't identify themselves, for chrissakes, we just opened up. They were wiped out. Ten were lost from my company, including a close buddy, a white guy from Denver. I guess I cried over that one. He was a good guy, had a wife and little boy back home, about the same age as Junior."

"Was anything ever done about it?"

"Sure, but it's too late now. That sergeant who sent out the patrol without the radio will be court-martialed someday."

"What's it like being back home?"

"Fine. A little quiet. Boring. But it's good to be back here. Killing people is not my—bag. Ha."

MAMA-SAN (VIETNAMESE WOMAN) AND KIDS

REMAINS OF A JEEP

THE SIOUX FLEXING HIS MOTORCYCLE TATTOOS

JOE WITH AN M-16 RIFLE ON HIS KNEES

"Did you, were you, forced to kill many civilians over there?"

"Tried not to, but we had a crazy lieutenant from Alabama. He really liked to get us mad, you know, in the mood to kill just about everything: chickens, pigs, dogs, ducks, women, kids, even babies.

"One night, when our squad was strafing a village, me and my Sioux buddy put an end to all that. We threw him a grenade, it wasted him."

"You killed the white guy?"

"Yeah, he was sick."

After a silence I ventured, "Guess you're a Bow Priest now?"

"Naw, before I left Stateside I was already initiated into that hunters' group, you know, the Coyote Society. But when I got back from Nam I was full of halow samu/*bad dreams,* you know."

"You mean nightmares? Hallucinations?"

"Something like that, with women and children screaming and running around with their clothes and hair on fire. It's awful, you know—the VC [Viet Cong] looked just like us Indians. I wasn't getting much sleep; I'd be polishing jewelry, hear screams, and see them running towards the Zuni River, on fire. Sometimes they turned round and chased me, got up on my chest, with their long hair and dirty nails on fire, and pushed down hard on my throat, cutting off my wind. That woke me up right there."

"Did you talk to anyone about that?"

"I told Rose."

"How is she?"

"Fine; well, I guess you've heard that we got back together. We had trouble before I went over there to Nam; guess I was drinking pretty hard. Did some fire-fighting for the Forest Service up in Washington. Went up there and made sixty bucks an hour on the chain saw. Sometimes I worked as a shooter."

"What's that?"

"When you get a really big wildfire the flames move ahead so fast it looks like surf. The bear, deer, antelope, squirrels can't escape—just catch on fire and run across the fire line into the brush and start up new fires. Shooters are spaced along the fire lines to shoot burning animals as they jump from the flames and race across the line.

"It's sad work killing animals that make it. I guess I prefer the sawing, but us Indians are usually the ones picked out for the shooting job. The pay's pretty good, as good as chain sawing, but it's sad.

"In the evenings us Indians of all tribes get together a case or two of beer, some corn chips and bean dip. We gamble with those Warm Springs Indians and by the time we finish fighting fires most of us come home with nothing. Even worse sometimes, we come home with debts to other guys.

"One time, when I came back from two weeks of fire-fighting, I found my favorite rifle—you know, the one with the deer inlay on the handle?"

"Sure thing, it's a handsome gun."

"Well, I found my gun, ammunition, moccasins, feather box, papers, photos—all that kind of personal stuff—stacked up out front the trailer. The guys who let me off really laughed when they saw my stuff outside like that. It sure was embarrassing.

"Right there I knew it was over between me and Rose. That's the way women get the divorce around here, you know. So I just gathered up all that shit, threw it in my pickup, and went back home to Mom. Pretty soon I volunteered for Nam."

"Sadie said you were still having real bad dreams. How's it going?"

"It's been bad all right. Couple of months ago Mom sent me in to the bosses of that Coyote group to get myself whipped. It was during a Comanche dance, and when those Salimopiya came out they scared all the little kids away.

"I told my dreams to each one of them; then they whipped

me, *hard,* four times on each arm with yucca whips. My arms got real bruised—couldn't even lift them for a whole week. But I guess it was worth it."

"How do you mean?"

"It worked out pretty good, I guess. You know how it is: after I told the Salimopiya my bad dreams, out there in front of everyone, they just went away, vanished. So, up till now, at least, I haven't joined that Bow Priesthood."

"Are you still bothered?"

"Kyamme, have you ever seen yourself?"

"What do you mean?"

"In broad daylight?"

"No, I never experienced that."

"Well, on Monday, last week, I stepped out of the shower here in the house and saw myself standing there in front of the mirror, already drying myself off."

"Have you mentioned that to Rose?" I asked.

"Yeah, and she told Mom about it. So I guess I'll be getting myself whipped again, or initiated, or something," he said, shuffling through his photos.

MAMA-SAN NURSING BABY

JUNGLE DOG WITH SKINNY KID

MASKED HEWA HEWA CLOWNS

"Now, wait just a minute, we thought it wasn't allowed to take pictures of masked dancers."

"It isn't."

"Well?"

"They're members of the family, and besides, I took it right here in the house. Look here, man, you can see it's a flash picture. Do you want it? It's a Polaroid. Maybe you could figure out how to make some bigger ones to give to the rest of the guys, Mom, and me."

"I'm not sure it's possible, but we'll ask at the camera shop."

We flipped through some more of Joe's pictures taken around the reservation: full-length portraits (mostly children), rock paintings, dead birds. They looked pretty good to me, so I asked him, "Have you ever thought about being a photographer?"

"No, I couldn't do that; nobody would pay me for my film. Jewelry or wages, if I could find a decent job around here, is about the best. Working nights at the school, I don't even get minimum wage. But I've got some money in the bank. You know, the part of my salary they withheld when I was on duty. It's not much, just enough to give Junior things I never had."

"What things in particular?"

"We had to make everything when I was small. We made toy cars by nailing bottle caps on blocks of wood, we never had any fireworks, and not much candy. Flora and me used to have to steal our candy from other little kids.

"I want Junior to have all the things white kids have—you know, things he sees on the TV. But I don't know if I can afford it, ever.

"After the war I was supposed to get some kind of veterans' benefits, like job training, finish high school, maybe even go to college. At least that's what they told us up in there in Gallup, at the recruiter's office—before we signed up, that is.

"But I guess when the war didn't work out too good they just canceled all that benefit stuff."

He gathered up his photos in silence, grabbed Junior by the arm, and walked out the front door to his wife's car.

12

STUCK IN THE MUD

■ ■ ■ ■

FLORA'S CERAMICS HAD EXCITED THE TRADERS, who immediately sensed an opportunity in the international antiquities market. It was her designs, which combined motifs from dance masks with geometric elements copied from photographs of nineteenth-century pots. But Flora herself wasn't especially pleased by her early attempts and couldn't understand why the traders took such a great interest in them. Why were they willing to pay her a hundred, even two hundred dollars per water jar or stew bowl?

Sadie, the shrewd one, had her suspicions, but she didn't want to speak them aloud, didn't want to hurt her little sister, the beautiful one, who had been unsuccessful in almost everything in her young life thus far. Besides, she was relieved to think that now Flora might be able to become a bit more independent; perhaps she would make the effort to find a husband, build her own home, and move out. After all, the subdivision house wasn't really big enough for all of them.

One afternoon, when Sadie and her family went to Gallup to

sell jewelry but Flora stayed behind watching TV, we dropped in. Eating popcorn and sipping Cokes, we chatted with Flora and asked to see her pottery. She reluctantly brought out a couple of small pieces, which were quite delightful: a tiny turtle with an even tinier deer painted on his back, and a cow-shaped pitcher with a braided-tail handle.

There was something whimsical about them, and I asked her if I might photograph them. Flora shrugged and walked over to Sadie's china cabinet, pulled up a chair, reached up on top, and retrieved a large ceramic bowl, which she gingerly handed down to me. I examined the pot; it was enormous, as large as any stew bowl ever produced at Zuni Pueblo, and the designs definitely had the feel of those on antique ceramics.[1] I was transported back in time. It was as though Zuni ceramic art had never gone into a steep decline—but it had. As the jars and bowls became smaller, and the designs simpler, losing both overall coherence and many-layered meanings, they had lost their market. And although I was aware that there had been a revival, of sorts, going on in the village, what I did not know was that anyone was already producing ceramics of such high quality.

Flora's extraordinary stew bowl was slipped in white with designs in red, black, and brown. On the inside center was a black crosshatched design element, normally reserved for the top of kachina masks, representing rain clouds gathering quickly from all directions. Emerging from this cloud motif, and climbing up the slope of the bowl, were four black-hatched flutes ending in scalloped gourd bells from which cascaded abstract flower designs in red. Alongside each flute were red-and-black rainbow arcs and lightning arrows, terminating in hooped drumsticks on which were poised, in profile, four mule deer circling round the bowl in a counterclockwise direction. Each dark-brown deer had a white rump and a blood-red breath line stretching from mouth to heart.

This bowl, which had already been used once to bring food

to the kiva for the masked dancers, was simultaneously a kachina's song for rain and a hunter's song over dead deer.

> *Dawn Boy goes along singing*
> *with rainbow arc and lightning arrows.*
>
> *"Yellow flowers sprout from my ears*
> *blue flowers from my nose*
> *red flowers between my eyes*
> *white flowers from my mouth.*
>
> *Each knee has flowers*
> *each elbow has flowers*
> *navel flowers*
> *heart flowers.*

Come, deer
come to my flowers
come to my all-colored flowers."

Though Flora was clearly working within the older pottery-making tradition, she had also produced a brilliantly original composition, which crossed the sensory domains of music and painting. Her design was the best illustration I had seen, thus far, of the full visual-auditory chromaticism the Zunis call "tso'ya," an aesthetic concept I had been studying.

As Flora brought out her large water jars and stew bowls, one by one, Dennis and I carried them outdoors into the sun and photographed them from several angles. I felt funny about showing so much interest in her work, when Flora herself seemed apathetic. Surely, showing a concern for her creative talent couldn't hurt any.

After we finished photographing all of her ceramics, Flora suggested that we drop by and visit her brother, who was living on the south side of the Zuni River. But on second thought, since it was already late morning, we would probably have better luck finding him over at Halona Plaza.

When we arrived at the dry-goods store, located in the big stone house Frank Hamilton Cushing had built for himself in the pueblo long ago, Joe greeted us at the entrance. We were shocked to find him working there, as a stock boy. Not only because he was much too bright for such a menial job, but also because we understood that *all* men in a host family had to give up their wage jobs for an entire year before the Shalako ceremony in order to help build the new house. There he was, starting up a brand-new job, while his sister Sadie was building her Shalako house.

Greeting us with a mischievous grin, he took us inside to meet his fellow employees, mostly young teenagers; but then, since it was nearly noon, he decided to invite us home for lunch. He was living with his wife and son in a battered house trailer parked on the south side of the Zuni River, in front of his mother-in-law's well-kept stone house.

Rose, who arrived home from her job just as her husband finished setting the table and putting out the food—fried hot dogs with mustard and pickles, canned hash with an egg on top, potato chips, and Pepsi—was introduced to us in English as "the one who has me." Joe, in turn, referred to us as his "Eastern aunt and uncle." Smiling broadly, Rose said that lunch would have to be "really fast," since she only had an hour.

She was working at the electronics factory on the north side of the village, a job she found immediately upon graduation from Zuni High. This was her best bet, since she could qualify for the U.S. government OJT (On-the-Job Training) program, which paid the minimum wage while she was learning. Although she already knew quite a bit about silversmithing, she decided not to become a full-time jeweler, since she couldn't afford to invest in silver, turquoise, and expensive jewelry-making machines. Besides, passing thin wires through tiny carbon beads in computer memory-storage panels was almost like stringing necklaces and soldering silver brooches.

She had started off on the assembly line back in 1970, and now, in 1973, was one of three supervisors. But because of her reluctance about promotions (they make you "show out" so that others envy you), she accepted each advancement only on a trial basis. Currently she was earning $175 a week, except for layoff periods during the summer. In high school she had had the best grades and SAT scores in her class and was offered a scholarship at the University of New Mexico, but declined it because there weren't many jobs for college graduates on the reservation, and she definitely wanted to live in Zuni. This way, at least, she figured that she had a good local job with a future.

At company meetings, up in Colorado Springs, she gave the bosses advice on how to run the plant. The firm had nepotism rules, but she explained that Zunis work best with their own relatives—husband and wife, or brothers and sisters—and that their hiring troubles were due to rules against this. "Why, you've just got to understand that *everyone* is a relative at Zuni."

Another problem was with the Navajos. She explained that, though it was good to let them work together in teams, family members shouldn't work in the same group, since their nine-day sings and curing rituals could occupy an entire extended family for up to two weeks at a time. With Zunis it was different, in that religious obligations mostly affected the men; thus, each work team should consist of more women than men, and no two men should ever be members of the same dance group. In this way a team could keep up their production rate even when one member had to be absent, or leave early, to prepare for a night dance.

But, Rose explained, under no circumstance should any work team ever consist of both Zunis and Navajos. Separate work teams made it possible for people both to speak their own languages and not to have to worry about witchcraft on the job. It's really important for people to feel at home, kind of relaxed, when they're working, if you want them to do their best for you.

Her husband had difficulty holding jobs and, as she phrased it, "It's a damn good thing I know how to make money." She's never late for work, and has never missed a day. She enjoys living near her mother, who takes care of Junior, and doesn't think she would much like having a kid if it weren't for her help.

"Joe doesn't enjoy living so close to my mom, but you know how the men are: they say they're interested in their kids, but then the woman just has to do all the dirty work. Yes sir, well, I decided that wasn't going to happen to me."

She glanced at her watch and excused herself, saying that she had to be back on the job at 1:00 P.M. sharp. She could never be late, for she was a boss now and had to set an example.

While shaking a hardy goodbye with me, she glanced down at our clasped hands, then impulsively stuck her ring finger into her mouth and loosened a large needlepoint turquoise ring, which she deftly slipped onto my right ring finger, with a wink but without a word. I responded with "Elahkwa/*Thanks*," and Rose smiled, touched my cheek softly, then turned and rushed out the front door to her car.

Joe decided that he would take the rest of the day off, "to relax some," and offered us each a beer. Dennis accepted, but I shook my head no. Joe turned on the radio and tuned it in to his favorite Gallup station, KGAK; but instead of rock they were playing Navajo Round Dance songs. He jerked it off with a grunt and complained about his loneliness, saying that he would have to wait around until 5:00 P.M., when Rose got off work, before they could drive up to Gallup "to have some fun."

I remembered our present and ran out to the car to retrieve a copy of *Alcheringa,* a magazine Dennis had founded with the poet Jerome Rothenberg back in 1970. This particular issue had a transcription of one of Hapiya's stories, and I thought Joe might enjoy reading it. Wanting to even things up, immediately, he walked over to his stereo cabinet, pulled out *Summer Songs from Zuni,* a new release from Canyon Records, and handed it to me. Such speed in reciprocation was startling.

There was an awkward pause during which we couldn't find a topic of conversation. Joe didn't seem to be interested in, well, anything, so we decided to go over to Sadie's place. When we walked in she was buffing a needlepoint necklace, but immediately shut off her machine in order to welcome us properly. She explained that Flora was napping and Sabin was over at her new house, with the boys, laying cinder block.

Dragging out a stack of ten-inch 78s, produced at the pueblo back in the 1950s by Pat Kelsey, a trader, she said she bought them for $3.50 apiece from her next-door neighbor: scratchy, but rare. She played one and hummed along with the song at first, but she fell quiet, then said she was worried because her father had been buying a lot of land recently, and if he died the family wouldn't know which pieces were his, and the people who had sold them to him might deny having done it.

When Dennis suggested that Albert might know about all this, she said, "Albert might know too much; he might add something to it."

She also didn't much like the manner in which Hapiya was trading jewelry for land. "He tries to do it in the old Indian way, bartering, but he just goes to the stores and buys the jewelries without first asking us, his own children, to make them for him."

We didn't respond, since we were sure Sadie would have given her father trouble over what he wanted the jewelry for in the first place. We were aware that neither Sadie nor Sabin much liked the country, and figured that they were supporting Hapiya's life-style by making most of the payments on his tractor and baler. As far as they were concerned, farming and sheepherding were a thing of the past. Nowadays they were just pastimes, giving old folks something to occupy themselves with, and young kids a place to run during the summer. Crafts, most especially the jewelry, were really the only way to make a decent living now.

Sadie was also worried about Hapiya's health, especially his chronic pneumonia; she tries to look after him, but he won't take it. He may be stepping out during the winter and she will say, "Why don't you wear a jacket?" But then he'll just get mad. Any sort of advice is especially hard for Sabin to give, because he's just an in-law. And whenever he asks his father-in-law for information about landholdings, Hapiya says, "You like the village. You're not interested in anything out in the country."

Her father had been having some problems with the rams,

several of which were ailing. She brought a medicine man out to look after them and paid him with an inlaid-silver bolo tie she made and four long-sleeve shirts from Gallup; her father gave him a pair of eagle tail feathers. The curer removed needles from about forty of the rams, and told them that's how many would have died because of jealous persons. She wishes her father wouldn't show out so much. He'd recently been elected to an important post in the tribal government. It was a difficult job with lots of politics. It seems he has to talk up about something at government meetings all the time now, and it's dangerous. But what can a daughter say?

Dennis was bored with all this worry talk and decided to drop in on the Shalako house construction. There were eleven guys there, including Kwinsi and Sabin, and so far all they had was the foundation and two rows of cinder blocks, on the east side. As we climbed out of the car we could see that they were hard at work, either making concrete or hauling blocks around. Dennis would have to pitch in and help, or split. He wasn't sure if it was appropriate for him to help out, since he only knew three of the guys in Kwinsi's kiva group; besides, neither Kwinsi nor Sabin had even looked up to acknowledge his arrival. They probably didn't want to have to explain who we were to the guys in Kwinsi's kiva group: having ethnographers as friends might lead to accusations that they were "selling their religion." We decided to leave, and drove back over to Joe and Rose's trailer.

When we pulled up, Joe was standing behind the living-room drape, staring out the window blankly, while drinking a beer. Hearing us open the front door, he stepped away from the drape and said, "This must be what it's like to live in a big house all by yourself," then suggested that we might as well drive up to the country to visit his father. When we agreed, he went next door to his mother-in-law's and got Junior, sending him to the back seat of the car. Then he returned to the trailer, and emerged with a brown paper sack concealing a six-pack and climbed in back with his son.

As soon as we hit the highway he popped a top, and after giving Junior a taste offered us some; when we declined, he simply consumed all of it. We guessed he didn't want his father to catch him drinking.

Hapiya and Albert were the only ones at the house when we arrived. Tola was down below in her squash patch, and the grandchildren were out with the sheep. Albert, who pointedly ignored his younger brother, not even looking his way, took immediate notice of Dennis' shirt—one with irregular areas of green, orange, dark red, and buff—calling it "hish tso'ya/*very beautiful*." Joe, who would later comment on the shirt as well (saying that Dennis looked like he was ready for picking up girls at the Scalp Dance), wandered off aimlessly in the direction of the tractor shed.

Albert was plucking his latest bird kills— three woodpeckers and a sparrow hawk. They were long overdue and beginning to stink. "Those religious guys down at Zuni need woodpecker feathers right away and sent up for them," he said.

He carefully wrapped the feathers—keeping them separate by species and by location on the bird, tail or wing—in neatly cut strips of newspaper. The strips had already been folded in four: all folds parallel and equally spaced. He placed a given bunch of feathers between two folds and parallel to them, then made a new small fold at right angles to the others, so as to create a pocket for the bases of the feathers. Next he folded the whole strip back up, using the old creases, leaving the feathers neatly enclosed and not in danger of falling out unless, of course, the pocket got turned upside down. He rejected feathers that had any blood in the quills, or had been damaged when the bird was shot. As he went about his task he seemed like nothing so much as a hobbyist, though the feathers were for religious purposes.

Hapiya complained that his shoulders were sore, because he had spent the previous day loading hay into the baler. He said he might sell some, but would keep most of it for feed and nesting for his animals next winter.

Tola returned from her gardens and prepared a pot of coffee. As we sat sipping our coffee, Hapiya said, "The old-timers, they were talking about this 'black water,' the coffee and the wine. Look how many dead persons we got out here, in this young generation. What's the Whiteman doing all over these United States? They came from the Old World; now they boss on us, us, naturalized citizens, *Indians*.

"What are they doing? They're making all kinds of laws, regulations. Do they obey their regulations, their bylaws? No sir, they violate themselves. Like season, deer-hunting season—guys shoot each other.

"These old-timers used to say, and it's true, that the White-man, when anything makes a motion, just start a little bit moving, then he shoots. But the Indian, he look at the side where the animal is, until he sees him move, then the Indian can shoot. Not like the Whiteman, who just goes ahead and shoots. That's the way old-timers used to do.

"And what I'm talking about, this old 'black water,' old-timers spoke about. I think they were talking about the coffee and about the wine. Look how many dead persons we got out here right now, this younger generation.

"Well, you know who opened that? Navajos. You didn't know that?"

"No," answered Dennis. "We've never heard *that* before."

"The Navajos were crying for the whiskey, crying for the wine. That old chairman, Chee Dodge, back in 1944 or 1943, well, he's the guy that coaxed for his Navajos to be open on the liquor. He drank himself, so he wanted his whole tribe to have a chance to drink; but not on the reservation, in the town only. You could go into Gallup, into the saloon, and if you're over eighteen, or twenty-one, you're eligible.

"This thing was put up by the Navajos, but look what the Zunis are doing. Look at the highway. You've been seeing the highway?"

"Ummm."

"It's all decorated up. They say they got no money, but once upon a time they called a general meeting about their water bills. And the councilman went to the BIA, over in Gallup, and the big boss from Washington told him, 'You've got to tell the tribe to pay their water bills.'

"Well, the councilman said, 'We're poor, we've got no money.' This word came up, about decorating the highway, and about the televisions, antennas on every roof, and about the cars, the cars are in their yards. And they say Indians are poor, they got no money.

"Then the first word that come out was, the Zunis are *rich,* because of their silversmithing, they've got a lot of money. All this Zuni Reservation, all the whole village, nobody's got a bank account with the jewelry yet; but these livestock owners, they've got some guys in the banks, but not all.

"This word came up in the general meeting, and I told them it's a shame to talk about it, but the BIA is telling you the *truth.* If you look at your roads, even at your house, like that pop bottle laying right over there [pointing to an empty aluminum can on the floor], sure, we've got money to buy the pop, same with the beer. Anything can be bought with the money. But probably we make jewelry, just enough to be able to buy those things, and maybe two dollars left over. Then what? Probably you'll think about the gasoline, and that might be all. Then you come home with pop on your roof, and the gas filled up. You'll probably come home drunk. And another month comes. The water bill

comes up again, the water. Well, this was what the head councilman was told once before.

"But these Navajos, they're crying for their liquor. Now, up
to date, we had this OEO [Office of Economic Opportunity]
meeting. A guy brought this liquor up before the governor; well,
the governor said he was just teasing. There's no such a word as
'teasing' when you're right before the public, in a general meeting. The governor can't tease—he's got to be straight and be
true. He's got to stand there strong and tall, so everybody will
mind him.

"They already got their certificate on the package liquor, already got the license. They're going to open this supermarket in
Zuni, and I'll bet package liquor will be put up in that joint
someplace. He's already got the license; I know it's approved
already in Santa Fe. A lot of the guys say it can't be done. He
will. He's got a chance to make money with it. Because they say
you make more money with the liquor than with anything else.
That's what they say.

"First they opened the Witch Wells bar, on Shalako night;
that was in '66. First night they make over thousand dollars.
The Zunis go over there and drink; just the Zunis themselves,
that whole night, Shalako night. Everybody goes there and brings
liquor out. They make over thousand dollars, just *one night*. Well,
suppose, end of the week, how much they make?

"So the governor knows that the liquor's got the money, but
he don't look at the people. He don't probably *realize* what might
happen to his own people.

"Well, look at what the Navajos are doing in town. The city
of Gallup is a dirty town. And why? On account of Navajos
laying out in front of the bars. And the people make complaint
on it, especially the tourists who drive back and forth. Then the
guys over there make reports on it. It's a dirty town, they say.
In order to make a good city, they hire more patrolmen, but

they can't stop the drinking. They got one place, a kind of penitentiary, where they put the drunk, a place to sleep. Getting to be a sanitation problem. They say Gallup is dirty, Gallup is drunkenness. You know how it is?"

"Yes, Gallup is full of drunks, all the time, not just on the weekends or holidays," I replied.

"And when they're *really* drunk, you know how they act? You know how it is when a dead person, really drunk, you know how they act?"

"I know. I went two years ago to Ceremonial. I think you came with us then?"

"Yes."

"After you left, I went into town to buy some gas; right at the Malco, across the railroad where the Gallup Mercantile is. I got the gas, and went another block to turn around, right close to the feed store, in that block. Just when we turned, and we went about fifty yards, we saw a Navajo woman and a man. The man started taking his pants off, he was all naked, and I told Albert, 'Looook, free show,' I said.

"Then we had that meeting, and I told this same story to the governor too. We don't know what will happen; because some of these guys, because it's right in the center of the village, they hog it up, drink too much, get real drunk. And up to date the wines are no good, they say it's no good. Somebody might get crazy for it, get out of control. Well, if that thing comes up, the people in Zuni will raise cain about it."

Hapiya stood up dramatically, abruptly ending his narrative, and went outside, down the hill, into the shed. When he returned with a gallon of gasoline, to fill the tank on his new irrigation pump, he asked Dennis to take him down below to his fields before it got dark. Since they would be going some distance in the muddy fields, he suggested that Dennis drive the pickup Kwinsi had left till he could afford to fix it up. Soon after they took off in the pickup, Joe said to his brother Albert, referring to Dennis, "Let's go see if Uncle Sam knows how to work that pump."

They jumped into our car and went flying out at top speed after Dennis and their father. Dennis later told me that he squeezed them out at the bridge, without seeing them. Then they came up alongside him, on the straight stretch, and wanted to race. He refused to go fast, so they just stayed alongside and followed on right into the fields. Hapiya warned him about a wet spot, and Joe somehow avoided the spot without the warning.

While Hapiya was filling the gas tank, one small can at a time, Joe tried to start the pump with the top off, the choke in, and the grounding lever against the spark plug. In the end it was Hapiya who got the thing going. Then Joe thought the end of the hose in the creek (the intake) might be stopped up, so he waded in to fish it out, and water came up over the tops of his fancy new cowboy boots, filling them. Hapiya told him,

in a restrained tone, to leave the hose alone; then he wandered
off into the field to see how the water was spreading.

Dennis drove over to meet him. Joe followed, making as if to
race, and took a shortcut that got him stuck in the wet place.
His solution was to tromp on the accelerator, again and again,
until the rear wheels were driven into the mud, up to the axles.
Once it was clear to him that he was thoroughly stuck, he said
he'd have to get the tractor to pull the car out, and asked Dennis
to drive him up to the shed to get it.

As they drew alongside the spot where Hapiya was (he had
taken no notice of the immediate events), Joe told Dennis just
to go on. But since Hapiya was the only one who could properly
work the tractor, Dennis stopped the truck. Hapiya was standing
there watching the water, as if he didn't know what he was going
to be asked. Joe remained in the cab of the truck while Dennis
got out and made the request.

Hapiya's only comment, in a low voice, was: "This just makes
too much messy work."

On the way back up to the shed, Joe's only statement was:
"Maybe if I'd been going faster I could have made it." Hapiya's
reply to this, in a sharp tone and in Zuni, was to the effect that
Joe simply shouldn't have driven in the soft part of the field.

Joe rode back to our stuck car, on the rear of his father's
tractor, and Dennis drove down in the truck. Kwinsi's son Harry
was already there, on his bicycle, talking with Albert. The other
herders, up at the foot of the hogback, had sent him down to
investigate.

Albert and Joe first tied the chain to a thin brace connecting
the front left fender to the frame, and it snapped immediately.
Then they tied it to the frame and it held. As soon as the car
was clear Joe took off in a hurry with the truck. Dennis and
Hapiya exchanged a glance; Hapiya shook his head slightly, no;
he didn't want a ride home. Dennis nodded at Albert and they

climbed into our car and drove up to the house. Hapiya chose to remain in his field for quite a while.

Back at the house, Joe Junior began to wonder why his grandpa didn't return, and begged his father to go look for him. Joe put his son in a small red wagon, and set out to find his father. As it grew dark, the squeak of the wagon could be heard near the old school. Some time later the lights of the approaching tractor were visible, and Dennis walked down to meet it at the bridge. It was coming very slowly, because the toy wagon was hitched on behind, with Joe and Joe Junior riding in it. This proved a great sensation, and everyone came out to see.

Tola and I had already started to fix dinner for the whole crew when Joe insisted that he had to return to the village, immediately, because Rose would be sitting there worrying and wondering if he had forgotten his promise to take her to Gallup. I apologized to Tola for running off like this. She smiled, shook her head, and told us to go on down to Zuni.

As we pulled up to the trailer, Rose was standing on the concrete stoop staring at us, with hard eyes, and before Joe could even get out of the car, she walked over to Dennis' window and asked us to stay with Junior, while she talked to her husband. Holding his head down, Joe followed her inside.

Soon we heard muffled shouts, followed by bumping sounds; then it was quiet, totally quiet. Rose and Joe emerged, and clambered into the back seat with Junior. The forty-mile trip to Gallup seemed longer than usual, since everyone was speechless; even Junior sat there without making a sound.

To mask the silence, Dennis tuned the radio to the Zuni FM station, KSHE, named for the standard greeting, "Kesshe/*Hello*." The disc jockey was playing an album put out by Canyon Records called *Zuni*, which featured Leo Quetawki's all-male choir singing "Comanche," "Red Beard," "Crazy Grandchild," as well as other kachina songs.

13

TOUGH MAMA

■ ■ ■ ■

WE STROLLED ALONG the still-hot blacktop past chicken-wire-and-orange-crate vegetable stands, illuminated by headlights and raw light bulbs, candied-apple and popcorn peddlers, enormous pastel bunnies with satin bows wrapped inside cellophane, plaster-of-paris burros, sombreros, jackalopes, painted black velvet bullfighters and bronco-busters. Rose bought two heads of cabbage, a bushel of peaches, and a candied apple for Junior. Joe bought a black velvet painting of a rampant mustang and a tiny toy pony for Junior, saying, "I always wanted a horse when I was small." After stuffing it all in the trunk, we continued our early-evening walk.

Four blocks down, after Bear Claw Tool Sharpening and Smith's Feed & Tack, we arrived outside the infamous Palomino Saloon. There were lots of folks gathered round their pickups drinking beer and wine, listening to Country Western on their radios: men in high-crowned, silver-banded black felt Stetson

hats with hawk- and eagle-feather trimmings, plaid or striped
cowboy shirts with green-snail snaps, tight freshly pressed faded
Levi's fraying over high-heeled dusty Justin boots; and women
in flowery rayon scarves, royal-blue, magenta, and purple velveteen blouses with silver buttons, over yards and yards of calico
skirts, and tennis shoes. They were laughing in that soft country
way, drinking together, oblivious to a middle-aged woman in a
long blue skirt who was alternately whimpering, belching, curs-
ing, and throwing up while rolling back and forth under a giant
billboard announcing, in both Navajo and English, a new Texas
pint-sized Garden de Luxe Tokay.

Rose jerked her head to one side, picked Junior up, and, closing
his nostrils with her fingers, turned his head away. She love-
hated Gallup, with its fine stores, Mexican food, and drunken
Indians. The Place by the Bridge, as it was called, once was a
meeting place for raiding parties. She remembered that her grandfather feared this gap between the iron-red mesas where Navajos

organized themselves, then swooped down south to plunder Zuni fields. Today truckers simply call it "Drunk City, U.S.A.."

Continuing along and then across a concrete-lined storm-sewer, up over the Rio Puerco (called "Perky" by local cowboys), across the Santa Fe Railroad tracks, and up Second Street. Right on Coal past Piggly Wiggly, Sand-n-Silver, a failed Woolworth's, to the Kiva Hotel, with its usual assortment of teenagers waving, smiling, and calling out to passing ranchers and cowboys.

Down past City Electric Shoes and Woodard's Indian Arts, with its basement museum of ancient arrowheads, stone hammers, pottery, baskets, and other artifacts, including a locked closet of sacred Indian art: kachina masks and dolls, icons, fetishes, and altars. Most items were copies, but some were not and were thus forbidden but, of course, available to any "serious collector," at inflated prices. A left turn and one block down to U.S. 66, past Murphy's Camera Shop, where only Indians must leave a deposit with any film they want developed, Windy Mesa Gallery, Sanchez Karate, El Charro Cafe, and into the Commercial Club.

Kwinsi was standing next to his brother Albert, leaning on the bar, near the front door. In his hand he held his usual Jack Daniel's with his Coors chaser before him. "Hey there, Kachinmana, Kyamme, Rose baby, and Joe ol' boy. Look here, Joe Junior, mighty grown up already. I'll bet you already drink ummo ky'awe/*foam water*. Right, Junior?"

"Right; gimme Tuush an Hepikkya Ky'awe/*Horse Piss*."

"Well, folks, I'm buying. So what will it be? Scotch. Whiskey. Martini. Margarita. Tequila Sunrise. Whatever fancy drink you like."

We ordered a pitcher of Coors.

"Kyamme, what's this I hear about your plans?" asked Kwinsi.

"We're doing research right here in Gallup, starting now. I received a grant from the University of Pennsylvania's Center for

Urban Ethnography, so I guess we'll be spending some time hanging out at Eddie's, talking with folks about life in town and back home—you know, work and trade and all."

"What? Are you two insane?" blurted out Joe. "Eddie's is as bad as Milan's, much rougher than the Palomino. Besides, them bars are filthy, never safe, you know that. None of us go in 'em. Only ones who do are down from the Big Reservation, and not all of them go near them neither."

Kwinsi grinned. "You crazy anthropologists, what's wrong with you is you're too damn curious. I sure as hell don't understand your line of work. When you tell me you get paid just to hang out in bars and saloons, I start wondering, you know."

"Kwinsi, how many times do I have to explain it to you?" I sighed. "This kind of fieldwork is called 'participant observation.' We hang out in public places in order to *meet* people and *talk* with them, informally, about their lives in town, out on the rez, and all. It's the only way we can learn personal things, important things. We sure as hell can't go door to door, like traveling salesmen, asking people to answer a long list of dumb questions. You know that."

"It still sounds weird, you know. Your kind's been coming round here for a hunnerd years, looking for secrets. What secrets you gonna get from a drunk?"

"Not everyone in a bar is drunk, right?"

"Right."

"Besides, we're not looking for secrets, never have been; you also know that."

"Okay, okay, but just the same, as them Navvies say, 'It's sure strainch.' "

"We already know quite a bit," I added.

"For example?"

"For example, did you know that Gallup has thirty-nine liquor licenses?"

"So?"

"So, that's thirty-two licenses too many, according to a New Mexico state rule of one for every two thousand population. And there were more than *ten thousand* drunk arrests here last year."

"Mostly Navvies, I'll bet," said Joe.

"Probably so," I admitted. "The sentence for drunk-and-disorderly here is *ninety days,* and sometimes there are thirty or more people crowded into the *same cell.* The police chief thinks that if the jail were enlarged there would simply be more people getting into it. I don't think so. Why, just look at Farmington—it has twice the space of Gallup and half the arrest rate. But, then, what can you expect with the mayor as owner of the Navajo Inn?"

Kwinsi, for the first time since I had known him, looked shocked. "Well, I'll be goddamned. I've heard plenty 'bout him, but I never heard that he owned *that* dive. So, he plays it both ways, liquor man and big in the GAARD."

"What's GAARD?" Dennis asked.

"Where you been, ol' boy? Haven't you heard about the Gallup Alcohol Abuse Rehab Design? G-A-A-R-D. They came to my American Legion Post a couple of months back and tried to round up some apples."

Dennis frowned and Kwinsi elaborated: "You know, red on the outside and white on the inside: Uncle Tomahawks, White-man's Indians. My group guessed right away they needed 'Indian support' so they could get federal money. But what I don't understand is how in hell the mayor balances owning the worst joint around—I've seen *minors* in there drinkin'—with helpin' drunks."

"Profits both ways," I suggested. "First by making them drunk, then by getting them sober. But somehow it doesn't sound legal to me; or maybe it's legal, but it's not right. You know, we should interview him."

"Better not, Kachinmana. Next thing you know, Tough Cop Rodriguez will be on your case. Better stay away from them guys if you want to get your study done."

"But if nobody questions those guys, then they'll think nobody's awake out there, and they'll do just about anything."

"I'm warning you, don't talk to him, or any other politician in this town. You're likely to get messed up."

"We'll see about that. I'm hungry, aren't you?" asked Dennis.

"Sure. It's nine-thirty and Pedro's closes at ten, so if we're gonna chow down we'd better make tracks," replied Kwinsi.

"Fine by me."

Dennis, Joe, Rose, and Joe Junior took off to get our car while Albert and I climbed into Kwinsi's brand-new pickup with a bumper-sticker proclaiming "I'M PROUD TO BE AN AMERICAN, INDIAN." Kwinsi popped a Cream album into his tape player and cruised down Highway 66; then up Coal Avenue with "Born Under a Bad Sign" blaring out the window in the Friday-night bumper-to-bumper go-to-town-and-look-at-one-another crowd.

Kwinsi caught sight of Sadie and tooted at her in her closed car, an emerald-green Buick. He said she was well off now, since she got the commission to make inlay-silver crowns for the Zuni Fair Queen and all her court. At Pedro's Mexican Restaurant the owner greeted us and escorted us over to an elegant table, in the very center of the big room; Pedro loved to display his Zuni friends.

As we drew near the table Albert objected: "No. How about along the side, or in back?"

Kwinsi sighed, then nodded. The busboys pulled together three tables along the far wall from the front door. When Pedro went looking for a kiddy chair, Junior climbed up into my lap, announcing loudly he'd eat with Tsilu, and proceeded to grab hold of my hair, hard, with both fists.

Rose said firmly, "Lesma! Lesma! Paniyu/*Don't! Don't! Get down.* Let go and get off Tsilu's lap right now!"

Junior giggled and slyly looked through my long tangled hair at his mother. Rose looked away, embarrassed. When I started humming a Zuni lullaby, he quieted down a little and asked for a tostada with red-chile sauce.

Lena and Nelson waved from a nearby table. She had lost a lot of weight recently, but at 185 pounds she was still much too heavy. She was the only one of Tola's daughters who used permanent waves—she knew her mother didn't like the way her hair looked, but she thought the curls made her appear more up-to-date, like the women she saw on television and in the movie magazines.

At the table next to them was Kosha, the head of the Neweekwe Clown Society, with his whole family. And over in the corner was One-O-One with his strange Apache wife.

Albert blurted out, "Let's go, get the heck out. Too many Zunis in here tonight."

Kwinsi chuckled. "What's the matter with you? Think Old One-O-One's strong enough to witch you or something? Or maybe that clown might trap and initiate you?"

Albert's fear was not unreasonable. After all, he'd recently killed a black bear in the cornfield, by mistake, and had tried to keep it a secret. It was the combination of his nearsightedness and the twilight that turned that bear into a deer. He didn't realize his mistake until he approached his kill. He immediately recoiled, because he knew that bears were dangerous power animals and that it would be better to have nothing to do with them. Then, after he did it, since bear killing is as serious as people killing, he should have been initiated; maybe not by clowns, but into some kind of medicine knowledge.

He didn't want to. His excuse was that it cost too much. But Kwinsi said he thought his younger brother couldn't join any society, because he just wasn't strong enough to handle the medicine way. By refusing, though, he was withholding himself, and

Kwinsi felt that was even more dangerous. In fact, he could easily get himself killed that way.

Our favorite waitress, Betty Jo from Oklahoma, approached and, seeing Kwinsi's eye patch, did a double take but decided not to question him about it. I'd almost said something myself about it, but figured that there must be something wrong with his glass eye and that he probably wouldn't want to talk about it.

Everyone but Kwinsi ordered chiles rellenos and refries, Spanish rice, small mixed salads, and extra green chile. He ordered the most expensive item on the menu, "Pedro's Nightmare," a New York strip, medium rare with fire-roasted whole green chiles on top, then nudged Betty Jo with his elbow, asking her how it was going down at Ruidoso.

"I've won eight hunnerd bucks on Flamin' Jet so far. You guys been down bettin' with them hot tips I tole you 'bout?"

"No, we can't. We got a Shalako house to build."

"Listen, honey, if you won some, it could help out with them expenses."

"Sure, but the main thing is, we can't travel all that far right now, you know."

Albert whispered to his elder brother, tightly between his teeth, "Not so loud, man. That clown over there in the corner is listenin' to you."

I involuntarily turned and looked directly into Kosha's eyes. He nodded, then smiled. Returning his smile, I walked over to his table.

"Aren't you going to call me sometime, sugar?" he asked. "I know some real pretty songs."

"Sure. Next time we're in Zuni I'll come by," I replied, gently touching hands with his wife and teenaged sons, and walked back to the table.

As I pulled out my chair Kwinsi demanded impatiently, "Well, so what does he want?"

"Nothing."

"Nothing? Come on, Tsilu!"

"He wants to talk about songs."

"He didn't ask you nothing about us?"

"No."

"Are you *sure*? You know we can't go to town this year. The only traveling we do is visiting shrines like A'ts'inna, or—what do they call it?—that sandstone butte with the writing on it—"

"You mean El Morro, Inscription Rock? Over there towards Acoma, past Ramah, with Indian pictographs and conquistador signatures all over it?"

"That's it, and from Inscription Rock and the Ice Cave in the east, over to Kachina Village in the west, that's as far as we go."

"But you guys have to come up north to Gallup at least once a week. How can you get your laundry done, jewelry supplies, fertilizer, groceries, and all that?"

"We just can't, since we're kind of valuable—you know, tehya—right now. The ladies should do all that for us."

"Since you're Shalako guys I guess you're valuable all year long and shouldn't help out with jewelry or sheepherding or anything like that?"

"You might say that. At least, they shouldn't *see* us doing any of that kind of stuff, unless it's for the Shalako. Well, since we're here in town and we've been seen, what about dancin'? We could warm up over at the Little Rock, then mosey on over to Manolo's when they're really rockin'."

"Sure thing, but we can't get in at Manolo's. You have to be *Zuni* to get into that joint," Dennis objected.

"You two speak Zuni pretty good, good enough to get by the bouncers; besides, didn't I hear that you're from an Eastern branch of our family?"

We laughed and Rose said, "Hey there, you're our aunt and uncle, aren't you? So why not? What do you think?"

We looked at one another and winked; I said, "Sure, it's pretty dark, so maybe we can pass. Besides Zuni, we can talk Spanish to the owner, who'd feel pretty funny about not letting us in. Who's playing?"

"The Sapphires, a Zuni rock-and-soul band."

"Great, sapphire's my birthstone; besides, I've heard they're one of the best groups in town."

"We gonna have Mexican puddin' [flan] or can we get the hell out of here?" Albert asked urgently, shoving himself out at arm's length from the table.

"Wait there just a minute, buddy. Who's gonna finish the pitcher?" asked Kwinsi.

Albert pulled back the table and Kwinsi poured beer all round. When Junior demanded a taste Joe looked at Rose and raised his eyebrows.

She replied, "Sure, give the kid a taste."

Kwinsi poured a little into Junior's empty Pepsi glass and he belted it down, the way he had seen men drink straight shots, then demanded a beer chaser. Rose firmly said no, that was all he could have.

Kwinsi laughed at Junior's imitation of him, then called over Betty Jo and pulled out his wad of bills, a hundred on the outside. "So, dear, what's the damages?"

"Fifty-three bucks altogether."

Dennis slid his American Express Gold Card across the table toward her as Kwinsi slammed a hundred-dollar bill down. She smiled at them both. "So who's the big guy tonight?"

"You paid last time," complained Dennis.

"Okay, okay. I'll pay at Manolo's, since they don't accept no plastic of any kind over there, only pure American money. American Indian bucks."

As we got up to leave Rose whispered to me, "Before we go to Little Rock, don't you want to pee?"

"Sure, I'd better, so I don't get into any trouble later on."

We walked over to the rest room together and Rose pulled a pint of Smirnoff out of her purse. I had forgotten that Zuni women never drink the hard stuff in public, and realized that this was Rose's only chance for a stiff drink before getting back to beer. I closed my eyes and belted mine down, nearly gagging.

After we emerged from the ladies' room, the five of us squeezed into the cab of the pickup with Kwinsi. I flipped over the cassette and "Sitting on Top of the World" played as we caravaned with Sadie, down U.S. 66 to the Little Rock.

When we got inside, there was Ruby, the queen of Zuni jewelers. She waved us over to her table with her turquoise-ringed hand. Her whole huge arm was loaded down with bracelets—sand-cast and chunk-coral, carved-cactus, and solid-silver snakes.

I had met her once before, briefly, at a masked dance down in Zuni. But tonight, for some reason, Ruby decided to tell us all about herself: how she has lived in Gallup for more than twenty years now, working as a highly paid jeweler at Tobe Turpen's. How she owns a big house down in the village, where her four daughters are living. How her old man works as a janitor at the PHS (Public Health Service) hospital. Tonight he left her at the Little Rock Bar and took the keys with him, which has happened before. She keeps an extra set at work but can't get at it before Monday, so she might have to stay in a hotel if he doesn't return. In the cab of the pickup, which he drove off in, were groceries that cost seventy-five bucks; if they spoiled she would charge him at least $150, since this would be the second time he wasted their groceries.

As she went on and on about how much money she made, how she had two cars and cleaned up her husband's bills, I became uncomfortable: I'd never seen a Zuni woman "showing out" like this before. Studying first her face and then her body, I noticed tattoos all over the insides of her arms, and decided that this was probably my very best opportunity, ever, to learn more about the practice.

"Ruby, I notice you've got tattoos, and a lot of other Zuni ladies have them too. I've been wondering how it's done and what it means and all."

Pulling her sweater down over her arm, she replied haughtily, "Maybe it's love, maybe it's magic."

Then, turning her back and looking directly at Dennis, she said, "Well, what do you say, Misho? What will it be?" She flicked an imaginary speck of dust off his Western-style corduroy-and-buckskin sport jacket and threw her huge flabby arm around his shoulders.

He was startled that she knew one of his Zuni names, especially since he had no idea what any of hers were, and replied cautiously, "Well, what's everyone else having?"

"Baby, you can have anything you'd like at Ruby's table. What will it be?"

"Coors."

"And how about you, honey? I'll bet you're drinking them beautiful Margaritas."

"No, I'll have a Coors too."

"Well, then, how 'bout a couple of pitchers of brew?" She snapped her fingers and the pasty-faced hillbilly waitress shuffled over.

"Yeah?"

"Two pitchers of Coors, and make it snappy!"

In walked a bizarre party consisting of two black men in their mid-thirties with two girls, one white and one black, both about eighteen. All four were wearing black leather jackets and square-toed low-heeled boots with noisy brass chains around the ankles. The guys wore Afros and silver studs in their left earlobes and rims. One gal wore an enormous Afro, and the other a Dolly Parton beehive hairdo together with purple-and-green glitter all around her eyes, and each fingernail painted a different color. Their identical hot-pink T-shirts blared "ENJOY COCAINE!" After ordering a pitcher of beer, the foursome went over to a pool table.

Other Zunis arrived, mostly men, and Ruby called them over to her table and bought them drinks. The table grew and grew until other tables were carried over to the great mother table. When the really big guys arrived, the ones who worked construction and wore fancy twelve-karat gold-overlay belt buckles, shell-mosaic watchbands, and giant spiderweb turquoise rings made for export (primarily to Texas), the Navajos at the pool table in the corner got skittish and left.

The Dolly Parton lookalike stood up and poured a beer over the head of a woman sitting nearby, saying, "Dirty Indian." The lady was dumbfounded and just sat there with the beer, which was hers, dripping down on her shoulders and onto the table.

One of the guys at Miss Parton's table jumped up and took her over to the corner where the rest rooms were, while the other guy brought the Zuni lady a new beer from the bar. Then they all sat down at the lady's table but Miss Parton upended the beer-soaked lady's chair, dumping her on the floor. Rose rushed over and helped her to another table. Again she showed no reaction whatsoever.

Kwinsi and Joe stood up and strolled over to the Zuni lady's table and sat down with the group; they talked quietly for a while, until Miss Parton jumped up, breaking her beer glass on the edge of the table, and lunged at Kwinsi. A bunch of guys leapt up from the nearby tables and surrounded him and the girl. The fellows she had come in with charged, grabbed her from behind, then carried her kicking and scratching out the front door and dumped her into their pickup bed. The black girl ran out without a word, and without paying.

"What in hell was that all about?" asked Ruby as she sauntered over to the bartender and paid their bill.

"I asked that tramp to apologize to the lady and she refused," Kwinsi replied. "I don't understand what's going on these days; things like that didn't use to come down in this place."

Dennis looked at me, I nodded, and he stood up, pulling out his credit card and saying, "Well, folks, it's time to go if we're to do some dancing."

"Wait just a minute, buddy; when you sit with Ruby, Ruby pays. Now, be a good boy and put that away. Besides, they don't take no credit here anyways. Seriously, honey, where're you two goin'? Maybe I'd like to join in with you and invite some of these fine men along too."

"Sure, Ruby, we're goin' to Manolo's—if we can get in, that is."

"No problem, baby; not if you take me along. And as you know, even though I'm Badger clan, I'm not mean and I'm not stingy. You can ask anyone round here about that."

"Ruby, we all know that, now let's mosey," Kwinsi said as he slipped his muscular arm around her waist.

The Zuni doorman at Manolo's turned out to be one of Kwinsi's buddies from Korea, but he decided to give us the Zuni test anyway.

"So, my good friend here says you're related to him in some way. Can you explain that to me?"

"Well, sir, I'm his kyakya/*mother's brother,* and she's his tsilu/ *mother's younger sister,*" said Dennis.

"And what clan are you?"

"Ky'aky'aliikwe/*Eagle.*"

"All of you?"

"No, just Sabin and me."

"Then what groups are the rest?"

"Rose and her little boy here are both Towaakwe/*Corn.* Kwinsi,

Albert, Ruby, Sadie, Joe, plus my wife here all belong to To-nashiikwe/*Badger*."

Laughing, the doorman said, "And since when do Zuni Badgers grow strawberry-blond hair?" But then, without any further questions, he let us in, saying, "Well, hell, whatever you guys are, you're sure as the devil not Navvies."

Inside it was dark, very dark. There were a few men at the bar, whom Kwinsi immediately joined, but every table in the house was full. When people saw Ruby they greeted her and offered space at their tables. She grabbed Junior's hand and escorted him and his parents to a table up front, near the band. Sadie and Sabin found a corner of a table near the dance floor, but since there was no room for us we went back to the front door and sat down next to a young woman on the long wooden bench in the waiting area. She was with a handsome guy with bowl-cut bangs in front and long hair tied up in back with a red-and-green woven belt.

I asked her, "Do you think they'll ever give us a table? The band's pretty well known, you know."

She nodded.

"Do you come in here often?" I continued.

"No, it's our first time. Had trouble getting in; he thought we were Navajo, or Apache, or something."

"We've never been in here either. So I guess we four are outsiders tonight."

"Where you guys from? By the cut of your hair it looks like Frisco," asked the man.

"I'm originally from Albuquerque," said Dennis. "But we met out in Berkeley."

"We're from Santo Domingo. Guess you know our village if you're from Albuquerque."

"Sure, we go there for the feast day every August 4 we can get away."

"Next time when you two come over for the fiesta, our house is in the second row from the east side of the plaza. It's the only one with a pink doorframe, and storm windows with screens. So don't knock, just walk right in," the woman said.

Her man leaned over and whispered to Dennis, "Do you guys ever go to the Thunderbird?"

"Yes, we have friends in Placitas. Why?"

"It's our favorite place to celebrate after we've sold a lot of heshe/*shell,* necklaces and things."

The woman leaned toward me and asked shyly, "I need to use the rest room. Maybe you could ask the bartender for the key?"

"Won't he give it to you?"

"No. I'm not Zuni."

"What? I'm not either, even though I speak a little of the language and I've got family down there. But I'll give it a try. Surely he's a Mexican?"

"Yes, and we tried speaking Spanish to him, but he wouldn't answer us."

I stood up, ran my fingers through my hair, straightened my belt buckle, one with a silver snake slithering through chunk turquoise, and sauntered over to the burled-oak bar. Standing next to Kwinsi, I greeted him, "Kesh*she.*"

"Kesh*she,* Kachinmana," he replied, putting his arm around my waist and smiling broadly. "And what may I do you for?"

"The key to the washroom."

"It's locked?"

"Yes indeed, and that girl over there says the bartender won't give her the key."

"We'll see about that. Hey there, Lucas, my relative here needs the key to the washroom."

"Sure, little lady," he said, giving me a smile. "Now, keep it nice and clean, and don't let anyone else in," he added, handing me the key. It was tied to a wooden dance wand with carved sun face, inset turquoise eyes, and coral mouth.

Circling round, I whispered to my new friend, "Just walk in after me."

When we were inside I asked the woman why the bartender was rude. As she replied, "Mexicans are mean, hard on women," a couple of young kids opened the bathroom door, and we headed back for the bench.

Our men were gone; they'd found a table near the band: six guys in beaded headbands, multicolored inlay chokers, skintight designer jeans, and hand-sewn moccasins. As we sat down the Domingo man asked Dennis what we did, volunteering that they were jewelers. They'd dropped out of sociology at the University of New Mexico a few years back, because there was a lot more money in jewelry than social work.

"We've seen that too, at Zuni. Lots of folks start college but get discouraged and drop out before they graduate, because the jewelry business is so good. Now, though, I guess it's starting to tighten up."

"You're right. On this trip we noticed that it wasn't so easy to sell, even in places like Palm Springs and Scottsdale. Some stores are afraid because of silver plate from Colorado, Japanese imitation turquoise, and Filipino machine-ground heshe. You'd think the tribes could get their lawyers on the case. It's probably too late anyway, since it looks like folks back east are getting kind of tired of Indian jewelry."

The band started up and the first song, dedicated to Ruby, was Creedence Clearwater Revival's "Bad Moon Rising." Ruby asked a big fellow to dance, and they were the first ones up. The floor slowly filled with dancers doing a great job, although it was hard to tell for sure, with strobe lights and prismatic colors. A second number, "Revolution," also dedicated to Ruby, was a Beatles number. Ruby asked a lady to dance this time.

Rose jumped up and stuck out her hand dramatically toward Dennis. The spins, turns, twists, and hand clasps were executed with precision, combined with a certain angularity, a sort of stiff elegance, that one never saw at the Avalon, Winterland West, or any other Frisco ballroom.

They stayed on the floor for the next song, "Sunshine of Your Love," by Cream, also for Ruby, who asked another guy to dance. I was starting to get uncomfortable, because I noticed that Sadie Hawkins seemed to be the rule. Up to that point, at least, no man had asked any lady to dance. I took a deep breath and asked Joe to dance.

Smiling, he said, "I guess you noticed this place works pueblo style, with ladies' choice."

Joe was a wonderful dancer, never missed a beat, moving from half-timing to double-timing. I realized that I liked him, a lot, despite his wildness, or maybe . . . He certainly was handsome.

Guiding me up close to Dennis and Rose, he grinned. The next number was a Dylan song, "Tough Mama," for Ruby, of course, and we kept on dancing. Ruby danced with a different person each song; whenever a number got near the end she left the guy or gal, walked over to the band, peeled off a ten-dollar bill, whispered her request, and asked someone else to dance.

At midnight bright lights turned on and everyone got up to leave. Our Domingo friends bid us goodbye at the door saying, "Sorry we don't have any grass right now or you could join us for a smoke over at our pickup. See you guys around Placitas sometime."

Late that fall, Sadie telephoned to tell us that her new Shalako house was almost ready and we were expected to be there for the blessing. She thought it would be the first Saturday in December, but we could get the exact date by calling her back. We should arrive at least one day before Shalako, because she wanted us to help decorate the interior.

She put her dad on the line with Dennis and he told him to be sure to get our ears pierced. He wanted both of us to be able

to wear fine-ground turquoise-bead ear loops during the ceremony.

Naturally we were pleased and excited to be invited to Shalako
by a host family. Most especially to be asked to participate in
house decoration, just like any regular member of the family.
Even more wonderful was the invitation to be dressed traditionally
in old-time earrings. The next morning we rushed out to the
shopping mall to buy two self-piercing earring kits.

14

SHALAKO

■ ■ ■ ■

IMAGINE A SMALL NEW MEXICO VILLAGE, its snow-lit streets
lined with white Mercedes, quarter-ton pickups, and Dodge vans.
Villagers wrapped in black blankets and flowered shawls standing
next to visitors in blue velveteen blouses with rows of dime
buttons and voluminous satin skirts. The men in black Stetson
silver-banded hats, pressed jeans, Tony Lama boots, and Pen-
dleton blankets. Strangers dressed in Day-Glo orange and forest-
green ski jackets, stocking caps, hiking boots, and mittens. All
of them crowded together gazing into new houses illuminated
by bare light bulbs dangling from raw rafters edged with Woolworth's red fabric and flowered blue calico. Cinder-block and
plasterboard walls layered with striped serapes, Chimayó blankets, Navajo rugs, flowered fringed embroidered shawls: black
silk from Mexico, purple and blue rayon from Czechoslovakia.
On poles suspended from the ceiling hang rows of Hopi dance

kilts and rain sashes, Isleta red-and-green belts, Navajo concha belts, and black mantas covered with silver brooches set with carved lapidary: rainbow mosaic, channel inlay, turquoise needlepoint, pink agate, alabaster, black cannel coal, and bakelite from old 78s, coral, abalone shell, mother-of-pearl, and horned oyster. Whitetail and mule-deer trophies wearing squash-blossom, coral, and chunk-turquoise necklaces circle the room on rampant buckskins above Arabian tapestries of Martin Luther King and the Kennedy brothers, the Last Supper, horses, a herd of sheep and haloed herder, peacocks in a formal garden.

Against the far wall stands a wooden tongue-and-groove slat altar, carved and freshly painted with mountain lions, coyotes, rattlesnakes, rainbows, sun, moon, morning and evening stars. A turquoise-studded meal painting swells outward before the icons in great white cumulus scallops with a cornmeal road emerging from the center, trailing off toward the front door. Scattered along the cornmeal path, pottery jars of mossy spring water, tadpoles, water skates, and baby water snakes; a crystal ball that snows when shaken; Pima, Papago, Apache, and Pakistani baskets of tinkling all-colored corn kernels; small-handled pottery jars containing strong meal of white corn, ground shell, and gems; tiny paint pots. On the linoleum floor before the altar stand perfectly kerneled unblemished yellow corn ears clothed in beadwork with olivella-shell, turquoise-nugget, and branch-coral necklaces, smothered in mallard, macaw, parrot, turkey, downy-eagle, blue-jay, and songbird feathers, butt ends nestled in rawhide cups wrapped with cotton in oat-straw basketry; inside a cavity filled with all-colored corn kernels, wheat, squash, watermelon, and muskmelon seeds, piñon nuts. Each one the breath-heart of a medicine person. Stuffed parrots, red-tailed hawks, and golden eagles in stone-fetish necklaces, jet bears and quartz mountain lions with tiny tight turquoise eyes line up one behind another along the meal road facing the front door.

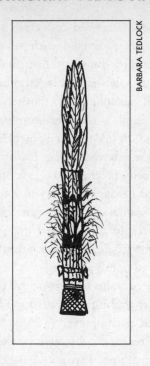

To the left of the altar stand an enameled white water bucket, a wooden bench, and a pottery jar with tautly stretched buckskin drum head, bent willow drumstick on top. Deer silhouettes, each with a thin red line from mouth to heart, circle the belly of the great medicine drum poised on wooden planks over the hollow earthen resonating chamber. Behind the drum hang ten red round gourd rattles and the dressed hide of an immense cinnamon bear stretched flat, stapled to the wall on top of a red Oaxaca blanket in a diagonal flying arc. Red downy-eagle feather tied to his forelock; turquoise and coral necklaces with a massive abalone pendant draped about his neck, protruding at an angle into the room. Before him yellow-gray fire-making Badger, sporting a coral choker, stapled to the wall in mid-flight; white furry breath-road leading from nose to forehead down the back, con-

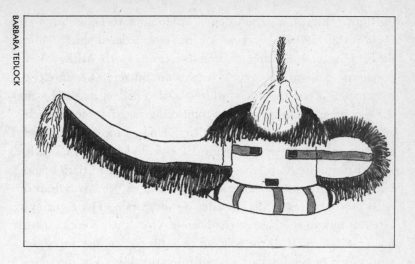

BARBARA TEDLOCK

necting Great Medicine Bear behind him to the Dance Hall of the Dead.

■ ■ ■ ■

Wind-strewn snowflakes, opalescent in pale sunlight, scatter as a man robed in white buckskin, with painted white face, carrying a basket full of feathers, brings a group of masks into the southern plaza. In the lead is the Little Fire God, Shulaawitsi, a Badger-clan adolescent. His body and helmet mask are blackened with cave darkness spotted yellow, turquoise, red, and white: flying sparks, corn kernels, shimmery stars of Orion's Belt, Pleiades, Big and Little Dippers. Each colored paint assigned an individual Badger-clan member; each dot that runs, a promise forgotten. Hanging diagonally from right shoulder to left hip a fawn skin, head and all, filled with wild and domestic seeds. In his right hand a string of speckled cottontails, green mallards with violet wing patches, gray-and-copper ring-necked pheasants. In his left hand a smoking juniper torch, friction-lit in the ancient way.

Right behind him, the Council of Gods, with Longhorn and Huututu in the lead. Each in a white embroidered shirt, white dance kilt, and rainbow-colored moccasins with Milky Way porcupine-quill-work anklets. Fawnskin quivers and antelope bags dangle across shoulders; white-elk-skin helmet masks, black slit eyes extending through and connecting to their wooden ears, are surrounded by Milky Way collars. Tied on top are feathered prayer wands with tips pointing backward. Longhorn's gently curved turquoise horn, the crescent new moon of initiation and rebirth, is hung with black goat's wool, Sun Father's path draped with the blessings of dark, male, big-drop rain. His right eye extends only to the base of the horn (a witch's dangerous path); his left eye extends all the way out onto his ear, connecting sight with sound (a good person's beautiful path). His right foot does the stepping and his left follows along, never advancing further than the right. The Yamuhakto twins in turquoise helmets with cottonwood sticks on top, balanced by multicolored yarn tassels, necks surrounded by striped Milky Way collars, bodies splattered with sunflower petals and ocher from Kachina Village, Land of the Dead.

Approaching from the dressing place at White Rocks, the stately masks stride forward in single file to the ghostly hooting of Huututu and the brittle scraping of antelope scapulas. They are met at the edge of the village by a muffled male crowd wrapped in black blankets. Entering the southern plaza, the masks drop their prayer plumes, tied to colored sticks, into an underground altar, then move on through the old village, planting prayer sticks in six excavations: each one a sacred Shrine of Emergence.

In the Beginning, when Earth was soft, Sun Father was not pleased with the people. They did not offer him prayer sticks or prayer meal, so he decided to bring new people up out of Earth

MUSEUM OF NEW MEXICO

Mother's fourth inner room into his daylight. But he did not know how; he was thinking and thinking; clouds were swelling, they were getting bigger, and the rain came. It rained and rained and rained, creating waterfalls. The water made suds and it was there that the Twin War Gods, the Ahayuuta, sprouted, received life. They were funny-looking; their hair was tangled and they had long noses and cheeks.

Four days after they sprouted they asked their father, "What are we to do?" He replied, "When I summoned the people in the first room they came out into my daylight, but they never offered me prayer meal, so I summoned the ones in the second room, but because of the ozone smell of the second ones, the first were killed. When the third ones came out, their smell killed the second ones. Those in the fourth room are still down there." He had decided to send the Twins down into the fourth inner room, the room full of soot.

They left and wandered around until they found, there in the southwest, the place of emergence. Then they drew their lightning arrow across their rainbow and shot. They entered the first room. It was filled with the color of dawn. Entering the second room, they found it filled with yellow. In the third room they could hardly make anything out, and there in the fourth room they could not see. When they found their footing they wandered aimlessly for some time until they met someone following a deer. The hunter offered to take them to where he lived. They made cedar-bark torches, but when they made them blossom, lit them, the one who had been in the dark so long could not see. They put out their torches and followed him. He took them westward to his village.

At the village they met the Sun Priest and told him that Sun Father had sent them to bring his people into daylight. He agreed, but did not know the way out, so he sent them to the North Priest, who lived at North Ocean. When they arrived the Twins told him that Sun Father had summoned them to help bring the people out into his daylight. They needed help and he agreed, but did not know how. He assembled his sacred things—his wild seeds, his garden seeds—and went along with them to West Ocean, to the home of the Evening Priest. He too did not know the way out, so he gathered his wild and garden seeds and took them to South Ocean, where they joined the Coral Priest. Finally they arrived at East Ocean, where the Morning Priest joined them, and they rested.

The Twins went on a bit to the place where they had descended and cut long yellow prayer sticks. They measured them off against their own arms, from fingertip to elbow. Then they went northward, tying feathers to their prayer sticks. When the sticks were finished they stood them up, and where they stood up a fir tree grew. It grew and grew until it reached the next level above, the third room, and stood sticking out there a little. They went back and got the priests and their people. Younger Brother shimmied up the branches and all the people followed; the last one out was Elder Brother. In the third inner room the Twins approached evening's direction, where they brought the blue prayer sticks to life. They stood them up and an aspen tree grew there. The aspen grew and grew until it reached the second room. They brought the people out into the second room. Next it was the red prayer sticks they made. They approached coral's direction and set them up on the ground: a cottonwood stood up, a narrow-leafed cottonwood grew. There in the next room they made the white prayer sticks and set them up, and a cane plant grew. It stood like an arrow. The people stepped from branch to branch and came out into Sun Father's blinding light. Tears of pain ran from their eyes, and from these tears yellow mariposa lilies and sunflowers grew.

Accompanying the council are two of six Salimopiya warriors, in cotton dance kilts embroidered with butterflies and lilies. Each carries bayonetlike broad-leaf-yucca whips with thick leaves edged in white threads; the right whip, with its tips forward, purifies nightmare-struck people, while the left, with its tips backward, conceals wild and domestic seeds for spring planting. Headdresses of sagebrush sticks wound in yellow parrot, green drake, and white sandhill-crane feathers point westward toward the Land of the Dead. Raccoon masks, raven ruffs, corn-kernel bandoleers, and war pouches thrust down and outward while multicolored pinwheel ears thrust up and inward.

As black and checkered masks run madly in place, jerking their heads from side to side, emitting deer calls, an ancient man in red silk headband and brown buckskin moccasins steps forward and whacks a feathered four-directional mobile. Eagle-bone piping, pottery drumming, lightning-quartz and turquoise-gourd rattling, shake the steel window sashes. Here and in five other houses the ceremony has begun.

■ ■ ■ ■

The night before, plastic trash bags bursting with multicolored textiles had been delivered to Sadie's new home. Women and men, young and old, family, kiva, and clan members, hammered up the cloth kaleidoscope: yards and yards of bolt fabric, buntinglike between women's triangularly folded flowered shawls. I mistakenly placed nearly identical blues next to one another and was whispered to by a child, "No, Tsilu, make it tso'ya, all different." Grabbing a maroon shawl and stapling it between the blues, I pondered, "Hish tso'ya/*Very tso'ya?*"

TSO'YA

Purple martin's iridescent hunting swoop
curled ebony plume & rust-brown pin-striped crown of Gam-
    bel's quail
killdeer's black breast bands & crimson eye rings
drake mallard's emerald helmet
antelope rump hairs ruffled by an evening wind
startled whitetail flags
swallowtail butterfly's indigo & vermilion shimmers
last stages of a New Mexico sunset
metallic green lizard scurrying along in his orange-and-black
    choker

At the west end of the long room men create a monstrous construction combining a dirty, limp, smelly rag-rug and several khaki, denim, and blue-jean jackets. When Dennis added a Mex-

DENNIS TEDLOCK

ican serape that had been through the washing machine, causing the colors to careen together in a medley of pastels, everybody laughed. A child, striking a theatrical pose before the display, giggled, "Pecho takit." I paused—perhaps this mugging at the camera revealed not humor but uneasiness, discomfort. Perhaps ugly, smelly displays were constructed only for visitors. But we weren't ordinary visitors—Sadie had telephoned, put her father on the line to instruct us to get our ears pierced, had invited us to participate in her house blessing. The more I rationalized our participation, the more self-conscious I became. This feeling intensified when a small wooden shelf, holding a carved cottonwood Shalako doll, was gingerly carried in, hammered to a rafter in the center of the room, whispered to, and lovingly sprinkled with jeweled cornmeal by the older people.

I asked Sadie for the Zuni word that best described the decorating process and learned that it was "teshkuna," a verb formed from the root "tesh," meaning *shrine, sacred, taboo, forbidden,* together with the causative "-u" and the static ending "-na," *shrine construction*. Recoiling, regretting having asked, wondering why Sadie had included us in the enshrining of her new home, I nonetheless committed the word to memory. In the past Sadie and her parents had abruptly told us to absent ourselves, or flatly refused to discuss a certain topic because it was "sacred." At such times they reminded me that, although we were adopted family, referred to by everyone as Kyamme/*uncle* and Tsilu/*aunt,* we could not be included because we were, after all, also Melika, a loan word from the Spanish "americano/*American.*"

Not until later did I climb out of my skittish mood and feel once more at home. When the men brought in their antlered trophies and sat down on the long wooden benches, snuggling them suggestively between their thighs, I giggled, along with all the other women. Kwinsi, Sadie's one-eyed, handsome older brother, grabbed a mountain-lion skin, placed it over his head, and pranced up and down the long dirt floor to the impromptu singing and potato-chip-canister drumming of teenaged boys. He ended his mountain-lion dance by bowing low before me and everybody guffawed. Guessing it was suggestive, I blushed.

Sadie diverted attention by suggesting to her younger brother GI Joe that he mount his eight-point mule deer directly on top of the head of a fully armed Aztec warrior woven into a Oaxaca blanket. And although the other trophies were mounted on rearing white buckskins, the family chuckled approvingly at her innovation. Flora jumped up, folding and stapling a Hopi dance kilt as a frame surrounding Mr. Deer. Joe pointed out with pride that his trophy's neck was turned slightly to the right side, which helped him really show out. Now the hunted was the hunter, and Aztecs, not only Zunis, might be reincarnated as deer.

Tola appeared in the doorway, cradling in her arms the enormous pelt of a cinnamon-colored bear, sacred hunter of the west. As she made her entrance she called out in a low gravelly voice,

"Attannnniiii," meaning *dark, muffled, shaggy, old, fearful, dangerous*. In the natural world the principal referents for the term "attanni" are the raven and the bear. Ravens, with their sharp Roman beaks, rip into and devour practically anything. Their raucous calls range from a series of hoarse melancholy croakings to lisps, buzzing noises, and gulps. These sable hunters riding the wind circle for hours in a flat eaglelike glide, suddenly somersaulting and dropping from the height of five hundred feet to grab a fawn or lamb for supper. Black bears, who range in color into blues and cinnamons, have poor vision but acute hearing and a keen sense of smell. Although generally sluggish, they can on occasion run very fast. Hunting primarily from ambush and

by surprise, black bears kill their victims by swatting them. Bearskin gloves and moccasins are an important part of the paraphernalia of medicine women and men.

After Bear was stapled to the wall behind the altar his heavy head—complete with skull, sharp teeth, glass eyes, turquoise and coral chokers, heshe necklaces—needed support, so Dennis hammered up a small wooden shelf under Bear's chin. Sadie smiled approval, saying that he had sure helped him to show out.

Some time later, after completing more research on the native peoples and cultures of the Americas, I realized that this prominent incorporation of a dangerous element within a primarily beautiful context has its roots in the hunting magic and bear possession of that ancient shamanic heritage Zunis share with other Native North Americans. Their complex expressions of the beautiful in Shalako wall decoration belong to another ancient heritage, the Mesoamerican-Puebloan tradition. And it is in the meeting and

DENNIS TEDLOCK

interplay between these two aesthetics that Zuni Pueblo articulates its own mythopoetic religious core.

With her characteristic twinkle Tola suggested that perhaps Bear might even scare some Navajo visitors; then, becoming serious, she caught my eye and, puckering her lips as though to kiss the air, twisted them sideways toward the next room, where women were kneading sourdough for bread. I dutifully left in order to help out, while Dennis was taken aside by Hapiya and instructed as to how properly to greet and give the blessing to gift-bearing visitors. He was a quick study, because he had spent so many hours over the years transcribing and translating mythic narratives. Hapiya was pleased: Oh, how his friends would be taken by surprise at hearing this old-time Zuni eloquence out of the mouth of a Melika!

Later we were assigned pantry duty: helping stack cases of

Coke and tons of flour, lard, sugar, and coffee, and dozens of baskets; hanging whole-dressed sheep and venison from steel hooks. Sadie had finished instructing me to keep a careful record of all the gifts and givers on the back of paper plates hammered up on a two-by-four inside the doorway when, looking at me strangely, she began rummaging through stacks and stacks of multicolored textiles.

On finding an emerald-green flowered shawl, she gently covered my reddish hair, then brought over a dish of fine-ground cornmeal mixed with petals of the evening primrose and powdered my freckled face pale white. This, I learned, was the reenactment of a sacred beautifying act initiated by White Shell Woman, Zuni patroness of beauty, who, like Isis of the ancient Egyptians, imparted loveliness to all those she breathed upon.

Long ago White Shell Woman, Mother of Sun Father and Goddess of West Ocean, taught the Corn Maidens to chew her white flowers and rub their necks, breasts, arms, and hands with her essence. Later, placing white-corn flour between her palms and applying it to the faces of young humans, she changed their countenances to appear as white as her own shell mantle and as smooth as the finest dressed doeskin. She also taught these women to sing the most beautiful of songs while grinding the Corn Maiden's sacred flesh, mixed with white flowers (uteya k'ohakwa/*flower of White Shell Woman*) and shell, in order to beautify themselves and tease their lovers.

Hapiya chuckled approvingly at the appearance of my powdered face and wrapped a red silk scarf around Dennis' head. After tying a big bow over his right ear, he slipped a two-strand turquoise necklace over his head and handed him a big black blanket with which to wrap himself.

Slowly turning toward each other, looking long and wordlessly, we smiled—so very pleased with our transformed appearance—but what would other Zunis, Zunis who weren't family, think? What if anyone we knew recognized us wearing Indian getup? Playing Indian is a dangerous business.

■ ■ ■ ■

With the twisting and untwisting of the star-cloud mobile which dangled above the medicine-society altar, the ceremony began. The ancient leader of the Red Ant Society moistened the long bumpy hand-spun string of his bullroarer, slammed the flat lightning-painted paddle on the hard earthen dance floor, and whirled it round and round and round his head. The nummm-nuuummmmm-nuuuummmmmmmm-nuuummmm of his num-numnanne roared for thunder. The tutsu-tususu-tususu of the pottery drum summoned the beasts. Flowing song strings brocaded with the chilili, chilili, chilhchi, chilhchi of gourd rattles lightly embroidered with eagle-bone melodies welcomed the masks. This was followed by the whisking of cleansing yucca-root water with foaming iridescence of corn kernels, embers, stars. The jammed room smelled of juniper logs, piñon nuts, sage, and expectation.

Gazing at the feathered medicine wands standing before the antique wood-slat altar, iridescent green drake, red-and-turquoise macaw, yellow parrot feathers—gleaming, glimmering, glistening, shimmering—each wand swelling and subsiding, swelling and subsiding, I whispered to Dennis, "They look like they're breathing."

"I was thinking the same thing," he replied softly.

Later, when we told Hapiya about the miracle, he chuckled and said, "Yes indeed, those miwe breathe all right. They're persons, you know."

Primary-wing feathers of the eagle, one in each hand of the

medicine leader, mark out the drum's rhythm: 1 2, 1 2 3,
1 2 3: 1 2, 1 2 3, 1 2 3. On and on, faster and faster they went:
1 2 3, 1 2 3, 1 2 3 chu'na/*sudden silence.* Soft sounds sifted in
from outside and the sansanaawe, sansanaawe; muusilili, muusilili; tsilili, tsilili, tsilili of large, medium, and small sleigh
bells announced the arrival of a giant Shalako mask. As everyone
turned, a tiny child, who had crawled into my lap, giggled and
begged to be let down. Tola leaned over toward the child, scold-
ing him in an uncharacteristically sharp tone: "Lesma, lesma,
lesma, LESMAA/*Don't, don't, don't, DONT!* Hold on to him, tight,
Tsilu!"

Two men in red silk head scarves and black blankets threw
open the front door for Elder Brother Shalako. So handsome with
his glistening warrior's black stripe from cheek to cheek across
his nose, white buckskin cap with silver buttons, plum-colored
velveteen shirt with many-colored rayon ribbons dangling from
shoulders, white short pants, blue breechclout with embroidered
belt, high blue moccasins with red-and-yellow turn-back cuffs,
a row of jingling sleigh bells encircling his ankles, and quill-
work heels. Bending down, he planted a double turquoise-and-
yellow prayer stick in the threshold while praying for the health,
wealth, and fertility of all those within Sadie's new home. Then
he sprinkled a handful of wild and domesticated seeds, together
with hard white-shell and turquoise-studded cornmeal, into the
threshold shrine. Straightening up, he rushed all around the
room, stopping at the center of each of the four walls and marking
the spot with his four widely spread cornmeal-coated fingers as
he chanted:

Ho' pishle lhahkwimokkya.
Ho' kyaalits'i lhahkwimokkya.
Ho' alahho lhahkwimokkya.
Ho' temak'o lhahkwimokkya.

I have rooted the north.
I have rooted the west.
I have rooted the south.
I have rooted the east.

Younger Brother Shalako, similarly dressed but with a crimson velveteen shirt, immediately followed, planting groups of prayer sticks and sprinkling prayer meal in the threshold. Then, racing around to each of the four walls, he struck the cornmeal streaks, the four sacred life-roads, with his long yucca whip. Each masker in turn then climbed an aluminum ladder and placed prayer sticks and prayer meal in the ceiling altar, Shrine of the Zenith. On descending, they sowed wild and domestic seeds in the circular hole located directly below it, in the exact center of the earthen floor: Shrine of Emergence.

■ ■ ■ ■

When the people from the fourth inner room emerged, they had to stop and wait until their eyes were strong enough to see. The Twins then took them along for some distance until Sun Father set. They stayed there four years, then they heard a rumbling sound, tuuun, something like distant thunder, back where they had emerged.

The priests who held the sacred things said, "Ahaa, there is someone else. It must be an extraordinary person to make such a rumbling."

The Twins ran to the place of emergence and there he sat, someone dangerous, someone unclean, a witch!

"Soooo it's you. What is your reason for coming out? Having you in this will not be good."

"Indeed, but that is just the way it is. I am a person with garden seeds."

They wanted to kill him but he said, "Very well, it's up to you, but first you must kill this, then you can kill me," and he showed them his ear of yellow corn. "These are my garden seeds. The others who have come out do not possess this kind of corn and their flesh will not be good. That is why I have come out. But if you are going to kill me, you must kill this first."

The Twins thought about it. And when they had thought about it, they did not kill him. They took him back to the people. But the people were not happy. "Having him in this won't be good," is what they said.

"But I live by these garden seeds. These yellow ones are my garden seeds; even with all your wild seeds, your garden seeds, the women's flesh will not be good. This ear of yellow corn will make their flesh heavy. That is why I have come out," is what he said.

"Indeed, but you must live a better life. The kind of person you are now—you must not be such a person." So they told him, and they lived on until the fourth day.

The sorcerer spoke: "Now you must give me one of your little ones and I will witch him."

House Chief had a child. "Go ahead, try this one," he said and gave up his little boy. Immediately the child was witched. His elders held him as he died. Preparations were made that he might return. On the fourth day the House Chief sent the Twin War Gods to the place of emergence. At the time they arrived the little boy was playing there by himself. When they entered upon his road they said, "So, you are living here, not far from us?"

"Yes, this is how I live. When you return tell my elders they must not cry, for when the time comes I will enter upon their roads."

They took the word back and spoke to the ones who held the sacred things: "Now, our fathers, our children, prepare yourselves, for we have been here four days," they said. They had stayed four years.

Starting out from there, they went on until they came to Moss Lake. When they arrived they still had tails of moss; their hands and feet were webbed. The Twins said to them there, "Now, my children, for a time you must settle here. The way you are made is not suitable, it will not do."

They sat down there and the Twins washed off all the people's moss. When they were finished washing them, they used their spearhead to undo the webs of their hands, and they cut off their tails. It seems we had testicles on our foreheads; they cut all of these off and made us the kind of people we are today. They completed us.

■ ■ ■ ■

Elder Brother Shalako rushed outside, where the mask stood directly in front of the door, and an attendant helped him climb inside. The enormous conical mask was draped with six embroidered Hopi wedding blankets and a pair of fox skins for arms. Once inside the mask, he held the seven-foot-long cottonwood central pole, surrounded by flexible willow hoops, with both hands at waist height. On top of the pole sat an ancient turquoise helmet mask with horns, backed by a fan consisting of twenty-four tail feathers from an adolescent golden eagle. The feathers were white at the base, with the terminal one-third brown. When an eagle is three years old these feathers are replaced by new ones with less basal white and only narrow dark bands at the tips; so, from the look of this mask, the feathers were those of a four-year-old. The wooden buffalo-shaped turquoise horns that framed the eagle fan had a fluffy eagle breast feather dangling from each tip, natural white on the right and dyed red on the left. Four small yellow parrot feathers were tied to the long black bangs.

On the back of the head, just behind the eagle fan, was tied a bunch of tail feathers from a scarlet macaw. A long hand-spun cotton string, dotted with fluffy eagle down, trailed along behind on the full length of the black wig, ending in an iridescent abalone shell. Protruding spherical black leather eyes, encircled with white paint, bobbed as the mask bowed and turned. Jutting out between and slightly below the eyes was a tubular turquoise foot-long articulated, snoutlike wooden beak, with painted black-and-white teeth along the sides and across the blunt-cut end. Around the neck hung dozens of the finest turquoise and coral necklaces.

From my distance I could just make out some small holes and rips in the mask. So, this was the Shalako captured long ago in the war with the Kyan'aakwe, hunters who were also called "White People," because they wore white cotton blankets. They emerged from a cave far to the southeast and lived in a large village fifty miles south of Zuni, near Salt Lake. Their leader was a female warrior who wore her hair half up in women's style and half down in men's style. Carrying male bows as well as female corn ears and wearing a man's cotton dance kilt on her left shoulder, she was a great hunter who corralled all the deer and antelope for hundreds of miles. Early in the battle she captured Kolhahmana, the androgynous firstborn child of an ancient brother-sister incest, along with Itsepasha/*Glum Clown,* Sayalhi'a/*Blue Horn,* Kokk'okshi/*Good Kachina,* and one of the Shalako. The masks escaped but were immediately recaptured. Only Shalako, running swiftly on a jackrabbit's zigzag path, got away.

Elder Brother Shalako quivered, turned, and bolted down the dance hall to the west end of the long room, where he stopped abruptly. Kneeling down, he rested the base of the giant conical mask on the floor. Helpers surrounded him with black blankets; he slipped out from underneath the mask, walked over, and sat down on the long narrow men's bench.

The room was filling up with Sadie's relatives, and with friends from other pueblos, when an Anglo family of four from Albuquerque, eager for entertainment, forced their way in the front door and elbowed up to the dance space. Kwinsi jumped up and kindly but firmly asked them to leave the room. At the front door the man nudged Kwinsi with his elbow, then moved as if to put out his fists. Kwinsi's silent reply was to smile and step forward, lightly brushing the man's desert boots with his buckskin moccasins. The man instinctively jumped backward and Kwinsi again stepped forward, forcing him to retreat out the front door and into the courtyard, where an amiable Zuni policeman befriended the guy. The cop tried to explain to him that he and his whole family were welcome at Shalako, but that the big fellow was right in asking them to leave the dance room.

They had missed the house-blessing ritual altogether, and thus did not realize that the dance floor had been consecrated. They were most welcome in the house that evening, but not within the dance space. In fact, as far as the hosts were concerned, they were more than welcome: they were important representatives of humans or "daylight persons" living on the face of this earth. Even witches are welcome on Shalako night, because long ago the Twin War Gods had allowed the first witch to join the people.

A frail older man in a bright-red cowboy shirt, with an elaborate turquoise-and-coral bolo tie, brown dress pants, and moccasins, strolled slowly up the cornmeal path toward the medicine-society altar. Standing there, solemnly facing the carved icon of Achiya Latapa/*Knife Wing*, he held out each arm and leg in succession as the Shalako priests struck them with yucca whips. Then he spat on the whips: a removal of bad luck and bad dreams. As he departed, the hosts, Sadie and Sabin, walked up the long meal road and stood with bowed heads before the altar. They repeated long prayers given them, line by line, by Elder Brother Shalako.

Shortly after they left the altar, a group of unmasked Mudhead clowns pushed open the front door, and their leader, Old Buck, launched into an outrageous anecdote about Sabin, who had been seen repeatedly driving up to Gallup.

"One day an Eagle clansman came by early in the morning in his closed car to the house of his friend's lover. 'Beep! Beep! Beep! Beep!' But his friend did not come out. 'Beeeeeep! Beeeeeep! Beeeeeep! Beeeeeep!' He still didn't come out. 'Beeeeep! Tosh kwayi? Tosh kwayi?/*Are you coming? Are you coming?*' "

Everyone laughed at Sabin, who stood accused of several wrongdoings at once. First, a member of a family hosting a Shalako should not visit Gallup at all during the year preceding the celebration. Even a quick business trip to purchase turquoise, or sell jewelry, weakens and defiles one through contact with drunkards, drug addicts, loan sharks, weekend cowboys, pimps, players, and the many hustlers and hookers who frequent the town. Sabin was also culpable in his friend's unfaithfulness, because he clearly knew that he would not be at home, but with his lover. That he was blameworthy was further demonstrated by his question, "Tosh kwayi?," which is a word play simultaneously indicating (in reverse order) that his friend was coming out of the house, emerging from his lover's body, and ejaculating.

Moments later the Mudhead clown known as Eshotsi/*Bat* peered through the door into the house, calling out to Hapiya, "Lewan tunati/*Look here*. Who was your first girl?"

"Your woman," Hapiya said, just loud enough for most people to hear, and there were chuckles all around the room.

Tola muttered, "He's supposed to keep quiet and be patient, but listen to him talk. If I had a rock I'd throw at him."

"He wasn't supposed to answer that guy?" I whispered.

Tola replied, tensely, "That's right, he's not supposed to say anything, nothing, not one word."

She seemed angry and I guessed she might scold him if it weren't Shalako. Feeling embarrassed, not knowing what to say or do, I left and went next door to watch the Council of the Gods. They had just begun the unison chanting of their origin story. In the narrative they name every spring they stopped at along their migration route to Zuni Pueblo, Itiwana/*Middle Place, Middle Time*. After listening politely for an hour, I returned to Sadie's and squeezed back into the vacant chair between Dennis and Tola.

Elder and Younger Brother Shalako had each pulled up a folding chair and sat knee to knee with Hapiya and Sabin. They passed a cigarette back and forth, a long reed filled with a mixture of wild tobacco and inner-bark shavings from red-willow stems, exchanging antique kin terms.

Tacchumo *Father*	Talemo *Son*
Papamo *Elder Brother*	Suwemo *Younger Brother*
Kyakyamo *Uncle*	Ky'assemo *Nephew*
Nanamo *Grandfather*	Aalemo *Grandson*
Toshlemo *Granduncle*	Uwakkyamo *Grandnephew*

Hapiya asked the Shalako maskers for what reason they had come and they replied in unison, telling of the ritual events that led up to this moment. Their monotone chant, with a rise at the end of each line, began as they transformed themselves into their gods:[1]

> *Lukkya telhinanne*
> *ho'n aatach illap'ona*
> *kokkwaa shiwani*
> *kokko temlha*
> *yam ky'awatulin yaana*
> *yam ky'awatulin koni*
> *holh chimikya'kona teliyana*
> *ho''i yaaky'ana.*

> This night
> the ones we have as fathers
> kachina priests
> all kachinas
> at their full lake
> at their shallow lake
> as they have since the beginning
> are becoming persons.

On and on and on the chant ran as our nieces and nephews squirmed and fidgeted, squirmed and fidgeted in our laps. When the children fell quiet, too quiet, we shook them and sang softly in their ears so they wouldn't slip off to sleep and end up with shortened life-roads. Humming, pinching, squeezing, and jostling the exhausted children, we noticed the New Mexico state archeologist and his artist wife at the threshold. We nodded and smiled slightly in their direction. They returned our greeting by smiling broadly and winking. Because they made annual Shalako pilgrimages, they knew how to behave, and would not presume to push into the main room just because they had seen other non-Zunis there.

The Shalakos chanted their list of prayer-stick plantings at dozens of springs south of Zuni: Snow Hanging, Rock Wedge, Painted Rock, Poison Weed, Mesa Wall, Rainbow Springs, and on and on for ten consecutive new moons at ten separate springs, beginning the previous year at the winter solstice.

I have come from the sacred lake to see my people.
For years I have heard about my people living here at the Middle
  Place
for years I have wanted to come.
I wish them to be happy.
Especially I want the women to be fortunate with their babies.
I bring my people all kinds of seeds
different kinds of corn
different kinds of fruit.
I have been praying for my people to have long life
and that whoever has an evil heart should stand up in the daylight.
I have been praying that the rooms may be full of corn of all colors
beans of all colors
all squashes
pumpkins
water gourds
watermelons
sweet melons.
That my people may have plenty of fresh water
that they may be healthy and handsome.
As I was coming by Rainbow Spring a frog with red legs was there.

I did not want anyone to be left behind
so I brought him with me.
I saw a little duck ready to come with me
so I brought him along too.
I did not want anyone to stay behind.
Everywhere someone was ready to come with me.
I did not want anyone to stay behind
they have all come here with me.
They will bring my people long life.
We have all come.
We are all here bringing you good fortune.
I wish you to be happy.
I wish you to be well and to have strong hearts.
I have brought you seeds to plant with your crops next spring.
I want your houses to be full of seeds.
I have prayed that you may be fortunate with your babies.
That no one in this house may drop down.
Yes, I have worked hard and prayed for all my people.
I do not want any roots to rot.
I do not want anyone to sicken and die.
I want everyone to stand up firmly on his feet all year.
This is how I have prayed for you.
I was poor when I was young but the priests have thought of me.
Someone wise has picked me out.
It was in their minds to pick me out and here I am.
I was poor but they have thought of me in their prayers
wanted me to come.
So I have come that you may all be happy here tonight.

Lost in sound, musing on what would happen later on, when the morning star rose, I was startled by sharp silence followed by scraping chairs, as Tola and her daughters slipped from the ceremonial room into the dining room. I jumped up and joined them in preparing to serve the masked gods and medicine-society choir great steaming bowls of barbecued deer, mutton, turkey, and beef plus a special old-fashioned soup called "k'alhiko sanna/*hot bowl*," consisting of venison jerky, ground chile, onions, and a mixture of fruits and herbs including wolfberries, chinchweed, and both mountain and coyote mints. Each woman carried over a bowl of food and handed it through a slot in the wall to the performers' helpers. Then came the beverages—coffee, tea, pop, and Kool-Aid. Breads included Hopi blue-corn piki, Zuni sunflower and wheat, Navajo fry, Pueblo sourdough, and Rainbo from the store. Piles and piles of jalapeño peppers and long green chiles, bowls of pinto and white tepary beans, boiled squashes, pumpkins, and potatoes. And finally, for dessert, apple, peach, and pumpkin pie, corn pudding, cattail-flour muffins, and Oreo Creme Cookies.

About midnight, when the men were done, we served the hordes of Hopi, Acoma, Navajo, Mormon, and Anglo guests. And although I kept my strawberry-blond head down and hazel eyes on the food while waiting on this multiethnic group of weary, hungry folks from all over, a rancher from west of the village, near Witch Wells, in his fine brown Laredo lizard-skin boots, with anaconda vamps and flame wing-tips, cracked what he thought was a cute joke. Nudging Tola with his forearm, he said, loud enough to turn heads, "Hey there, sister, yer sure got one goodlooker white girl. Ain't seen her round here before. What's 'er name? She married in or jest sleepin' round? Haw. Haw."

If he had been a Zuni, such crude and shameless behavior would have meant that he was a witch, and thus to be treated with circumspection. Although he was clearly Anglo, Tola decided to take no chances and was extremely polite to him, waiting patiently for him to quit laughing at his own joke. Then, softly, but oh so firmly, with a forced smile and an edge in her voice, she replied, "She's our aunt, cowboy. Sit down. Eat."

Over the years I had learned to be silent, even downright impassive, around bad-ass rodeo types—looking straight out ahead past and through the interaction in a respectful open-closed way. But it was no use; I was humiliated and angry. The steer jerker didn't seem capable of understanding that all those within a host home should display the Apollonian mildness and moderation Ruth Benedict described as the key cultural configuration of Pueblo peoples. Benedict was wrong, insofar as she thought Apollonianism was the essential nature or psychology of Pueblos, but right, in so far as it was the required etiquette during religious festivals, such as Shalako. At this special time, if everyone remains serene, kind, and cheerful, then the host family, village, nation, and even the entire world can know the end of anger and the beginning of profound peace.

Ashamed to look, be, white like this shit-kicker—having so much trouble controlling myself—I bolted from the dining room. My Southern upbringing, with its stress on maintaining composure and good manners even in the most difficult of situations, had momentarily failed me. I was afraid I might let loose a stream of verbal abuse that would ruin the ritual for everyone. Trying to calm myself, I rearranged my shawl so as to hide my face partly, then stood up tall and walked slowly into the main room, where the all-night celebration was once more getting under way.

Settling down between Dennis and Albert, I decided to calm myself by taking careful mental notes. The unmasked Shalako danced the sun's annual north-south arc while scuffling sideways along an east-west path. Simultaneously the masked Shalako trotted east to west, giving the ik'ok'u deer call while clapping his foot-long articulated snout and bending down to tease the clowns. One Mudhead darted back and forth with small quick steps, holding his body bolt upright in perfect imitation of the room-long rushes of the Shalako. Another caught his hand in Shalako's wooden beak and got dragged along for some distance, crying out in mock terror. Two Mudheads sat in the same chair, one in the other's lap, and the masked Shalako rushed down upon them, knocking both them and the chair onto the floor in a heap. Albert leaned over to Dennis, chuckling: "Now, this is what I call fun." Everyone giggled when the Shalako managed to strip a clown of his kilt, leaving him standing there stark naked, shivering as he clutched at his tied-down penis.

Far in the night, fourteen Pakokko/*Navajo Kachinas,* with rows upon rows of crisp new dollar bills pinned to their velveteen shirts and blouses, arrived with a merry crowd of dancers. The dance, based on the Navajo Yebichai, was first performed at Zuni during the 1850s, when Navajo traders arrived during an epidemic of mumps. Because they had successfully rid themselves of a similar epidemic by performing a Yebichai, they offered the dance. After performing their healing rite, they paraded all night long through the pueblo until the following morning, when sick people spat upon them, asking that the sickness be removed. Some years later, during another epidemic, Zunis performed the dance successfully for themselves, and ever since then they have been doing it.

Tonight a slightly tipsy Navajo visitor, bouncing in time with the music, tugged at the edge of Dennis' blanket, asking him, with her eyes, to dance. He returned her smile, nodded, but declined her invitation. Albert bragged that he had already been with a Navajo girl who, tired of the boy she arrived with, had followed him out of a house. She had some sort of drink with her, and she and he, according to him, spent about an hour in a corral. "Then I just don't know where she went. She thought I had some money, I guess, but I didn't."

It was nearly three in the morning when Tola approached me, motioning with her lips toward the front door as she gently pulled her daughter's favorite flowered shawl up from my shoulders, to cover my hair. Then she redusted my ruddy cheeks with fine-ground cornmeal flour, took hold of my hand, and guided me out the front door. We stood together on squishy, muddy snow in a long line of women, scattering the gift of White Shell

Woman on the heads and shoulders of departing maskers. Then, with heads bowed, we prayed in low voices for home, village, visitors (including cowboys), and the nation, as well as all non-human or raw persons on, in, and over the earth. When we were done we returned, refreshed, to our kitchen duties.

As the dark sky was pierced by the first red beams of sunlight in the east and the visitors left, we looked for a place to sleep. Opening an unfamiliar door, we blundered into a room where Tola and Sadie were carefully washing the sacred paint off the bodies of Shalako performers. We stood there, stupidly staring, until Ramona noticed us. She widened her eyes and rolled them, gasped, then laughed out loud, and quickly covered her mouth with her hand. When Tola, Sadie, and all of the performers looked up and saw the two of us awkwardly standing there, we beat a quick retreat followed by chatter, giggles, and then gusty laughter.

At six in the morning, the breathy warbling of Payatamu flutes awoke the Shalakos. After quickly repainting their bodies and rushing into their courtly masks, they emerged from the houses and paraded through the narrow, crowded streets. As they wound through the village, in the peacock-blue-and-apricot glow of early morning, people coated them in fluffy soft cornmeal blankets. After crossing the Zuni River, they lined up east to west on the ceremonial grounds and on signal dashed back and forth, depositing prayer sticks, while praying in their hearts for rain. As they finished, men burst from the crowd and chased the giant masks upriver; when they had caught them and wrestled them to the ground, each man shouted triumphantly in Zuni, "I've killed a DEER!" Then, after sprinkling the six downed masks with cornmeal, shell, and turquoise bits, breathing in deeply from them, and talking with them as though they were dead deer, they thanked them joyously for all future luck in hunting and child begetting.

DENNIS TEDLOCK

15

THE GUN AND THE PAINTBRUSH

■ ■ ■ ■

TWO YEARS SLIPPED BY before we returned to Zuni. When we stopped in at Sadie's, with our bushels of peaches and apples, both she and Sabin seemed quite a bit older: they were only in their early forties, but looked closer to fifty. It's strange about aging, I thought, how it's not in smooth increments but, rather, in sudden leaps.

During the winter of 1974 there had been a recession in the jewelry business; because dealers didn't sell what they anticipated, they didn't buy any new jewelry. The situation was so bad that Sadie hadn't been able to afford to put a kitchen or bathroom into her new Shalako house. There they were, still living in the wretched subdivision. Sadie blamed the Arab traders. They'd gotten started at Zuni by bringing in Arabian tapestries to trade for jewelry. Everyone at the pueblo really liked the tapestries, and before they knew it the Arabs were setting the prices and buying up all their jewelry. Recently they'd been working together as a cartel, and pushed the prices down so low that it was almost not worth making the jewelries—but what was one to do? She and Sabin had separate budgets now: she was responsible for the closed car and the Shalako house, he was responsible for the pickup truck and subdivision house.

There had been an increase in crime at the village, especially up at Black Rock; a woman was buried today who died from injuries she received from two female hitchhikers who beat her for her money and jewelry. Last week a drunk hanged himself in jail, with his own belt. A while back the son of Short Man hanged himself in the same place, with his bootlaces; but he wasn't drunk, so he must have been witched.

Sadie can't stand being anyplace now where there are too many people: that's why she doesn't vote, and when they go to the store she sends Sabin in—"He's my errand boy."

Last year Sabin felt tired all the time and suddenly began losing weight, but he wasn't dieting or anything. Then he started having trouble with his eyes. Whenever he looked up from soldering or polishing jewelry and tried to see something across the room, his vision would become blurry. They became concerned, he went up to Black Rock to check it out, and they flew him over to Albuquerque. It was the blood sugar—he was a diabetic and they didn't know it.

At first he had to take his insulin shots every couple of days and they put him on a special diet. A doctor from the Public Health Service had hit upon a culturally appropriate way to describe the diabetic diet for Zunis: "It's just like Teshkwi for you from now on, no fats." This appealed to Sabin, since it reminded him of the Shalako pilgrimage. Over the past several months he had managed to stay on the diet, and had reduced his insulin needs dramatically.

He joked that now he was "a holy man for life," since the only meat he ate was deer, and only a small taste after each kill.

The hardest thing about the diet, though, was giving up beer and pop. Hapiya was pleased that his son-in-law could kick the sugar habit and said he hoped more Zunis, in the future, would turn away from the drinking and overeating they learned from TV commercials.

Sadie's family had taken up exercising; each evening they ran around the peach orchards at the foot of Towa Yalanne mountain. They were lucky that Sabin was still active, since they'd heard that many diabetics develop gangrene and loose their toes, feet, legs—even their lives.[1]

One night, about a month ago, when they were driving to visit friends, they saw a big buck, an eight-pointer, just west of Ramah; Sabin pulled his .30/30 off the gun rack and shot it. But they couldn't get his buck down through the ditch and out onto the road. "We didn't have a knife or cornmeal or anything," said Sadie. So they went up to Tola's for help. Everyone was asleep there, but when they gave their news, Hapiya and Albert left with Sabin to get the deer while Sadie waited with her mother.

Sabin has a permit to hunt on the reservation, not elsewhere in New Mexico; nevertheless, they got the off-reservation deer without mishap. The meat was in the freezer and the head was in Albuquerque, at the taxidermist's.

Dennis announced that we planned to drop by Joe's, and asked if he could use the phone.

Sadie rolled her eyes upward strangely, as if Dennis had said something he shouldn't have.

Sabin moved over next to Dennis on the couch and spoke softly. "Kyamme, he shot himself, or was shot, with a hand gun, not long after you left. Over there at the trailer, in his closet. He and Rose were having . . . a party. They had wine punch. It was one-thirty in the morning. They were drunk. She accused him of . . . playing around . . ."

"But he worked nights, so how *could* he?" Sadie interrupted vehemently.

"But *she* was. Earlier that same night, in Gallup, we saw her with another guy, ducking out of sight at Pedro's."

"Oh *no*. Oh my *God*," said Dennis.

"How's Flora?" I asked.

"She took it hard," replied Sadie. "Had to use black cornmeal, again and again, to darken the road—you know, to become invisible. But he still visits in her dreams. Sometimes he wears his uniform. Guess he wants his sister to follow him over to Kachina Village."

"But that's *dangerous*," I blurted out.

"Sure is," Sabin replied. "Rose got married again right away, almost the next day. She should have waited at least four days. So now the one who passed away visits her every night, screaming and screaming at her. Her belly has been swelling up, but she's not pregnant. Before long she'll probably be going west too. Junior got sick right after it happened, and almost followed his dad. He has lots of nightmares too; wakes up talking to his dad over there in the west."

"If he visits him a lot in his dreams, he probably won't return," added Sadie. "You know how that goes."

"You mean he'll pass away young? Or take his own life?" I asked, remembering a graduate-school friend of Dennis' who, on his first teaching job, hanged himself in his office. He thought he was a fraud, couldn't face the students. When his only son, also called "Junior," grew up and went back east to college, he had some problems and shot himself.

"We don't know what might happen," replied Sabin. "But one thing is that it's not too good with his father wailing and yelling all the time. Guess he's lonely and wants company out there in those ruins west of the village."

"Rose didn't throw the black cornmeal, the way she should have, on the fourth day after he passed away, and she didn't leave the front door open to help his 'wind'—well, you know, kind of like his 'spirit'—to leave the house. Junior didn't know how to make the prayer sticks for his dad, and nobody in Rose's family came over to help out.

"In our way, Mom and Dad couldn't touch the body; so, *her* parents should have washed him. When Kwinsi found out that nothing was being done right, he and his wife went over there. They washed the one who was, wrapped him in his blanket, and carried him to the graveyard. Albert helped Kwinsi bury him there, on the south side. Then they gathered up his radio, rifle, military decorations, and all his pictures, took them over to the riverbank and buried them there.[2]

"Would you like to see Flora's baby?" asked Sadie.

"What? But we didn't know she was pregnant!"

Sadie smiled and called her younger sister into the living room. As she walked down the long hall toward us, holding a fluffy pink blanket, I noticed that she had gained weight, a lot of weight. Handing the blanket to me, she told me the name of the baby: Lorinda.

I admired the chubby little girl, with her tiny silver-and-turquoise needlepoint bracelet, and asked, "How old?"

"Three months; she was born just after Teshkwi. You remember Teshkwi?"

"Sure. It's those ten special days right after the winter solstice when you can't eat fatty things or take fire outdoors," I replied.

"I was scared that I might have her during Teshkwi, at night; then, if I had any trouble, complications, I wouldn't be able to get to the hospital."

"Why not?"

"Because the streetlights are all turned off in the village, and since the priests say that car headlights are fire too, you're not allowed to use them during Teshkwi. So, there's just no way you could see to drive to the hospital at night."

Noticing a large beautiful water jar on top of the color TV, I asked her, "Are you still making pots?"

"I was, until that bad thing happened, and I started having trouble with the clay. After that, all the pots I made broke during firing. I'm waiting for my luck to change. Did Mom tell you about the one who has gone away?"

"Yes, it's tragic. He was a young guy and had so much more life ahead of him."

"He had really changed. He was trying to make something of himself. We talked a lot about all kinds of things, and he decided to finish high school—then that happened."

"Do you ever see Junior?"

"No, Rose won't let him come over here. She blames me."

"How does she figure that?"

"I was his closest sister, almost like a twin, and as we say, 'Ayyu'yaana tewan koholh leyati tun'ona/*She knows what will happen tomorrow.*' And since I knew, I could have, should have, stopped him."

"But *did* you know?"

"Kind of; he was in a hurry, wanted to catch up for the time he lost fooling around in the military. Quit drugs, quit drinking, went back to school, and was a good worker on the job. I know that may seem impossible to you, but he changed himself, straightened out. I still can't believe he suicided himself," she sobbed.

"He didn't," said Sadie grimly.

"Either way, he who was, is over there now, somewhere in the ruins there at Wind Place. He has to wait till he finishes his life-road; then he'll walk on further west to Kachina Village," Sabin said over his shoulder on his way out the front door.

Sadie slid over on the sofa next to me and asked, "Remember that time you took Albert to the medicine man?"

"Sure."

"He almost died. It was a good thing you two drove him down there that day. The medicine man took something out of him. The next morning, when Sabin went out herding in his place, he got kind of sick too. There's something wrong with the rams. Some witch guy is trying to kill—to get to—Old Man, you know, by killing someone close to him, one of his sons."

"Tsilu, remember that time you took all those pictures of the pots?" asked Flora.

"Yes."

"I bet this one wasn't one of them," she said, pointing with her lips to the beautiful water jar on top of the TV.

Circling round the neck, standing on the breath-road, were four whitetail deer, in profile, each one captured inside the outstretched wings of a fat swallowtail butterfly. On the belly of the vessel were two large asymmetrical designs composed of various elements, including feathers, flutes, hooped drumsticks, stormclouds, and the Milky Way clown path across the sky.

"No, I've never seen that pot before. Hish tso'ya/*Very beautiful.*"

"It won a ribbon at the State Fair in Albuquerque, and a trader wanted to buy it right away, but I remembered you said you might like to have one for yourself sometime."

"I'd love to. It's a wonderful pot."

"It's not whole; it's got a little nick in it. Go look around the neck."

I got up, with the sleeping baby in my arms, walked over to the TV, and looked for the nick. I looked hard, and when I finally found it, it was tiny, truly tiny. Since it didn't bother me, I asked, "How much?"

"He said he'd give me two hundred for it, if I didn't sign it."

"That's disgusting. He just wants to cheat people. It's a prize-winning pot, isn't it? I'd like you to sign it for me, and I'll pay the two hundred."

BARBARA TEDLOCK

"No, Tsilu, I'll sign it for you, but it's nicked now, it's not worth two hundred—maybe one hundred?"

"Sure."

She went into the bedroom and returned with a tiny clay paint pot and yucca brush. After she had signed the bottom of the jar, I handed her back the baby, pulled out five twenties, and passed them over to her.

Later I realized that the design was one from *Finding the Center*, a book of traditional narratives Dennis had published. Since he'd given the family several copies of the book just after it came out in 1972, I thought it must be the source for this wonderful design, which appears on the page just before "The Women and the Man," a strange tale about Payatamu, the Sun Father's eldest son, and the murderous K'uuchinina women.[3]

One morning, when Payatamu went to bring out his Sun Father, one of the K'uuchinina women accosted him, demanding to know where he was going. He said that he was on his way to bring out his Sun Father.

"He's going to come out *anyway*. Just the way he's *been* coming up," she said.

"No, it's because of me that he comes up," is what he told her.

They kept on arguing this way until she got the better of him and he said, "Well, then, if that's the way you feel I won't go."

She led him into her cornfield and challenged him to play hide-and-seek with her. "Whoever is found must be *killed*," the girl told him.

"Indeed."

"You go ahead," she said.

"Why should I go first? You're the one who wanted this, you go first."

The girl entered her cornfield and, when she came to the middle, started counting cornstalks. At the fourth one, she fastened herself onto a stalk and became an ear of corn.

The young man followed her footprints, and when he got to the fourth stalk, her footprints ended. But he couldn't find her. He went all over the field and couldn't find her. When he gave up, she came out of the ear of corn.

"Now it's your turn," she said.

He entered the field and did what the girl had done, going past the cornstalks to the middle, then on past the fourth cornstalk, but he didn't turn into anything. He stood facing south.

It was noon and his father was in the center of the sky when he spoke to him: "Tísshomahhá! My son, surely you'll be *killed now*."

The young man took out his cornmeal and sprinkled it toward his father. The cornmeal made a road, and he followed it up.

When he got there his father said, "There will be a lot of trouble now; she will surely kill you. Even so, sit behind my back."

Payatamu sat behind his father's back.

The girl came out looking for him, she followed his footprints and, when she got to where he had stood, unfolded an abalone shell from her blanket and filled it with milk from her breast. The sun was reflected in the milk, and she saw Payatamu's headdress sticking out from behind the Sun.

"Haaaa, hurry on down, for I've found you," she told him.

His father said, "That's all. I must go in, for I've been rising each day because of you. She's going to kill you. You must go down, and I will go right in."

The young man came down. She unfolded her blanket, and there was a large spearhead inside. "Look at your Sun Father for the last time," she said.

She made the young man look up and she cut through his throat. His body fell dead. She held his head while the blood drained out, then set it down. Now she went into the field, dug a hole, and carried the young man's body there and buried it.

After wrapping up his head in her blanket, she took it home to her sisters and put it in a water jar. During the day his headdress quivered, and at night it became still. This was a sign for them, and they slept through the night.

When four days had passed by without the sun coming up, or Payatamu returning, Payatamu's brothers and sisters, the members of his medicine society, decided to ask their grandfathers to help look for him. They sent for Mountain Lion, Bear, Badger, Eagle, Vulture, Coyote, and Crow. One by one they came and tried, but none of them could find him.

Finally they sent for Mole, who found Payatamu's head in the water jar, and the place in the cornfield where it had been cut off. Multicolored tenatsali flowers,[4] medicinal flowers, were blooming there.

Then he found where the body was buried; there were a lot of tenatsali flowers there too. He went back and gave Payatamu's brothers and sisters the news.

They sent for Hawk and Owl. Four Payatamu men took plain blankets and Mole led them, together with Hawk and Owl, until they arrived at where Payatamu had talked to the woman. There Owl gave Mole his root to chew. When he had chewed it Mole went up with the root and spit the root on the women. The women, who were weaving basket plaques at the time, suddenly became sleepy. They put Payatamu's head in the jar on a shelf, with the flowers all around it, and went to bed. Mole saw it and, when the women were sleeping, went in and pulled all the flowers, and took them outside to the medicine people, saying, "You must take all of these, so that his flesh will be whole." Then he told Hawk, "Now you must go in."

Hawk went in and flew out with the head. The headdress was still on it. He gave it to the men, and they went down to the place where he was killed. They picked all the flowers, bundled them up in a blanket, and dug up the body. They put him in the blanket and carried him back to the house where the medicine society met.

They laid him out on the floor with his head to the east, put the flowers on top, sat down at their altar, and sang their string of songs. They drummed and sang, drummed and sang, and on the fourth song Payatamu arose.

"I'm not even tired," he said.

Their elder brother had come alive, but instead of a headdress at the back of his head, he had a hair knot on his forehead, just the opposite of where a hair knot should be. He was saying the opposite of what he meant, he was Ne-payatamu.

It was getting light as he spoke. "Now, my younger brothers,

I've come alive, but I'm not the same person. They cannot do wrong and get away with it. We must have *revenge*."

When he finished speaking he took out his flute and blew. A big swallowtail butterfly came out. Hish tso'ya/*So very beautiful.* Then he sucked on his flute, and the swallowtail went back inside.

"Now we will go, for they cannot do wrong and get away with it. Rise up," he said to the beasts: Mountain Lion, Bear, Badger, Coyote, and Mole. He took them along with him. When he blew his flute, the swallowtail came out, and he said, "When they try to catch you, you will sprinkle them with your wing powder, and then the beasts can do whatever they wish."

The swallowtail flew to the K'uuchinina women's home and came down the ladder, lighting on each and every rung. He landed on the basket plaque the killer herself was weaving. She liked his design and tried to catch him. He sprinkled her with his wing powder, and she went crazy.

Then he sprinkled all of the women with his powder and flew back up the ladder. They followed him, tried to catch him, threw their capes at him; he led them along toward Nepayatamu, hidden in the top of a cottonwood tree. By now they were naked. They got to the tree, lay down in the shade to rest, and fell asleep.

Nepayatamu summoned the animals, calling them his "grandfathers," and they had pleasure with the flesh of the women. Another wrong was done.

When they had all gone, the women awoke and found themselves naked. They looked up and saw Nepayatamu, and demanded something in return.

He tore leaves from the tree, wet them, and threw them down. They became blankets. The women dressed themselves, and Nepayatamu took them home to his society sisters, who fed and clothed them.

Next day Nepayatamu took them out in the direction of where the Sun rises and sucked on his flute. One by one he sucked them inside, and as he blew out, flocks of moths emerged. He went on his way until he came to the ocean. There, in the midst of the waters, the Sun Father came out and asked his son to sit on his left side. He told him, "Now we shall go and look at the world."

At noon they came to Zuni—Middle Place, Middle Time—and then Nepayatamu was taken by his father to his shrine there at Ash Water. It was in this way that the Neweekwe clowns, and their initiation rituals, were created at Zuni.

Flora's water jar, with her special combination of fat Rocky Mountain swallowtail butterflies enclosing deer, drumsticks, flutes, and the Milky Way, became, for me, an illustration and interpretation of this tale of magical transformation, death, reincarnation, revenge, and initiation: strains of *The Magic Flute* and *Orpheus* sounding together in a distinctly Zuni key. The magical death and rebirth of the hero in "The Women and the Man" is parallel to the Orpheus tale. Like *The Magic Flute*, the Zuni narrative contains an initiation ritual, but, unlike the Masonic initiation, the Zuni ritual involves the ingestion of a mind-altering substance, tenatsali flowers. This narrative is also an etiological tale, telling of the origin of an important sacred clown society.

■ ■ ■ ■

Sadie stood up. "Are you going to check on Mom? She's up at Lena's."

"How *is* Tola?"

"Her health's pretty good, but she's been dreaming a lot lately. It started up just after the funeral. She dreamed she saw a line of Nahalisho/*Crazy Grandchild* kachinas, and the one who died was in the middle of the line, holding a bundle of prayer-stick offerings for the dead. The kachinas filed out of the plaza, and as they did, the last one in line gave the ik'ok'u—you know, that deer call the Shalakos make?"

Nodding, I replied, "Has she done anything about that dream?"

"Well, she told it to us, so it won't be yuk'iis mowa'u/*completed*, she won't die."

"Why would she die? Just because she saw Crazy Grandchildren in a dream?"

"Seeing the kachinas is okay, it probably means it will rain, but to recognize a person dressed as a kachina is, as you know, hish attanni/*very dangerous, frightening.* If you don't tell anyone, then maybe you end up following that dead person to Kachina Village. You know how dead persons like to get the living to come back with them to their homes?"

"Yes. If a person dies during a kachina dance people say that they just couldn't help themselves. The dancers were hish tso'ya/*very beautiful, exciting,* and so they blacked out, died."

"And then they followed the dancers to Kachina Village."

We said goodbye, carefully nestled Flora's beautiful pot into the back seat with an old towel, and drove over to the center of the village. There were no cars outside Lena's house and the front door was locked, so we guessed she had gone to Gallup.

Late the next morning we found Tola at Lena's, beading a pincushion. It was nearly lunchtime, and Lena was warming up something in a big enamel pot on the electric stove. She complained that she hadn't expected company so she hadn't made any oven bread. Also, since she hadn't been shopping recently, she didn't have any store bread. When I offered to make fry bread, Lena seemed pleased and got out her fifty-pound sack of Bluebird flour. She measured out six cups and mixed it together with two tablespoons of baking powder, a half-cup of instant nonfat powdered milk, and one tablespoon of salt. Then she sifted these dry ingredients by tossing them up into the air with both hands and letting them fall back into her metal pudding pan.

I stepped outside to the woodpile, where I found some dry piñon branches. I brought them inside, rustled up some matches, and got a fire started in the wood stove. Once it was good and hot I heated the water, added it to the flour mixture, gradually blended it together with my fingers until it was soft, and kneaded it until the texture was fine and the dough was elastic. I covered the dough with a piece of cloth, to let it set for five minutes.

At this point Lena placed a cast-iron skillet on the stove, and melted enough lard to produce about an inch or so of liquid fat. While the lard was heating, we pinched off palm-sized balls of dough, then flattened and stretched them, by pulling gently with one hand and moving in a circle with the other, until they were thin and about six inches in diameter. After slapping the dough back and forth, from hand to hand, until the lard was bubbling, I lowered them, one by one, into the grease.

I let them fry until the floating dough filled with air bubbles and turned a rich yellowish-brown on both sides. As I took them out I let the fat drain off them for a moment and then stacked them on paper towels.

Just as I finished, Hapiya walked in. "Kesshe/*Hello;* well, how's it going? Haven't been seeing you for a while now."

Before I could respond, Lena said, "Itonaaway." And everyone sat down to lunch: piping-hot fry bread, rewarmed mutton stew, cilantro, scallions, radishes, raw jalapeño peppers, and weak, sugary coffee.

Hapiya was in a mischievous mood. He decided to embarrass Tola by talking about an adulterous episode dating from a long time ago. He was invited by a certain woman "to come to her house," and did so. Another man knew about this, and went to Tola that same night, telling her about her husband's behavior,

DENNIS TEDLOCK

suggesting she get even. That man spent the night with Tola, and Hapiya spent the night with the other woman.

Next day, when Hapiya returned to Tola, she demanded to know why he had been out all night. But he had seen the other man go into her house, and told her so. Then he said it would be best simply to tell the truth. He told her everything, and she admitted spending the night with the other man.

"And that was the end of having other friends, wasn't it?" he asked his wife with a big grin.

Tola said nothing, kept her head down, eating.

After a long pause, Hapiya asked if we had heard about "the one who passed away." We said we had. He replied, "Guess that one had a short road."

Dennis explained to Hapiya that, once again, our visit would be brief: it was our spring break, and we still had more teaching to do. We'd be leaving right after lunch.

Hapiya said he understood about our work, but wondered if we could spend a summer again sometime, or else the Christmas break, in New Mexico. "Don't your folks over in Albuquerque miss you sometimes too?"

"Yes, they do, and we'll try to come around more," Dennis replied.

As we started to leave, Tola jumped up from the table and ran back into her bedroom. She brought out a beaded basket for me, and a beaded rabbit-foot key chain for Dennis. We both said, "Elahkwa," and Dennis put his keys on his new chain.

16

TIED TO THE CRADLEBOARD

■ ■ ■ ■

WE WERE MAKING OUR GOODBYE ROUNDS when we entered Sadie's subdivision home. Walking in without knocking, we found Flora watching a soap on TV while her baby napped in the next room. When she went back to bring her baby out, we heard a cry followed by high-frequency wailing. Then, shaking and shaking the baby, Flora came running down the long hall toward us, her aunt and uncle, frozen before the color TV.

She placed the baby, strapped to an ancient cradleboard, on the couch, and knelt down beside her to untie the leather laces. But by the time she got the baby girl off the board, her stiff outstretched arms and legs had lost their color, her eyes were rolled up inside her head, and she was barely breathing.

Or not breathing.

I flipped the TV off, and as I knelt down next to Flora on the crimson carpet, Dennis dangled his rabbit-foot key chain, suggesting a quick trip to the hospital. Flora shook her head no.

She cradled the baby in her arms, placed her mouth over the tiny mouth and nose, and pushed in four short breaths in rapid succession, paused, then gave her four more breaths, and four more, and four more.

She grabbed the wall phone, dialed, spoke rapidly in Zuni, stopped, breathed into the baby's mouth, let out a low howl, hung up, started wailing, then breathing for the baby, then wailing again, and breathing again. I reached out toward her, or thought I did, but Flora didn't notice me.

Velma, Tola's sister, rushed in the front door with two of her daughters. Rummaging around in the kitchen cabinets, they located a small brown paper bag. They folded back its neck and placed it over the baby's nose and mouth, an improvised respirator.

Praying quietly in Zuni, Velma rolled up her sleeves and breathed into her hands, then massaged the baby's stomach, back, and limbs and the soft spot in her skull. I had seen medicine men do this type of deep massage before and realized, for the first time, that she must be a healer. After about five minutes of massage Velma blew into the baby's fontanel, and she let go her first burbles, followed by a low gasp.

Velma had a brief exchange in Zuni with Flora, who then called Black Rock Hospital and explained in English that "the baby had dif-fi-culty breathing."

When Flora hung up, a soft whirring sound caught her and she went into the back bedroom to shut down her grinding wheel and acetylene torch. She'd been spot-soldering and buffing her needlepoint necklaces with matching earrings, waiting for the Arab to pull up outside in his new air-conditioned Volvo and beep for this week's orders. He provided her with silver and turquoise and set the prices; in return she gave him everything she made. Or at least as far as he knew she did.

As Flora walked back into the living room the siren and lights of an ambulance bounced off the ceiling. A Zuni woman about thirty, with long uncut hair, jumped down out of the cab of the rescue van. She rushed into the house with her bottle of oxygen and greeted us, "Kesshe!," which almost means *hello* but really means *now*. Velma alone replied, "Kesh to' iya/*Now you've come*," as the rescue lady approached and knelt down beside her and the baby.

She placed a small clear plastic mask over the baby's nose and mouth and twisted on the oxygen while holding the respirator in place. Then she asked that someone call the police, since she would need a driver to help her take the baby to the hospital.

A white sedan with flashing lights and Zuni tribal seal pulled up and a young cop in a short-sleeved shirt with an embroidered Knife Wing Bird patch on his left sleeve, the insignia of the handsome male, swaggered over. He pulled the screen door open, doffed his two-toned blue motorcycle helmet with a flourish, and coolly surveyed the living-room tableau. Then, slowly, and in English, he said, "Good afternoon, ladies and gentlemen. Is everything under control in here?"

Nobody replied.

Flora, who'd been standing in the corner with both hands over her mouth, her face like a puckered seam twisted down the middle, walked over and opened the metal kitchen cabinets. Fumbling around, she found and unfolded two dried corn husks, then placed them on the ironing board. She crossed the room to the bookcase, picked up a pottery prayer-meal bowl—the kind with Milky Way handle, cut-out stepped-cloud sides, painted feathered serpents, dragonflies, and tadpoles—carried it over to the corn husks, and pulled out a mint twenty-dollar bill from her hip pocket. I was sure it was one of the five I'd given her the previous evening for the pottery jar with encircling band of deer silhouettes enveloped in fat Rocky Mountain swallowtail butterflies.

By now the baby was blowing bubbles. Then she let out a single whimper.

Flora walked over to the ironing board and, while praying quietly, breathed into her own right palm. Grabbing a fistful of mixed cornmeal and turquoise grains from the prayer-meal bowl, she filled each corn husk: folding the first one into four parts, leaving the second one open with the twenty-dollar bill on top.

A young guy in a blue-flowered silk headband, turquoise earrings, long medicine-man necklace, and Western shirt arrived: a Mountain Lion Man. He walked in silently, right past us and over to the baby—never even caught our eyes. Flora handed over the corn husks.

He pulled up a folding chair, then, placing the husks between his feet, carefully removed the plastic respirator and breathed four times into the baby's mouth and nose. With a soft growling sound, he sucked at the baby's throat until, with a strangling cough, he ejected something dark and raggy-looking into his left hand and rubbed his hands together. He began pulling dark masses of hair and rag out from under the baby's chin, from behind her ears, her cheeks, her forehead. He placed this damp smelly stuff, including what looked like bits of thin slate-blue hair (deer hair?), on the cornmeal in the open husk. When he was satisfied he had removed it all, he gently replaced the respirator and prayed in a low voice.

I caught only a bit of his prayer: "Today, because of some foolishness, some envy felt by a two-hearted person, our child became ill. . . . Daylight Priests, Beast Priests, with your hands, with your breath, hold her fast."

He got up, holding the corn husks and twenty-dollar bill, turned around stiffly, and brushed by me out the open door. He walked four steps, turned back, and, while looking up at the Sun Father, began to pray rapidly. Spitting on the open husk, spinning it around his head four times with his left hand, he tossed it directly behind him into the corner of the yard near the doghouse, next to the chain-link fence. He breathed from the closed corn husk, then the twenty-dollar bill, and walked off down the road toward the Zuni River.

The rescue woman asked Flora for blankets; they bundled up the baby and walked over to the ambulance. We left to notify Sadie.

When we walked in the side door of the big Shalako house we found Sadie at her jewelry bench. She was holding a pair of chrome tweezers, placing small bits of green-snail shell into grooves on a silver pin. Her mother, Tola, was there too, singing a lullaby while sewing on her beadwork and bouncing a baby boy, strapped to a cradleboard, on her knee.

When she noticed us Tola stopped singing, put her sewing down, placed the cradleboard upright against the arm of the sofa, and stood up. Looking hard at our faces, she asked slowly, and in English, "Why have you come? Has someone passed away?"

"No, well, not yet," I replied. "It's Flora's baby; somehow, when she was napping, her cradleboard flipped over. Flora had the board propped up on a pillow next to the wall in the bedroom, and when she found the baby, her face was pushed into the mattress, she wasn't breathing. Velma massaged her and blew wind back into her head while Flora breathed for her till the ambulance lady arrived with the oxygen. Now they're all up at Black Rock Hospital."

"Where was my sister? What was she doing? Working on her potteries, or what?" asked Sadie.

"Watching TV."

"Ummm. So, the baby was all alone in that next room?"

"Strange, isn't it? I thought that the whole point of using a cradleboard was to be with the baby more."

"That's right. You've seen how sometimes I work on my jewelry with my little one here hung on the wall, so I can look at him?"

"Sure, and I've noticed that Flora and her baby are both really fat. The seams of her T-shirts and blue jeans are splitting, and Lorinda's cheeks look like she's got nuts in them."

"I don't know what's wrong with her. Four years ago, at the Tribal Fair, she was runner-up in the Miss Zuni contest, and that takes some thought, some attention to how you look. You've got to wear a blanket dress, high moccasins, dress your hair in the old way, and tell stories, or sing something; then make jewelry, paperbread, or potteries for the judges.

"But ever since her— Well, you remember the one who passed away?"

I nodded, remembering Flora's brother.

"All she ever does now is watch TV, eat, and sleep. She isn't interested in her little girl the way she should be. Let's go."

We arrived at the hospital about three-thirty and stood around outside the emergency ward, peeking in whenever a nurse or an orderly left or arrived. The baby cried now and then, so we all relaxed some, but I worried about how long she had been smothering. It couldn't have been too long or they couldn't have revived her, but had it been long enough for complications, like brain damage?

After more than an hour the doctor came out of the emergency room. Ten minutes later the nurse stuck her head out and invited us into the room, where she started grilling Flora.

"How did this happen? Where were you when your papoose was smothering? Were you at home? Was anybody at home?"

Tola interrupted her question chain: "You can talk with me about this."

"We're trained to talk to mothers."

"I am a mother, Flora's mother."

"Oh, well, okay, then," she said with a sigh. "This has sure been a close one, as close as I've seen in my thirteen years of practice. When they brought that poor little creature in here, it took more than twenty minutes to get her to be responsive."

"How much longer will she need to be in here?" asked Tola, firmly.

"It all depends on how it goes. Now, could you please tell me how this happened?"

"My daughter was watching TV while her baby napped on the cradleboard in the next room. Somehow the board flipped over. We found her when our aunt and uncle here arrived."

"What do you mean, your 'aunt' and 'uncle'?"

"We call them 'aunt' and 'uncle' because they're our relatives, to our way of thinking."

"Anything you say, lady. But I hope from this bad experience you've learned something about how the weight of a cradleboard can push a papoose's head into the mattress. The poor little thing can't get free. It's unnatural to tie an infant to a board. It's just like putting it in jail. Babies have to kick and move around some, you know. When they're strapped down papoose-style twenty-three or twenty-four hours a day, they don't learn to walk when they should.

"Now, don't you think it's about time to get rid of that old cradleboard and move into the twentieth century?"

"We all use boards; my father made that one before I was born. The cradleboard is our Indian way, and this is the very first time there's been any problem with one," Tola replied, uncompromisingly.

"Well, but now you know better, don't you? You know what can happen?"

"Yes, but, *why* did this happen to this particular child? That's the question we're asking ourselves right now. Over the years we've had dozens of babies on this cradleboard; it keeps them calm, helps them sleep. Up till now no baby ever got fussy and flipped the board."

"I really don't understand how it happened. But here's some grippe water to help her sleep better in the future, and if I were you I'd get rid of that cradleboard, just to be sure," the nurse replied, then walked out of the room.

She'd left her clipboard with the case history on the cabinet next to the sink. I picked it up.

August 13, 1975

Lorinda Tsipana, age three months, arrived at 3:02 p.m. by ambulance. She was found by her young mother, Flora Tsipana, smothering on the bed in the next room strapped down to one of those heavy cradleboards Zunis still use. The infant was nonresponsive until 3:26 p.m. when she cried for the first time. I spoke with the family about getting rid of the old-fashioned cradleboard. They were uncooperative.

As soon as the nurse reappeared I said to her, in what I had hoped was a neutral tone but which actually turned out to be quite curt, "Miss, your report says nothing about what the family did for the baby. They provided artificial respiration and massage before the ambulance arrived. They're the ones who revived the baby."

The nurse replied, "The infant was nonresponsive and very near death when she arrived at the hospital. She would have died without the doctor."

"You don't want to know how the baby's life was really saved, do you?"

"I know how that papoose was saved," she replied curtly and left the room again.

The baby was sleeping now in her oxygen tent and it was dinnertime, so we left for Velma's. When we got inside the big stone house, which had been built back in the 1930s for the great winter Shalako ritual, the long table was already set with pitchers of iced tea and lemonade, loaves of Indian sourdough bread, homemade mint jelly, raw jalapeño peppers, scallions, cilantro, radishes, cooked squash, pinto beans, posole, purple-corn-dough tamales filled with venison and chile, platters of mutton ribs, and small conical piles of the body of Old Lady Salt.

We were formally asked to sit and eat. Cutting off a tiny piece of mutton, tossing it into the piñon fire in the corner fireplace, I said, "Nanaakwe itonaawe/*Grandparents, let's eat.*"

We passed the food around as Velma, Sadie, and Lena spoke. Flora had been too smart and too popular at Zuni High; not only did she have the highest math score on the reservation, but her pottery had attracted too much attention at the Santa Fe Indian Market: why, all those museums bought her out!

Then the witchery began. She was always tired, started eating during her difficult pregnancy; now the cradleboard had flipped over and, why, they almost lost the baby! But somehow their thoughts and prayers kept the baby's breath nearby long enough to get it back down inside her heart. Who knows how long before the witch shoots at her again?

The silly nurse thought it was the cradleboard; pretty dumb when anyone can see that what that baby needs is a new heart. The healer called Lorinda "my child." Don't you think his medicine society will be wanting to adopt her in a few years?

As for Flora, it's high time for her to be settling down and getting married.

Softly, slowly, from the far end of the long table, Flora replied, "But I don't want to marry. I want to go to Albuquerque, get an office job or something. I can come home once in a while, on weekends and holidays, to visit, just like our aunt and uncle here—I can be visiting family too."

Tola replied evenly, "If that's what you want, to run away, why, that's yours. But as for Lorinda, you'll be leaving her here with us."

Velma reached over and touched Flora's hand. And although we've never been particularly good at knowing when to go, we knew it was time to be off to the Albuquerque Sunport.

As always, we promised to call, to write, and, most important, to return as soon as possible. Then, as Tola presented us with two warm loaves of sourdough bread, I cried, silently.

■ ■ ■ ■

Later, in the quiet of my study, I read over the sketchy field notes I'd written the following afternoon.

AUGUST 14, 1975

Stopped by Sadie's subdivision house, on our last day, and found ourselves in the midst of a medical emergency. Flora's baby, Lorinda, nearly smothered to death. Flora did artificial respiration and phoned Velma, who came and "pressed" (*hets'u'ati*) the baby. A medicine person trained in massage is called "one who presses" (*ahets'u'ak'een'ona*). Velma summoned a medicine man (*ak'waamossi*) or "curing boss" from Uhu-huukwe Medicine Society, order of "magicianship" (*itsepcho*), with the knowledge of "sucking" (*iwenashnaawe*). Counting Flora's and the ambulance driver's first-aid, the doctor's and nurse's procedures, Velma's "pressing," and the medicine man's "sucking," there were four health-care systems operating simultaneously. Medical pluralism in action. The nurse was aloof, secure in her vision of what native peoples needed. But her behavior nicely demonstrates the cultural hegemony of Western biomedicine.

From these handwritten traces of experience and interpretation, the departure scene stood right up before me so powerfully that I felt the need to narrate: to flesh it out, give it breath. I ran upstairs and pounded rapidly on the gray keyboard of "The Hulk" (an enormous out-of-date IBM Displaywriter). Watching my chartreuse words lighting up across the charcoal screen—bits of dialogue, thick description, relived emotional response—I was pleased, momentarily. But when I ran the spell check, printed out my hard copy, and read it over for accuracy, I became agitated.

It seemed inevitable that nurses hired and trained by the PHS would always believe that child-rearing practices and healing traditions that differed from those sanctioned by the Western biomedical system were somehow unnatural or old-fashioned. I had read that the swaddling of infants had once been a respected Western practice, but that it had disappeared in Europe shortly before industrialization. And although the reasons for its decline were not clear, it did seem to correlate both with nineteenth-century ideas about personal liberty and with the increasing use of pharmacological means, including sedatives and alcohol, of pacifying babies.

While my college friends were giving their infants sips of beer to quiet them, PHS nurses were using watered-down alcohol in amber bottles, the so-called grippe water, to quiet infants living on Indian reservations where both the sale and consumption of alcohol are prohibited. Why hadn't I spoken up? Warned my Zuni family that the nurse was trying to substitute cheap drug-store alcohol for traditional swaddling? By that time I should have been an expert in negotiating conflicting cultural realities, not just making mental notes on them, like a character in an objectivist novel.

I might have been, at the very least, of some value in defending the use of the cradleboard before that nurse who insisted on referring to Lorinda as a "papoose." I could have explained to her that Zunis never call their own babies (or for that matter anyone else's babies) "papoose," a word that came into English from Narraganset, an Algonquian language. Zunis reject the term, not only because it is not their own, but also because of its use in Western films and dime novels, where Indian "squaws" (another Algonquian import into English) are nearly always portrayed as having infants strapped onto their backs.

In psychological studies comparing the motor development of infants raised on the board with those raised without the board, it has been found that the age of walking was identical in both groups. Furthermore, swaddled babies sleep more, have fewer startles, and lower heart-rate variability.

But I had very little to say to that nameless nurse that cool spring day at Zuni Pueblo.

17

PUT IT AROUND YOURSELVES

■ ■ ■ ■

IT HAPPENED IN THE FLAT, between the reservation line and the Gallup Y, where the pavement was broken. It was winter and just starting to snow when a pickup came out from behind a trailer-truck, Dennis slammed on the brakes, and we swerved off on the shoulder, just in time.

When we arrived at Sadie's we told the story of our near miss, remarking that we were so scared that our hearts tried to jump right out.

Hapiya was concerned. "That's serious. It can make you sick five or ten years from now. The cure is to put it around yourselves. Here, take this napkin and scrape off a little grease from underneath the car."

We went outside and Dennis got down on the ground and rubbed a bit of grease off the differential. When we went back inside, Hapiya removed live coals from the stove with a shovel, saying, "Put that grease on them.

"Okay, Tsilu, take Tola's shawl and cover yourselves with it. Sit right here and cover up your heads." We leaned over the coals so that the shawl caught the smoke.

"Now, breathe, breathe it in hard, get it all." We did what we were told, but it smelled so awful I nearly choked.

"Kyamme, since you were the driver, put your hands in the smoke. That's enough. Good."

Now he brought over a glass of water. "Drop all the little coals in here. Okay, take them out. Now, both of you, wet your fingers and rub them all over your foreheads.

"Good. Wet them again, reach in underneath your clothes, rub them over your chest, over your belly. Like this. That's right. It's good you did it today; five or ten years from now, it might've been too late. You can do this in the future too, whenever something like that happens to you."

He grabbed the glass and stood on the threshold, praying in a low voice, then tossed the contents out into the dirt road. We were cured. Or, rather, a future illness, caused by the fright we had experienced, was prevented.

We had never expected to be treated by Hapiya—or any other Zuni medicine person, for that matter—since it was common knowledge that they only helped their own people. Not because they were selfish and didn't want to help others, but because they had learned that their methods and medicines weren't respected by outsiders.

We hadn't told Hapiya about our near accident in the hopes of being cured. In fact, we had no idea that Zuni medicine people had a treatment for fright, an illness Mexicans call "susto." Now that we knew, I was excited and wanted to ask Hapiya all sorts of questions about what had just happened.

But I kept quiet. Partly because I couldn't bring myself to objectify the situation so quickly, and partly because of Hapiya. He had not only cured us, but he had also taught us how to cure fright, or, rather, how to prevent the illness that fright can cause. He had given us some of his sacred medicine knowledge, a bit of his own life, his own breath. There was something about him, something that reminded me of Sabin's strange intensity years earlier, after his pilgrimage to Kachina Village, Land of the Dead.

I also kept quiet because we had something difficult to tell Hapiya. We were starting up new fieldwork, and this time it was far from the Southwest, in Guatemala. It was hard to find the words to explain to him why we would study elsewhere. Dennis and I had talked about this moment at length, and he had hit upon a way of explaining.

"Hapiya, we will be leaving soon to visit people in a country to the south of here, called Guatemala. That's an Indian word meaning *Many Trees*. Like the Zuni, they crossed a lake. Their village stands in the Middle, and the place of their dead is also in the west. Instead of burning meat for the dead they burn tree resin. Flowers are feathers for them, and breath—well, it's the same thing. They also talk about roads and look for the long straight Good Road.

"Maybe these are the ones in the story of 'The Beginning,' " Dennis offered, "who chose the macaw eggs, when the people were divided. You remember the story."

Looooing ago, when the earth was still soft, Payatamu's twin younger brothers struck the ground with their staves hung with shells and plumed with yellow, blue-green, red, white, black, and dappled feathers.[1] When they blew upon them there appeared amid the plumes four seeds of living beings: two speckled blue-green and two dull brownish-white.

"Now, my fathers, my children, we must test you. Perhaps you will be wise. You must choose between these eggs." That's what the twins told the people.

On this side, in the direction where the middle of the world would be, were the raven eggs, beautiful, spotted blue-green. Those who were to come this way chose the raven eggs. The macaw eggs were plain, dull, not beautiful. Those who were to go south, in coral's direction, chose the macaw eggs.

When the beautiful eggs cracked and chicks came forth, their downy pin feathers were yellow and blue, red and green. The people were so happy. But when the baby birds molted and took on their adult plumage, those from the beautiful dappled eggs became dangerous black ravens, while those from the plain eggs became beautiful multicolored macaws.

Hapiya wasn't feeling well and didn't eat much at dinner. He said his stomach hurt and asked Dennis to drive him over to his daughter Lena's house. No one was there, so we stood in her back yard, waiting. Hapiya looked up toward the southwestern hill, called White Rocks, and said there were ruins up there. Three weeks before, the Shalako maskers had costumed themselves there, prior to coming down into the village. In two or three years, perhaps, his youngest daughter, Flora, would be well enough off financially so that she could build her own Shalako house. He certainly hoped so.

It was windy, cold, and trying to snow. Then, even though Lena had not yet arrived, Hapiya dismissed us, saying simply, "Well, goodbye, Kyamme; goodbye, Tsilu; see you." We hesitated a moment, then, guessing that he either had a key or else knew where his daughter hid a spare, we drove off.

Early the next morning Dennis awoke saying that he felt Hapiya was cold, shivering, freezing to death: he needed a jacket. On the drive back down to the village he just couldn't get it out of his mind.

When we arrived Hapiya was gone.

The previous evening, when Lena got home from town, she had found her father lying on her couch, sweating profusely, complaining of chills and a stomach ache. She took his temperature, 104 degrees, and drove him to the hospital at Black Rock. Later his fever hit 106, and an ambulance took him to the PHS hospital in Gallup.

We found him there in the surgery ward. He had a tube taped to his nose, with a drainage pump on the floor; another tube taped to his right wrist, with a bottle of dextrose hanging over him. But his body was radiant; we both saw it. He awoke for a moment and noticed us, saying, "Kesshe! Good to see you." Dennis looked at him and for a long moment felt angry that he might let himself die. When he dropped off to sleep we talked with his doctor, who said Hapiya had stones in his gallbladder, with a massive infection all around it. He had removed the gallbladder, but shortly after they wheeled him out of the operating room, his kidneys failed. That had been attended to, and his condition was now stable.

Hapiya woke up and spoke a few words in Zuni with his daughters. Then a Catholic priest entered the room, looked at the tag on the foot of his bed, and went right back out. There, under his name and date of admission, next to his age and address, in the space for religion, were the letters "N.S." When Dennis asked the nurse what that meant, she replied, "Nonsectarian. I guess that's for people who don't have any."

Hapiya raised his head a little off the pillow and widened his eyes, saying, "What?!" We all laughed and he slipped off to sleep.

Lena offered us his bed at her house, but we declined; it was somehow too intimate. As we headed east out of Gallup, late that evening, a yellow star arced across the sky, falling long and slow across the highway toward the north, Mountain Lion's home. It burned out before it hit the ground.

Far away, in the highlands of Guatemala, we dreamed of Hapiya. I dreamed that I was reading his obituary in the Gallup *Indepen-*

dent, but that it was wrong; it said he was eighty-seven, not seventy-two. On the same night, Dennis dreamed that Hapiya was discussing the text of the story of the Beginning with him, saying that two of the lines were two ways of saying the same thing. Then he awoke with a start, thinking he'd been with a man who was already dead.

We asked Don Andrés, our Mayan teacher, to help us to understand our dreams. He asked for the date when Hapiya entered the hospital. It was the day Two No'j on the Mayan calendar, and he divined for us by combining the meanings of the calendar days, which he counted out with his bright-red divining seeds and sparkling crystals, with the lightning that raced through his blood.[2]

"Come here, Lord Two No'j, Three Tijax, Four Kawuq, Five Junajpu, Six Imöx"—on through the calendar—"Four Kan, Five Kame. Oh, Lord Five Kame, Five Death. Yés, after he came to the hospital he was a little better. But then his condition became more grave. He was in agony. Already he is dead."

Don Andrés looked down at his right shin and said, "What happened was not a simple sickness, nor was it sent by God or the earth, it was the deed of a man. We humans envy what another possesses, we put our word into the shrines. Yes, some neighbor or friend is to blame."

"Don Andrés, we know who it was, a neighbor who tried to kill his sheep."

Glancing toward his right armpit, he said, "The one who envied him is imprisoned, he does not walk on this earth, he died even before Hapiya did, but his deed remained."

Then he pointed behind his right knee. "Yes, it is so, my lightning speaks."

NOTES

▪ ▪ ▪ ▪

▪ **CHAPTER 1: PAGES 1—17** ▪

1. The orthography used here, for the Zuni language, is a practical one in which the vowels (a, e, i, o, u) should be given their continental values; double vowels (aa, ee, ii, oo, uu) should be held longer than single ones; most consonants should be pronounced as in English, except that "p" and "t" are unaspirated, the sounds in "lh" should be pronounced simultaneously, and "ts" is like the "ts" in English "bats." The glottal stop (') is like the "tt" in the Scottish pronunciation of "bottle." Double consonants are either held a bit longer than single ones or else repeated.

2. Dennis Tedlock is referred to by all Zunis in this large extended family, regardless of age, by the kinship term "kyamme/ *uncle*," or, more specifically, *mother's brother*.

3. The archeological project at the Mission of Nuestra Señora de Guadalupe (begun in 1966) was a joint project of the Franciscan Mission, National Park Service, and the Bureau of Indian Affairs (Caywood 1972). By "Catholics" Zunis do not mean baptized, practicing Roman Catholics but, rather, a political faction dating from the early 1920s, when the Roman Catholic BIA agent facilitated the reestablishment of the mission at Zuni (see Parsons 1939b:337–38; Smith and Roberts 1954:35; Leighton and Adair 1966:56–57; Roberts and Arth 1966:31–33; Pandey 1977:202–3). Likewise, the anti-Catholic faction, sometimes referred to as the "Protestants," are not necessarily followers of the Dutch Reformed Church; rather, their faith is in the Zuni religion (Trotter 1955:107; Leighton and Adair 1966:149). The proper analogy here is with political parties: Republicans and Democrats.

4. The best account of the history and techniques of Zuni jewelry making remains John Adair's (1944) careful study. Color photos of Zuni jewelers, plus examples of their excellent work, can be found in two hardback sources: a three-volume set published by Squaw Bell Traders of Grants, New Mexico (Bell and Bell 1975–77), and a single volume called *Who's Who in Zuni Jewelry* (Levy 1980). For a discussion of the change in perception of Southwestern jewelry from "costume jewelry" to "art" see Rosnek and Stacey (1976).

5. Though it is generally true that a house and its dooryard are thought of as belonging to women of the household, upon occasion men have controlled the power of alienation of houses. See Smith and Roberts (1954:78–82) for a thorough discussion of Zuni legal principles and practices concerning the division of property between individuals.

6. Because Hapiya so eagerly volunteered first-person anecdotes of this sort, in many informal social situations, we decided to collect and archive tape recordings formally.

▪ CHAPTER 2: PAGES 18–39 ▪

1. On this occasion I was referred to, for the first time, as "Tsilu/*Aunt*." More specifically, in proper technical kinship terminology, "tsilu" indicates *mother's younger sister*, or *mother's brother's wife* (see Schneider and Roberts 1965:3). From this point on everyone in this family, regardless of age, referred to me as their "aunt" and directly addressed me as Tsilu. As John Roberts (1965b:42) has pointed out, when Zunis wish to indicate close friendship they will use kin terms as a courtesy; thus, for example, in his own case, he was called both "suwe/*younger brother*" and "ky'asse/*sister's son*."

2. In contemporary Native American culture "the Whiteman" is a key social category and cultural symbol of what "the Indian" is not. For an Apache illustration and discussion of this category see Basso (1979).

3. On April 27, 1979, the tribe filed suit against the United States government in the U.S. Court of Claims to seek compensation for tribal lands taken without payment between 1846 and 1946 (Docket No. 161–79 L). President Bush, on October 31, 1990, signed the Zuni Land Conservation Act, which authorized twenty-five million dollars for the purchase of land in Arizona surrounding Kachina Village and the rehabilitation and restoration of reservation lands. For more information about these important land settlements see United States Congress House Report No. 95-953, Zuni Claims Settlement Act of 1990, Senate Report 101–306, and Senate Bill 2203, passed as Public Law

101-486 (United States Congress 1976, 1978, 1984, 1990; United States Laws and Statutes 1978, 1984, 1990), Hart (1983), and Dubin (1990a).

4. I have transcribed this narrative from a tape recording Dennis and I made in 1972.

5. For Zuni drawings of the Anahoho mask, see Ruth Bunzel (1932d:plate 29b, 993–94) and Barton Wright (1985:63). The elder-brother Anahoho mask, pictured in the text, is right-handed: the palm covers the face, and the eye holes are concealed within the fingertips (forefinger and ring finger).

▪ CHAPTER 3: PAGES 40–55 ▪

1. For an excellent overview of Zuni witchcraft beliefs see Simmons (1974:106–26).

2. This is a summary of the sacred stories concerning the origin and location of Zuni Salt Lake. These myths, variously titled "The Origin of Zuni Salt Lake," "Salt Old Woman," and "The Migration of Salt Woman," can be found, respectively, in M. C. Stevenson (1904:58–60); Bunzel (1932d:1032–35); and Benedict (1935:vol. 1, 272–73). For a humorous tale about two badgers, two coyotes, and two foxes who decided to visit the Salt Lake in order to gather salt for their food, but who were tricked by the Twin War Gods into thinking that they were unable to do so, see Handy (1918:459–61). The Salt Woman, or Ma'lokatsiki, is impersonated annually in the Mixed Animal Dance, or Wootemlha. For illustrations of her costume see Bunzel (1932d:plate 42a) and Wright (1985:plate 28c).

3. Clan membership at Zuni interlocks with the kinship and religious systems to regulate all important socioreligious behavior (Kroeber 1917; Cushing 1920:127–28; Eggan 1950; Ladd 1983a). A child is born into a clan and is the child of its father's

clan. When the child grows up she or he should not marry anyone from his or her own clan, and agricultural land as well as houses are inherited within clans. There currently exist fifteen clans: Dogwood, Eagle, Sun, Badger, Turkey, Corn, Frog, Crane, Coyote, Bear, Tobacco, Tansy Mustard, Deer, Chaparral Cock, and Yellow Wood (Ladd 1979a:487).

4. Kivas are subterranean or semisubterranean chambers built and maintained by pueblo societies, clan groups, and individuals. These rooms are used as locations for members to congregate in order to engage in weaving, mask and moccasin making, storytelling, as well as song and dance rehearsal. At Zuni there are six kivas, one for each of the six dance groups and sacred directions.

5. A discussion of Zuni medicine-society songs can be found in my entry on Zuni music in *The New Grove Dictionary of American Music* (B. Tedlock 1986a).

6. Zuni six-point sacred orientation is described in greater detail in D. Tedlock (1979:499).

7. This is an abstract of the Crazy Grandchild myth, published by Ruth Bunzel (1932d:1078–79).

8. The Zuni phrase for a person with sacred power and authority can be translated into English as "one who knows how" (Benedict 1934:88).

9. For a photograph of a mosaic-inlay pin of a masked Nahalisho dancer, made by another well-known Zuni jeweler, Ida Poblano, see Wright (1988:127).

10. More information on the history and distribution of the Kachina Society among the Southwestern pueblos can be found in Adams (1991). At Zuni, young boys are first initiated into

the Kachina Society when they are between five and nine years of age (see M. C. Stevenson 1887:547–53; Bunzel 1932a:516–21).

11. There is a traditional narrative about another mask, that of the White Shumeekuli, sticking to the face of an impersonator, causing him to go crazy and die inside the mask (D. Tedlock 1972:217–22).

■ CHAPTER 4: PAGES 56–75 ■

1. The Molaawe impersonators of the Corn Maidens come six days before Teshkwi, or the Fasting, and six days after Shalako. For a detailed description of the Corn Maidens and the Molaawe ceremony see Cushing (1920:40–54), M. C. Stevenson (1904: 277–83), and Parsons (1916d).

2. This type of placard, indicating strong tension and even violent disputes between adherents to Catholicism and Protestantism, has also been found in rural Mexico (Bernard and Salinas 1989:21–22).

3. In 1976, after Hapiya's death, the country house was inherited by Kwinsi, who used it strictly as a sheep camp; Albert left Zuni to work for the Martinez family on their ranch north of the reservation.

■ CHAPTER 5: PAGES 76–93 ■

1. For an early account of a visit to Zuni Salt Lake published by an ethnographer, see M. C. Stevenson (1904:354–61). A first-person narrative account in Zuni, with English interlinear and free translation, of a large Zuni-Hopi pilgrimage to the Zuni Salt Lake was recorded and published by Bunzel (1935:420–29).

2. See M. C. Stevenson (1915:45) and Camazine and Bye (1980:375–76) for discussions of the many medicinal uses of *Croton texensis* at Zuni.

3. For more information concerning the use of zinnias in healing see M. C. Stevenson (1915:45).

4. Among the Zuni names reported for flannel mullein are amidolan kwiminne/*rainbow medicine*; and kwimi shipba/*sour root* (Camazine and Bye 1980:378). At Hopi, flannel or common mullein is called wupaviva/*tall tobacco* and is gathered and dried in the same manner as tobacco leaves (Whiting 1939:92).

5. During the time when Cushing lived at Zuni a Mormon bishop by the name of Ammon M. Tenney resided on a nearby ranch. Tenney preached to the Zunis that all their land belonged to the Mormons, who not only were not Americans but did not even like Americans (Green 1990:365 n. 72). To this day Zunis do not include Mormons in their category Melika/*Americans* but instead place them in the unique category of Muumaakwe/*Mormons*.

6. For identification and discussion of the three types of saltbush found in the American Southwest see Lamb (1975:54). Zuni ethnobotanical sources report the use of a powder, consisting of saltbush flowers and roots, used in the treatment of inflammation caused by ant bites (M. C. Stevenson 1915:44; Camazine and Bye 1980:374).

7. M. C. Stevenson (1915:69) reports apilhalu/*hand many seeds* as the Zuni name for Rocky Mountain beeplant. Parsons (1919a: 333) reports that Rocky Mountain beeplant and jackrabbit meat are taboo to members of the Shiwanaakwe medicine society at Zuni Pueblo as well as to the cognate Shikani society at both Laguna and Cochiti. For a discussion of the many uses of beeplant,

in various pueblos, see Robbins, Harrington, and Freire-Marreco (1916:58) and Whiting (1939:77–78).

8. Marcos Farfán's account of his 1598 visit to Zuni Salt Lake can be found in Crampton (1977:25).

9. According to a note in M. C. Stevenson's (1904:357) ethnography, Mexicans first settled and took up mining at Zuni Salt Lake in 1902. Until that time Zunis and other Southwestern Indians (mainly Hopis, Acomas, Navajos, and Apaches) gathered salt there. In 1978 a congressional act, Public Law 95-280, directed the secretary of the interior to purchase the land around the salt lake for the tribe (United States Laws and Statutes 1978; see also Ferguson and Hart 1985:99).

10. This description of the preparation of yucca-pod conserves is abstracted from M. C. Stevenson's (1915:72–73) Zuni ethnobotany, which is one of the earliest, and most thorough, published works on Native American plant knowledge and use.

■ **CHAPTER 6: PAGES 94–111** ■

1. For a discussion and critical review of early studies of Zuni music see B. Tedlock (1980).

2. For a discussion of the dynamics and meaning of Zuni dream sharing see B. Tedlock (1987). The photograph in the text, made in 1972 by Dennis Tedlock, shows a pictograph of a deer painted on a cave wall at the Zuni archeological site of the Village of the Great Kivas. The most thorough description and analysis of Zuni rock art to date can be found in Young (1988).

3. Translations of somewhat longer, more elaborate, Zuni prayers, used during the manufacture and offering of prayer sticks, can be found in Bunzel (1932c:626–31). For the best discussion

concerning the manufacture and meaning of prayer sticks at Zuni see Ladd (1963).

■ **CHAPTER 7: PAGES 112–131** ■

1. For a detailed, step-by-step discussion of the gathering, soaking, and screening of clay, plus the grinding of potsherd temper, see Rodee and Ostler (1986:87–88).

2. Today Zuni women are building clay bear figures (Rodee and Ostler 1986:38).

3. See illustrations in Cushing (1883). A 1966 reprint of this essay on fetishes, in pamphlet form with an introduction by Tom Bahti, was made available by K. C. Publications of Flagstaff, Arizona. See also the 1988 reprint of Ruth Kirk's 1943 study of Zuni fetishes. More recently Zuni fetishes, together with the Cushing reprint, have been sold nationwide in upscale shopping malls by firms such as The Nature Company.

4. From Cushing (1883:11).

5. For a discussion of the categories "raw" and "cooked" persons see D. Tedlock (1979:499).

6. This deer-hunter's song was collected in the Zuni language, and translated into English, for my M.A. thesis work on Zuni music (see B. Tedlock 1973).

7. The Coyote Society, or Sutikyanne, is an all-male hunting society closely allied to the Kachina Society. The principal patrons of the Coyote Society are the prey and game animals of the six directions (see D. Tedlock 1979:502–3).

▪ CHAPTER 8: PAGES 132–141 ▪

1. For more about sacred clowning see Parsons and Beals (1934), Coze (1952), Hieb (1972), B. Tedlock (1975, 1979), Handelman (1981), Bouissac (1990), and Sweet (1989).

2. See Greenblatt (1981) for a discussion of allegory, which he sees as arising in periods of loss of theological or political authority.

▪ CHAPTER 9: PAGES 142–156 ▪

1. Ruth Bunzel (1933:3–4) recorded a text, in Zuni with English translation, concerning the building of an outdoor oven and the making of bread in it. Both Matilda Coxe Stevenson (1904) and Frank Hamilton Cushing (1920) described the preparation and cooking of loaves of wheat bread in such an oven. Whereas Stevenson describes the opening of the oven as being sealed with "a piece of sheepskin, the wool outside, held in place by a stone slab" (M. C. Stevenson 1904:365), Cushing describes it as being "closed with a heavy stone and plastered" (Cushing 1920:376).

On this particular occasion sackcloth was used, but on other occasions I have seen old sheets, blankets, and pillowcases, as well as sheepskins, together with wooden planks and stone slabs, covering the opening. Some women also plaster the opening as well, to make the loaves cook faster; without plastering, the baking takes anywhere from half an hour to an hour.

2. The first permanent Catholic mission established in the Zuni Valley, in 1629, was abandoned in 1821 because of Navajo raids and the "small attendance of the inhabitants at church" (Parsons 1939b:337). In 1916 a proposal for establishing a new Roman Catholic mission was vocally opposed in a general meeting, but the Catholics persisted, and in 1922 St. Anthony's Mission Church was constructed on a plot of land the BIA obtained (Eggan and Pandey 1979:478).

3. Individuals receive many names during their lives, relating to their personal appearance, characteristics, and habits. This tradition is extended to include traders and anthropologists who have lived for extended periods of time in the pueblo. Thus, for example, Douglas Graham, a trader at Zuni from 1879 until 1900, was called Tsibon K'winna/*Black Beard* (Pueblo of Zuni 1973:14). The ethnologist Frank Hamilton Cushing was known as both Tenatsali/*Medicine Flower* (Cushing 1920:11) and Hetsilhto/*Cricket*; this latter name he said he acquired because of his habit of whistling, singing, and jumping about (Green 1990:9). His publicist, Sylvester Baxter, was given the name Lhi"akwa/ *Blue Medicine Stone* or *Turquoise* (Green 1990:406 n.15). Matilda Coxe Stevenson was called Tims Okya/*Stevenson Woman*, and Ruth Bunzel was known as Hopaanso/*Grandmother Bunzel* (D. Tedlock 1983:329). The archeologist Frederick Hodge was called Teluli, from a mouse's warning in an animal story, "teluli teluli/*dig your cellar*" (Smith, Woodbury, and Woodbury 1966:3–4), and another archeologist, Mark Raymond Harrington, was given the name Tonashi/*Badger*, because of his burrowing ability (Harrington 1929:16). The seven-year-old son of Mr. Nusbaum, Frederick Hodge's field assistant during the excavation of Hawikuh, was given the name Techa'le/*Pottery Child* (Nusbaum 1926:viii). George Herzog, who recorded music in 1927, was known as Poklhi Ky'ayu/*Smoke Youth* (Bunzel 1932d:891). One of Dennis Tedlock's Zuni names, Ts'imaawe, is the name of a story character.

4. The majority of Zuni narratives are either part of the chimiky'ana'kowa/*origin story*, which can be told in any season at any time of day, or else they are telapnaawe/*tales*, which are told only during winter nights (D. Tedlock 1983:159–60).

5. Since a transcription of this narrative has already been published in a lined poetic format (D. Tedlock 1983:305–10), when

I listened to the tape I decided to keep the same arrangement for the story proper, but to use a prose format for my transcription of the informal discussion which followed.

▪ CHAPTER 10: PAGES 157–169 ▪

1. For fuller renditions concerning the birth of Koyemshi/*Mudhead* clowns see Cushing (1896:401–3) and M. C. Stevenson (1904:32–34).

2. Recordings of this genre of Zuni rain-dance music can be found on the Folkways album *American Indian Dances*, the Canyon Records albums *Zuni* and *Summer Songs from Zuni*, and on a tape entitled *Music From Zuni Pueblo* marketed by Rainbow Cassette Studio of Taos, New Mexico (see discography).

3. On page 162 is a detail from an early-twentieth-century photograph located in the Anthropological Archives of the Smithsonian Institution in Washington, D.C. The four dancers are wearing Kokk'okshi/*Good Kachina* masks, the most sacred dance masks of all, and the only ones appropriate for opening the summer rain-dance season.

4. This Mudhead song (part of a song string), performed once every four years when the pilgrims return from Kachina Village, is my translation of the Zuni text collected by M. C. Stevenson (1904:68).

▪ CHAPTER 11: PAGES 170–187 ▪

1. See M. C. Stevenson (1904:204).

2. In September and October of 1978 Zuni Tribal Council Resolutions M70-78-991 and M70-78-993 adopted the statements of religious leaders as the official position of the tribe and gave council support to these leaders' efforts to protect and secure proper care for, or the return of, items of key religious significance to Zuni people (see Zuni Tribal Council 1978a and 1978b). At

this point the Pueblo of Zuni, with the help of the Department of Justice and the Federal Bureau of Investigation, began an active campaign to recover all War God carvings located in either public or private collections (see Eriacho 1978, Eriacho and Ferguson 1979, Canfield 1980, Stephens 1982). To date, thirty-eight War God icons have been returned to a specially fortified open-air shrine at the pueblo (Ferguson and Eriacho 1990). Unfortunately, however, individuals continue to steal them from the reservation (Dubin 1990b).

3. See Cushing (1895).

4. This is a section from the draft of a letter, now located in the Southwest Museum in Los Angeles, that Cushing drafted to Baxter. It has been published by Jesse Green (1990:181–82).

5. *Kia-pin-a-hoi* is Cushing's rendering of ky'apin aaho"i/*raw people*, one of the two Zuni key categories of living beings: cooked, or daylight, people and raw people. Whereas daylight people live off cooked food, raw people do not: they eat raw food or food that has been sacrificed to them by daylight people. Also, raw people, unlike cooked people, can change form and are considered people because one of their potential forms is anthropomorphic. Mother Earth, Sun Father, and White Shell Woman are all raw persons (see D. Tedlock 1979:499).

6. In a lecture, "Life in Zuñi," delivered in Buffalo on December 10, 1890, Cushing described the way in which the scalping of an Apache was faked as a requisite for his initiation into the Priesthood of the Bow (see Green 1979:153–56; Green 1990:393 n. 50).

■ **CHAPTER 12: PAGES 188–204** ■

1. For illustrations of antique Zuni ceramics see J. Stevenson (1883) and Cushing (1886).

▪ CHAPTER 14: PAGES 224–255 ▪

1. The Shalako chant passages quoted in this chapter were collected in the 1920s by Bunzel (1932c:762–76); I have retranslated them.

▪ CHAPTER 15: PAGES 256–272 ▪

1. During this century adult-onset diabetes has grown to epidemic proportions on American Indian reservations (West 1974, Knowler et al. 1978, Nabhan 1982:101–10). Today more than 33 percent of all Zunis older than forty-five have the disease (Long 1978, Harbert 1990).

2. See D. Tedlock (1975) for more detail on Zuni death ritual and burial practice.

3. For the full narrative of "The Women and the Man," see D. Tedlock (1972:85–132).

4. Tenatsali flowers are medicinal and come in various colors, including yellow and blue. When Dennis asked Hapiya to identify the tenatsali plant he said, "If you are a medicine man, then you know what kind of medicine that is."

▪ CHAPTER 17: PAGES 285–290 ▪

1. More comprehensive narratives about the Beginning can be found in Cushing (1896), M. C. Stevenson (1904:23–26), Parsons (1923b), Bunzel (1932b), Benedict (1935, v. 1:1–10), and D. Tedlock (1972:223–69).

2. For a discussion of Mayan calendrical divination see B. Tedlock (1982). The orthography for the Quiché language used here is the new one adopted in 1988 by the Academia de las Lenguas Mayas de Guatemala.

BIBLIOGRAPHY

■ ■ ■ ■

Abarr, James
1980   "Zuni: An Indian Tribe Wins Control of Its
        Schools." *Albuquerque Journal Magazine* 3, no.
        23:4–8.

Aberle, S. D.
1948   "The Pueblo Indians of New Mexico: Their
        Land, Economy and Civil Organization." *Memoirs of the American Anthropological Association*,
        no. 4, pt. 2:1–93.

Adair, John J.
1944   *The Navajo and Pueblo Silversmiths*. Norman:
        University of Oklahoma Press.
1960   "A Pueblo G.I." In *In the Company of Man*, ed.
        Joseph B. Casagrande, pp. 489–503. New
        York: Harper and Row.

BIBLIOGRAPHY

Adair, John J., and Vogt, Evon Z.
  1949   "Navajo and Zuni Veterans: A Study of Con-
                trasting Modes of Culture Change." *American*
                Anthropologist 51:547–61.

Adams, E. Charles
  1991   *The Origin and Development of the Pueblo Katsina*
                Cult. Tuscon: University of Arizona Press.

Albert, Ethel M., and Cazeneuve, Jean
  1956   "La Philosophie des Indiens Zuñis." *Revue de*
                Psychologie des Peuples 2:1–12.

Basso, Keith H.
  1979   *Portraits of "The Whiteman."* Cambridge: Cam-
                bridge University Press.

Bell, Barbara, and Bell, Ed
  1975–77   *Zuni: The Art and the People*, 3 vols. Grants,
                N.M.: Squaw Bell Traders.

Benedict, Ruth
  1934   *Patterns of Culture.* New York: Mentor
                Books.

  1935   *Zuñi Mythology*, 2 vols. Columbia University
                Contributions to Anthropology, no. 21. New
                York: Columbia University Press.

Bernard, H. Russell, and Salinas Pedraza, Jesús
  1989   *Native Ethnography: A Mexican Indian Describes*
                His Culture. Newbury Park, Calif.: Sage.

Bohrer, Vorsila L.
  1960   "Zuni Agriculture." *El Palacio* 67:181–202.

Bouissac, Paul
  1990   "The Profanation of the Sacred in Circus Clown
                Performances." In *By Means of Performance*,
                ed. Richard Schechner and Willa Appel,
                pp. 194–207. Cambridge: Cambridge Univer-
                sity Press.

Bunzel, Ruth

1929   *The Pueblo Potter: A Study of Creative Imagination in Primitive Art*. Columbia University Contributions to Anthropology, no. 8. New York: Columbia University Press. (Reprint: New York: Dover Publications, 1972.)

1932a   "Introduction to Zuñi Ceremonialism." In *Forty-seventh Annual Report of the Bureau of American Ethnology for the Years 1929–1930*, pp. 467–544. Washington, D.C.: U.S. Government Printing Office.

1932b   "Zuñi Origin Myths." In *Forty-seventh Annual Report of the Bureau of American Ethnology*, pp. 545–610. Washington, D.C.: U.S. Government Printing Office.

1932c   "Zuñi Ritual Poetry." In *Forty-seventh Annual Report of the Bureau of American Ethnology*, pp. 611–836. Washington, D.C.: U.S. Government Printing Office.

1932d   "Zuñi Katchinas." In *Forty-seventh Annual Report of the Bureau of American Ethnology*, pp. 837–1086. Washington, D.C.: U.S. Government Printing Office.

1933   *Zuni Texts*. Publications of the American Ethnological Society, vol. 15, ed. Franz Boas. New York: Stechert & Co.

1935   *Zuni*. New York: Columbia University Press.

Bureau of Indian Affairs (BIA)

1973   *The Zuni Indian Reservation: Its Resources and Development Potential*. Report no. 207. Billings, Mont.: United States Department of the Interior.

Camazine, Scott M.
1980   "Traditional and Western Health Care Among
               the Zuni Indians of New Mexico." *Social Science
               and Medicine* 148:73–80.

Camazine, Scott, and Bye, Robert A.
1980   "A Study of the Medical Ethnobotany of the
               Zuni Indians of New Mexico." *Journal of Eth-
               nopharmacology* 2:365–88.

Canfield, Anne Sutton
1980   "Ahayu:da . . . Art or Icon?" *Native Arts
               West* 1, no. 1:24–26.

Caywood, Louis R.
1972   *The Restored Mission of Nuestra Señora de Guad-
               alupe de Zuñi.* Saint Michaels, Ariz.: St. Mi-
               chaels Press.

Cazeneuve, Jean
1957   *Les Dieux dansent à Cibola: Le Shalako des Indiens
               Zuñis.* Paris: Gallimard.

Coze, Paul
1952   "Of Clowns and Mudheads." *Arizona Highways*
               28, no. 8:18–29.

1954   "Twenty-four Hours of Magic." *Arizona High-
               ways* 30, no. 11:10–27, 34–35.

Crampton, C. Gregory
1977   *The Zunis of Cibola.* Salt Lake City: University
               of Utah Press.

Cushing, Frank Hamilton
n.d.   Letter to Sylvester Baxter, October 1881.
               Hodge-Cushing Collection, Southwest Mu-
               seum, Los Angeles, Calif.

1882–83   "My Adventures in Zuñi." *Century Illustrated
               Monthly Magazine* 25, no. 2:191–207; no.
               4:500–511.

1883   "Zuñi Fetiches." In *Second Annual Report of the Bureau of American Ethnology for the Years 1880–1881*, pp. 3–45. Washington, D.C.: U.S. Government Printing Office.

1886   "A Study of Pueblo Pottery as Illustrative of Zuñi Culture Growth." In *Fourth Annual Report of the Bureau of American Ethnology for the Years 1882–1883*, pp. 467–521. Washington, D.C.: U.S. Government Printing Office.

1895   "Katalog einer Sammlung von Idolen, Fetischen und Priesterlichen Ausrüstungsgegenständen de Zuñi—oder Ashiwi-Indianer von Neu Mexiko (U.S.A.)." *Veröffentlichungen aus dem Königlichen Museum für Völkerkunde* 4, pt. 1:1–2.

1896   "Outlines of Zuñi Creation Myths." In *Thirteenth Annual Report of the Bureau of American Ethnology for the Years 1891–1982*, pp. 321–447. Washington, D.C.: U.S. Government Printing Office.

1901   *Zuni Folktales*. New York: Alfred A. Knopf.

1920   *Zuni Breadstuff*. Indian Notes and Monographs, vol. 8. New York: Museum of the American Indian Heye Foundation.

Deloria, Vine, and Lytle, Clifford

1984   *The Nations Within: The Past and Future of American Indian Sovereignty*. New York: Pantheon Books.

Dubin, Margaret

1990a   "Zunis Celebrate $25 Million Land Rehab Award." Gallup *Independent* 103, no. 287 (Dec. 5, 1990):1.

1990b   "Zuni War Gods Stolen." Gallup *Independent* 103, no. 295 (Dec. 14, 1990):3.

Dutton, Bertha P.
1963   *Friendly People: The Zuni Indians.* Santa Fe: Museum of New Mexico Press.

Eggan, Fred
1950   *Social Organization of the Western Pueblos.* Chicago: University of Chicago Press.

Eggan, Fred, and Pandey, T. N.
1979   "Zuni History, 1850–1970." In *Handbook of North American Indians: Southwest*, ed. Alfonso Ortiz, vol. 9, pp. 474–81. Washington, D.C.: Smithsonian Institution.

Ellinger, Edgar
1952   "The Zunis and Their Jewelry." *Arizona Highways* 28, no. 8:8–13.

Eriacho, Wilfred
1978   Statement of Religious Leaders of the Pueblo of Zuni Concerning Sacred Zuni Religious Items/ Artifacts. Sept. 20 (U.S. House of Representatives Process).

Eriacho, Wilfred, and Ferguson, T. J.
1979   "The Zuni War Gods: Art, Artifact, or Religious Beings: A Conflict in Values, Beliefs, and Use." Paper presented at the New Directions in Native American Art History Symposium, Albuquerque, New Mexico.

Ferguson, T. J., and Eriacho, Wilfred
1990   "*Ahayu:da* Zuni War Gods: Cooperation and Repatriation." *Native Peoples* 4, no. 1:6–12.

Ferguson, T. J., and Hart, E. Richard
1985   *A Zuni Atlas.* Norman: University of Oklahoma Press.

Ferguson, T. J., and Mills, Barbara J.
1982   *Archaeological Investigations at Zuni Pueblo, New Mexico, 1977–1980.* Zuni Archaeology Pro-

gram Report no. 183. Zuni, N.M.: Pueblo of Zuni.

Fewkes, J. Walter

1890a   "On the Use of the Phonograph Among the Zuñi Indians." *American Naturalist* 24:687–91.

1890b   "A Study of Summer Ceremonials at Zuñi and Moqui Pueblos." *Bulletin of the Essex Institute* 22:89–113.

1891   "A Few Summer Ceremonials at Zuñi Pueblo." *Journal of American Ethnology and Archaeology* 1:1–61.

Finnigan, Fr. Joyce

1953   "The Zuñi Tribal Band." *New Mexico Magazine* 31, no. 7:16, 35.

Green, Jesse

1979   *Zuñi: Selected Writings of Frank Hamilton Cushing*. Lincoln: University of Nebraska Press.

1990   *Cushing at Zuni: The Correspondence and Journals of Frank Hamilton Cushing, 1879–1884.* Albuquerque: University of New Mexico Press.

Greenblatt, Stephen J.

1981   *Allegory and Representation*. Baltimore: Johns Hopkins University Press.

Handelman, Don

1981   "The Ritual Clown: Attributes and Affinities." *Anthropos* 76:321–70.

Handy, Edward L.

1918   "Zuñi Tales." *Journal of American Folk-Lore* 31:451–71.

Harbert, Nancy

1990   "Zuñis Exercise Option for Good Health." *New Mexico Magazine* 68, no. 4:23–24.

Hardin, Margaret Ann
1983   *Gifts of Mother Earth: Ceramics in the Zuni Tra-
            dition*. Phoenix: Heard Museum.

Harrington, M. R.
1929   "Ruins and Legends of Zuni Land." *The Mas-
            terkey* 3:5–16.

Hart, E. Richard
1973   *The Zunis: Experiences and Descriptions*. Zuni,
            N.M.: Pueblo of Zuni.
1983   "Zuni Relations with the United States and the
            Zuni Land Claim." In *Zuni History*, pp. 29–
            32. Sun Valley, Idaho: Institute of the American
            West.

Hieb, Louis A.
1972   "Meaning and Mismeaning: Toward an Under-
            standing of the Ritual Clown." In *New Per-
            spectives on the Pueblos*, ed. Alfonso Ortiz, pp.
            163–95. Albuquerque: University of New
            Mexico Press.

Hill, G. Richard
1983   "The Zuni Land Claim Litigation." In *Zuni His-
            tory*, p. 36. Sun Valley, Idaho: Institute of the
            American West.

Hill, Gertrude
1947   "Turquoise and the Zuñi Indian." *The Kiva*
            12:42–52.

Hinsley, Curtis M.
1989   "Zunis and Brahmins: Cultural Ambivalence
            in the Gilded Age." *History of Anthropology*
            6:169–207.

Hodge, Frederick W.
1921   *Turquoise Work of Hawikuh*. Leaflets of the Mu-
            seum of the American Indian Heye Foundation,
            no. 2. New York: Heye Foundation.

Hodge, Frederick W., and Cushing, Frank H.
n.d.   Manuscripts, letters, and papers pertaining to fieldwork at Zuni. Southwest Museum, Los Angeles.

Hofmann, Charles
1968   *Frances Densmore and American Indian Music.* Contributions from the Museum of the American Indian, vol. 23. New York: Heye Foundation.

Kenagy, Susan G.
1978   "Deer-and-Medallion Style Pottery at Zuni Pueblo: Iconography and Iconology." *New Mexico Studies in the Fine Arts* 3:46–52.

Kirk, Ruth F.
1943   "Introduction to Zuni Fetishism." *El Palacio* 50:117–29; 146–59; 183–98; 206–19; 235–45. Reprinted in 1988 as a booklet entitled *Zuni Fetishism*. Albuquerque: Avanyu Publishing.

Klett, Francis
1874   "The Zuni Indians of New Mexico." *Popular Science Monthly* 5:580–91.

Knowler, William C.; Bennett, Peter H.; Hamman, Richard F.; and Miller, Max
1978   "Diabetes Incidence and Prevalence in Pima Indians: A 19-Fold Greater Incidence than in Rochester, Minnesota." *American Journal of Epidemiology* 108, no. 6:497–505.

Kroeber, Alfred L.
1916   "Thoughts on Zuñi Religion." In *Holmes Anniversary Volume*, ed. F. W. Hodge, pp. 269–77. Washington, D.C.: James William Bryan Press.

1917   "Zuñi Kin and Clan." *Anthropological Papers of the American Museum of Natural History*, no. 18, pt. 2, pp. 37–205. New York: Trustees of the American Museum of Natural History.

Ladd, Edmund J.

1963   "Zuni Ethno-Ornithology." M.A. thesis, University of New Mexico, Albuquerque.

1979a   "Zuni Social and Political Organization." In *Handbook of North American Indians: Southwest*, ed. Alfonso Ortiz, vol. 9, pp. 482–91. Washington, D.C.: Smithsonian Institution.

1979b   "Zuni Economy." In *Handbook of North American Indians: Southwest*, ed. Alfonso Ortiz, vol. 9, pp. 492–98. Washington, D.C.: Smithsonian Institution.

1983a   "Zuni Religion and Philosophy." *Exploration: Annual Bulletin of the School of American Research* (*Zuni & El Morro* issue), pp. 26–31.

1983b   "An Explanation: Request for the Return of Religious Objects Held in Museums and Private Collections." *Exploration: Annual Bulletin of the School of American Research* (*Zuni & El Morro* issue), p. 32.

Lamb, Samuel H.

1975   *Woody Plants of the Southwest*. Santa Fe: Sunstone Press.

Leighton, Dorothea C., and Adair, John

1966   *People of the Middle Place: A Study of the Zuni Indians*. Behavior Science Monographs. New Haven, Conn.: Human Relations Area Files Press.

Levy, Gordon

1980   *Who's Who in Zuni Jewelry*. Denver: Western Arts Publishing.

Li, An-che
1937   "Zuni: Some Observations and Queries." *American Anthropologist* 39:62–76.

Long, T. P.
1978   "The Prevalence of Clinically Treated Diabetes Among Zuni Reservation Residents." *American Journal of Public Health* 68:901.

Nabhan, Gary Paul
1982   *The Desert Smells Like Rain: A Naturalist in Papago Indian Country*. San Francisco: North Point Press.

Newman, Stanley
1955   "Vocabulary Levels: Zuñi Sacred and Slang Usage." *Southwestern Journal of Anthropology* 11:345–54.

1958   *Zuni Dictionary*. Indiana University Research Center in Anthropology, Folklore and Linguistics Publication no. 6. Bloomington: Indiana University Press.

1965   *Zuni Grammar*. University of New Mexico Publications in Anthropology, no. 14. Albuquerque: University of New Mexico Press.

Nusbaum, Aileen
1926   *The Seven Cities of Cibola: Zuñi Indian Tales*. New York: G. P. Putnam's Sons.

Ortiz, Alfonso
1972   "Ritual Drama and the Pueblo World View." In *New Perspectives on the Pueblos*, ed. Alfonso Ortiz, pp. 135–61. Albuquerque: University of New Mexico Press.

Pandey, Triloki Nath
1968   "Tribal Council Elections in a Southwestern Pueblo." *Ethnology* 7:71–85.

1972   "Anthropologists at Zuni." *Proceedings of the American Philosophical Society* 116, no. 4:321–37.

1974   " 'Indian Man' Among American Indians." In *Encounter and Experience: Some Personal Accounts of Fieldwork*, ed. André Béteille and T. N. Madan, pp. 194–213. Honolulu: University Press of Hawaii.

1977   "Images of Power in a Southwestern Pueblo." In *The Anthropology of Power*, ed. Raymond D. Fogelson and Richard N. Adams, pp. 195–215. New York: Academic Press.

1979   "The Anthropologist-Informant Relationship: The Navajo and Zuni in America and the Tharu in India." In *The Fieldworker and the Field*, ed. M. N. Srinivas, A. M. Shah, and E. A. Ramaswamy, pp. 246–65. Delhi: Oxford University Press.

Parsons, Elsie Clews

1916a   "The Zuñi A'doshle and Suuke." *American Anthropologist* 18:338–47.

1916b   "The Favorite Number of the Zuñi." *Scientific Monthly* 3:596–600.

1916c   "A Zuñi Detective." *Man* 16:168–69.

1916d   "The Zuñi Mo'lawia." *Journal of American Folk-Lore* 29:392–99.

1917a   "Notes on Zuñi." *Memoirs of the American Anthropological Association* 4:151–327.

1917b   "Ceremonial Friendship at Zuñi." *American Anthropologist* 19:1–8.

1918   "War God Shrines of Laguna and Zuñi." *American Anthropologist* 20:381–405.

1919a   "Census of the Shi'wanakwe Society of Zuñi." *American Anthropologist* 21:329–35.

1919b   "Increase by Magic: A Zuñi Pattern." *American Anthropologist* 21:279–86.

1919c   "Mothers and Children at Zuñi, New Mexico." *Man* 19:168–73.

1922   "Winter and Summer Dance Series in Zuñi in 1918." *University of California Publications in American Archaeology and Ethnology* 17:171–216.

1923a   "Zuñi Names and Naming Practices." *Journal of American Folk-Lore* 36:171–76.

1923b   "The Origin Myth of Zuñi." *Journal of American Folk-Lore* 36:135–62.

1924   "The Scalp Ceremonial of Zuni." *Memoirs of the American Anthropological Association* 31:1–42.

1930   "Zuñi Tales." *Journal of American Folk-Lore* 43:1–58.

1933a   *Hopi and Zuñi Ceremonialism.* Memoirs of the American Anthropological Association, no. 39. Menasha, Wis.: Collegiate Press.

1933b   "Spring Days in Zuni, New Mexico." *Scientific Monthly* 36:49–54.

1939a   *Pueblo Indian Religion*, 2 vols. Chicago: University of Chicago Press.

1939b   "The Franciscans Return to Zuni." *American Anthropologist* 41:337–38.

Parsons, Elsie C., and Beals, Ralph L.

1934   "The Sacred Clowns of the Pueblo and Maya-Yaqui Indians." *American Anthropologist* 39:491–514.

Pueblo of Zuni

1966–73   "Zuni Tribal Newsletter," mimeograph, Zuni Tribe, Zuni, N.M.

1969   *Zuni Comprehensive Development Plan for a Better Zuni by '75: Presented by the Pueblo of Zuni with the Cooperation of Local, State, and Federal Agencies.* Zuni, N.M.: Pueblo of Zuni.

1972 *The Zunis: Self-Portrayals*, trans. Alvina Quam. Albuquerque: University of New Mexico Press.

Robbins, Wilfred William; Harrington, John Peabody; and Freire-Marreco, Barbara

1916 *Ethnobotany of the Tewa Indians.* Bureau of American Ethnology Bulletin no. 55. Washington, D.C.: U.S. Government Printing Office.

Roberts, Helen H.

1923 "Chakwena Songs of Zuñi and Laguna." *Journal of American Folk-Lore* 36:177–84.

Roberts, John M.

1961 "The Zuni." In *Variations in Value Orientations*, ed. Florence Kluckhohn and Fred L. Strodtbeck, pp. 285–316. Evanston, Ill.: Row, Peterson and Company.

1965a *Zuni Daily Life.* New Haven, Conn.: Human Relations Area Files Press.

1965b "Kinsmen and Friends in Zuni Culture: A Terminological Note." *El Palacio* 72:38–43.

Roberts, John M., and Arth, Malcolm J.

1966 "Dyadic Elicitation in Zuni." *El Palacio* 73:27–41.

Roberts, John M., and Gregor, Thomas

1971 "Privacy: A Cultural View." In *Privacy*, ed. J. Roland Pennock and John W. Chapman, pp. 199–225. New York: Atheton Press.

Rodee, Marian, and Ostler, James

1986 *Zuni Pottery.* West Chester, Pa.: Schiffer Publishing.

1990 *The Fetish Carvers of Zuni.* Albuquerque: Maxwell Museum of Anthropology.

Roscoe, Will

1991   *The Zuni Man-Woman*. Albuquerque: University of New Mexico Press.

Rosnek, Carl, and Stacey, Joseph

1976   *Skystone and Silver: The Collector's Book of Southwest Indian Jewelry*. Englewood Cliffs, N.J.: Prentice-Hall.

Schaafsma, Polly, and Schaafsma, Curtis F.

1974   "Evidence for the Origins of the Pueblo Katchina Cult as Suggested by Southwestern Rock Art." *American Antiquity* 39:535–45.

Schneider, David M., and Roberts, John M.

1965   *Zuni Kin Terms*. New Haven, Conn.: Human Relations Area Files Press.

Simmons, Marc

1974   *Witchcraft in the Southwest*. Flagstaff: Northland Press.

Smith, Watson, and Roberts, John M.

1954   *Zuni Law: A Field of Values*. Papers of the Peabody Museum of American Archaeology and Ethnology, vol. 43. Cambridge, Mass.: Peabody Museum.

Smith, Watson; Woodbury, Richard B.; and Woodbury, Nathalie F. S.

1966   *The Excavation of Hawikuh by Frederick Webb Hodge*. Contributions from the Museum of the American Indian Heye Foundation, vol 20. New York: Museum of the American Indian Heye Foundation.

Stephens, Michael

1982   "The Ahayu:da File: A Case History of Negotiations for the Return of Sacred Objects from the Millicent Rogers Museum to the Pueblo of Zuni." *Collection* 4, no. 4:3–13.

Stevenson, James

1883 "Illustrated Catalogue of the Collections Obtained from the Indians of New Mexico and Arizona in 1879." In *Second Annual Report of the Bureau of American Ethnology for the Years 1880–1881*, pp. 307–422. Washington, D.C.: U.S. Government Printing Office.

Stevenson, Matilda Coxe

1887 "The Religious Life of the Zuñi Child." In *Fifth Annual Report of the Bureau of American Ethnology for the Years 1883–1884*, pp. 533–55. Washington, D.C.: U.S. Government Printing Office.

1904 *The Zuñi Indians: Their Mythology, Esoteric Fraternities, and Ceremonies.* Twenty-third Annual Report of the Bureau of American Ethnology for the Years 1901–1902. Washington, D.C.: U.S. Government Printing Office.

1915 "Ethnobotany of the Zuñi Indians." In *Thirtieth Annual Report of the Bureau of American Ethnology for the Years 1908–1909*, pp. 31–102. Washington, D.C.: U.S. Government Printing Office.

Stoffle, Richard W.

1975 "Reservation-based Industry: A Case from Zuni, New Mexico." *Human Organization* 34, no. 3:217–25.

Sweet, Jill D.

1989 "Burlesquing 'The Other' in Pueblo Performance." *Annals of Tourism Research* 16, no. 1:62–75.

Tedlock, Barbara

1973   "Kachina Dance Songs in Zuni Society: The
        Role of Esthetics in Social Integration." M.A.
        thesis, Wesleyan University, Middletown,
        Conn.

1975   "The Clown's Way." In *Teachings from the Amer-
        ican Earth*, ed. Dennis Tedlock and Barbara
        Tedlock, pp. 105–18. New York: Liveright.

1979   "Boundaries of Belief." *Parabola* 4:70–77.

1980   "Songs of the Zuni Kachina Society: Compo-
        sition, Rehearsal, and Performance." In *South-
        western Indian Ritual Drama*, ed. Charlotte J.
        Frisbie, pp. 7–35. Albuquerque: University of
        New Mexico Press.

1982   *Time and the Highland Maya*. Albuquerque: Uni-
        versity of New Mexico Press.

1983   "Zuni Sacred Theater." *American Indian Quar-
        terly* 7:93–110.

1984   "The Beautiful and the Dangerous: Zuni Ritual
        and Cosmology as an Aesthetic System." *Con-
        junctions* 6:246–65.

1986a   "Zuni." In *The New Grove Dictionary of Amer-
        ican Music*, ed. H. Wiley Hitchcock, vol. 4,
        pp. 597–98. London: Macmillan Pub-
        lishers.

1986b   "Keeping the Breath Nearby." *Anthropology and
        Humanism Quarterly* 11:92–94.

1986c   "Masking." *Conjunctions* 9:166–76.

1986d   "Crossing the Sensory Domains in Native
        American Aesthetics." In *Explorations in Eth-
        nomusicology*, ed. Charlotte J. Frisbie, pp. 187–
        98. Detroit Monographs in Musicology, no. 9.
        Detroit: Information Coordinators.

1987   "Zuni and Quiché Dream Sharing and Interpreting." In *Dreaming: Anthropological and Psychological Interpretations*, ed. Barbara Tedlock, pp. 105–31. Cambridge: Cambridge University Press.

1989   "The Gleam in the Butcher's Eye." *Conjunctions* 13:179–94.

1991   "From Participant Observation to the Observation of Participation: The Emergence of Narrative Ethnography." *Journal of Anthropological Research* 47, no. 1:69–94.

Tedlock, Dennis

1968   "The Ethnography of Tale-Telling at Zuni." Ph.D. dissertation, Tulane University. Ann Arbor: University Microfilms International.

1972   *Finding the Center: Narrative Poetry of the Zuni Indians*. New York: Dial Press.

1975   "An American Indian View of Death." In *Teachings from the American Earth*, ed. Dennis Tedlock and Barbara Tedlock, pp. 248–71. New York: Liveright.

1979   "Zuni Religion and World View." In *Handbook of North American Indians: Southwest*, ed. Alfonso Ortiz, vol. 9, pp. 499–508. Washington, D.C.: Smithsonian Institution.

1983   *The Spoken Word and the Work of Interpretation*. Philadelphia: University of Pennsylvania Press.

Trotter, George A.

1955   *From Feather, Blanket and Tepee: The Indians' Fight for Equality*. New York: Vantage Press.

United States Congress

1976   *Zuni Land Claims: Hearing Before the Subcommittee on Indian Affairs of the Committee on Interior and*

Insular Affairs, House of Representatives, Ninety-fourth Congress, Second Session, on H.R. 4212 and S. 877 . . . Held in Washington, D.C., September 10, 1976. Washington, D.C.: U.S. Government Printing Office.

1978   *Directing the Secretary of the Interior to Purchase and Hold Certain Lands in Trust for the Zuni Indian Tribe of New Mexico, Conferring Jurisdiction on the Court of Claims with Respect to Land Claims of Such Tribe, and Authorizing Such Tribe to Purchase and Exchange Land in the State of New Mexico and Arizona: Report to Accompany H.R. 3787.* Washington, D.C.: U.S. Government Printing Office.

1984   *Zuni Indian Tribe Lands Bill: Hearing Before the Select Committee on Indian Affairs, United States Senate, Ninety-eighth Congress, Second Session, on S. 2201 . . . April 9, 1984.* Washington, D.C.: U.S. Government Printing Office.

1990   *Zuni Claims Settlement Act of 1990: Report to Accompany S. 2203.* Washington, D.C.: U.S. Government Printing Office.

United States Laws and Statutes

1978   *Zuni Indian Tribe: New Mexico Lands in Trust* (PL 95-280, May 15, 1978). United States Statutes at Large 92, pp. 244–45. Washington, D.C.: U.S. Government Printing Office.

1984   *An Act to Convey Certain Lands to the Zuni Indian Tribe for Religious Purposes* (PL 98-408, Aug. 28, 1984). United States Statues at Large 98 (2), pp. 1533–35. Washington, D.C.: U.S. Government Printing Office.

1990   *Zuni Land Conservation Act of 1990* (PL 101-486, Oct. 31, 1990). Signed into law by President Bush.

Vogt, Evon Z., and Albert, Ethel M.

1966   *People of Rimrock: A Study of Values in Five Cultures.* Cambridge, Mass.: Harvard University Press.

Walker, Willard

1974   "Palowahtiwa and the Economic Redevelopment of Zuni Pueblo." *Ethnohistory* 21, no. 1:65–75.

West, Kelly M.

1974   "Diabetes in American Indians and Other Native Populations of the New World." *Diabetes* 23, no. 10:841.

Whiting, Alfred F.

1939   *Ethnobotany of the Hopi.* Museum of Northern Arizona Bulletin no. 15. Flagstaff: Northland Press.

Wilson, Edmund

1956   "The Zuni Shalako Ceremony." In *Red, Black, Blond, and Olive,* ed. Edmund Wilson, pp. 3–4, 9–12, 23–31, 33–42. New York: Oxford University Press. Reprinted in *Comparative Religion: An Anthropological Approach,* ed. William A. Lessa and Evon Z. Vogt, pp. 171–80. New York: Harper and Row, 1965.

Woodward, Arthur

1939   "Frank Cushing—'First War-Chief of Zuñi.' " *The Masterkey* 13:172–79.

1950   "Concerning Witches." *The Masterkey* 24: 183–88.

Wright, Barton

1985   *Kachinas of the Zuni*. Flagstaff: Northland Press.

1988   *Patterns and Sources of Zuni Kachinas*. Phoenix: Harmsen Publishing.

Young, M. Jane

1981   "We Were Going to Have a Barbecue, But the Cow Ran Away: Production, Form, and Function of the Zuñi Tribal Fair." *Southwest Folklore* 5, no. 4:42–48.

1988   *Signs from the Ancestors: Zuni Cultural Symbolism and Perceptions of Rock Art*. Albuquerque: University of New Mexico Press.

Young, M. Jane, and Williamson, Ray A.

1981   "Ethnoastronomy: The Zuni Case." In *Archaeoastronomy in the Americas*, ed. Ray A. Williamson, pp. 183–91. Ballena Press Anthropological Papers, no. 22. Los Altos, Calif.: Ballena Press.

Zuni History Project

1983   "Zuni History." Sun Valley, Idaho: Institute of the American West. (Tabloid.)

Zuni Tribal Council

1975   *Constitution of the Zuni Tribe, Zuni Reservation, Zuni, New Mexico*. Zuni, N.M.: Zuni Tribe.

1978a   Tribal Council Resolution M70-78-991: Statement of Zuni Tribal Council Adopting Statement of Zuni Religious Leaders as Official Tribal Position on Sacred Religious Items. Sept. 23.

1978b   M70-78-993: Statement of Religious Leaders of the Pueblo of Zuni Concerning Sacred Zuni Religious Items/Artifacts. Oct. 5.

DISCOGRAPHY

■ ■ ■ ■

American Indian Dances. Folkways Records FD 7510, 1959.

Music of the Pueblos, Apache, and Navaho. Taylor Museum, Colorado Springs Fine Arts Center R 611317, 1961.

Music from Zuni Pueblo: Featuring Chester Mahooty and Family. Tribal Music International, Rainbow Cassette Studio, 1990.

Summer Songs from Zuni. Canyon Records 6077, 1971.

Zuni. Canyon Records ARP 6060, 1970.

Zuni Fair Live: 1971. Indian House 1401, 1972.

INDEX

■ ■ ■ ■

Page numbers in *italics* refer to illustrations.

INDEX

Mother Earth, 26, 115, 116, 228–29, 303
Nepayatamu, 267–68
Payatamu, 173, 264–66, 287
Salt Woman, 33–34, 42, 76–77, 91, 92–93, 294
Shulaawitsi/*Fire God*, 160, 165–67, 227
Sun Father, 41, 43, 76, 107, 108, 228, 230, 231, 238, 241, 264–65, 268, 303
Turquoise Man, 42
White Shell Woman, 238, 253–54, 303
Yamuhakto twins, 228
Department of Justice, U.S., 303
diseases, 19, 65, 79, 81, 195, 253, 289
diabetes, 257–58, 304
divorce, 2, 66, 130, 170, 185
Dodge, Chee, 198
dogs, 5, 12, 13, 16, 22, 27, 60, 62, 67, 82, 164, 180, 184, 186
dreaming, 7, 19, 53, 103, 107, 124, 125, 164, 288
daydreams, 159
hallucinations, 184, 186
interpretation of dreams, 289–90, 298
nightmares, 16, 184–86, 231, 246, 259, 268–69
duck (*see also* mallard), 5, 48, 184, 225, 227, 232

eagle, 29–30, 43, 78, 105, 225, 239, 265
feathers, 43, 48, 51, 70, 77, 196, 206, 226, 239–40, 243–44
ethnographers at Zuni, 99, 117–18, 173–181, 196
ethnography, xii–xiv, 136–41, 282–84
Center for Urban Ethnography, 207–8
field notes, 16–17, 282
fieldwork, 69, 169, 208
interviewing, 141, 209–10
participant observation, 208
trip log, 79–92
etiquette (*see also* gift exchange), 2–4, 9, 34, 50, 59, 69, 75, 136, 251–52
asking questions, 51, 122–23, 128
calling, 40, 132
eating, 3–4, 9, 34, 47
feeding, 3, 48–49
greeting, 6, 18, 92, 95, 164–65, 237

helping, 8–9, 22, 33
pointing with the lips, 35, 68, 175, 237

Farfán, Marcos, 87, 298
farm equipment, 23, 57, 58, 195, 203, 204
farming (*see* agriculture)
Fence Lake, 83
fetish (*see also* icons), 117, 118, 125, 174, 178, 181, 299
necklaces, 225
fieldwork (*see* ethnography)
fire fighting, 63–64, 144, 184–85
flowers, 51, 123, 124, 190–91
mariposa lilies, 231
sunflower, 228, 231
tenatsali, 266, 268, 301, 304
white, 48, 123, 190, 238
zinnia, 80, 297
food, traditional
blood pudding, 64, 100
cattail-flour muffins, 251
corn, 58–59, 63, 85, 172
cornmeal, 28
dove chile, 79
flatbread, wheat, 47
hapnuskinne/*haggis*, 64
Indian oven bread, 9, 33, 47, 75, 93, 129, 142–43, 146, 251, 269, 280–281
k'alhiko/*hot bowl*, 251
Navajo fry bread, 251, 269–71, *271*
paperbread or *piki*, 9, 28, 251, 278
piñon nuts, 49, 172, 225, 239
sunflower bread, 251
tepary beans, 251
venison, 3, 8, 46, 47, 92, 121, 127, 128, 129, 145, 238, 251, 257
yucca pod conserves, 90–91
fox pelts, 102, 161, 243

Gallup, Ceremonial, 62, 102, 105, 133, 201
ghosts, 36–37, 172
gift exchange, 3, 12, 14–15, 17, 56, 93, 94–95, 129, 158–59, 194, *237*, 238, 256, 272, 282

Halona Plaza, 144, 191
Hano, 86

INDEX

sports
  basketball, 55
  kick stick races, 45–46
  swimming, 68–69, 91, 183
Spring Canyon, 152
stars and planets, 27, 41, 135, 137–39,
    225, 227, 289
Stevenson, Matilda Coxe, 173–76, 297,
    298, 300, 301, 302, 304
stinkbug, 121
stories (see narratives)
suicide, 104, 175, 257, 261
Summer Songs from Zuni, 194, 302, 327

taboos, 13, 16, 86, 111, 165, 180, 233,
    260, 297
tape recorder, 172, 182
tattoo, 68, 99, 183, 215–16
tehya/*precious*, 110, 213
television, 1, 19, 41–43, 105, 187, 189,
    199, 211, 258, 260, 262, 273, 277,
    278, 279
teshkwi (see rituals)
textiles, 12, 47, 50, 91, 232–33, 238
tobacco, wild, 47, 81–82, 118, 247
torch, bark, 27, 160, 227, 230
trading, 23, 63, 195, 256
tribal fair, 102, 210, 278
tribal government, vii, 130, 134–35, 144,
    180, 196, 199, 200, 302–3
tropes
  allegory, 101, 137–40, 141, 300
  irony, 61, 74, 141
  metaphor, 48, 90, 93, 110, 230
  metonymy, 128, 207
  symbol, 79, 109
tso'ya/*beautiful*, xi, 51, 55, 89–90, 100,
    139, 191, 197, 232, 262, 267, 269
turkey, 50, 51, 67, 105, 110, 225, 251
  feather, 51, 107–8
turtle, 121, 160, 168, 189
twins (see also Ahayuuta, Yamuhakto), 7, 13,
    16, 29, 129, 261

U'ky'ahayan El'a/*Where Downy Feather Stands*,
    78
Ute, 33

Vietnam War, 78, 130, 170–72, 175, 182–
    187
Village of the Great Kivas, 298
volcano (see also Sitting Mountain), 86–87

Warm Springs Indians, 185
Washington, D.C., vii, 7, 22, 24, 179, 199
willow, 56, 106, 109, 226, 243, 247
witchcraft, 9, 28, 36, 41, 70–71, 129–30,
    193, 211, 228, 241–42, 246, 251,
    257, 262, 281, 290, 294
  whiteman's, 32–33, 40–42, 45, 71–72
Witch Wells, 72, 200, *201*, 251
Where Downy Feather Stands, 78
Whiteman, the, 23, 45, 133, 139, 144,
    176, 181, 198, 293
Wind Place, 261
wolf, 49, 117, 119
women
  ritual knowledge of, 42, 51, 59–60, 77,
    79, 92, 96–98, 120, 181, 233–36,
    238, 254
  work of (see also crafts), 6, 9, 33, 34, 59–
    60, 98–106, 114–17, 142–46, 193

Yamuhakto (see Deities)
yucca, 53, 64, 114–15, 186, 231, 239,
    241, 263, 298

Zuni, 204, 302, 327
Zuni Craftsmen Cooperative, 130
Zuni language, 2, 6, 17, 19, 26, 31, 33,
    34, 36–37, 46, 50, 52, 93, 95, 113,
    120, 124, 125, 128, 137–39, 146,
    153, 155, 158, 171, 173, 178–80,
    184, 207, 210, 233–34, 291, 301
Zuni reservation, 23–26, 52, 61, 66, 82,
    110, 187, 199, 258, 293, 298
Zuni River, 158, 191, 192, 254, 277
Zuni Tribal Newsletter, 130–31